ARMAGEDDON
IN THE
MIDDLE EAST

ARMAGEDDON IN THE MIDDLE EAST
by Dana Adams Schmidt

THE BLACK DILEMMA
by John Herbers

CONFLICT AND COMPROMISE:
THE DYNAMICS OF AMERICAN FOREIGN POLICY
by Richard Halloran

EASTERN EUROPE IN THE SOVIET SHADOW
by Harry Schwartz

MADMAN IN A LIFEBOAT:
ISSUES OF THE ENVIRONMENTAL CRISIS
by Gladwin Hill

OUT OF THIS NETTLE:
A HISTORY OF POSTWAR EUROPE
by Clyde H. Farnsworth

THE USSR TODAY
by Harry A. Rositzke

The New York Times
SURVEY SERIES

THEODORE M. BERNSTEIN
GENERAL EDITOR

THE NEW YORK TIMES Survey Series comprises books that deal comprehensively yet comprehensibly with subjects of wide interest, presenting the facts impartially and drawing conclusions honestly.

The series draws on the great information resources of *The New York Times* and on the talents, backgrounds and insights of specially qualified authors, mostly members of the *Times* staff.

The subjects range from the relatively particular problems of civilized life to the broadest conceivable problems concerning whether civilized life, or any kind of life, will continue to be possible on this planet.

The hope is that the books will be essentially informative, perhaps argumentative, but beyond that stimulative to useful, constructive thinking by the citizens who ultimately must share in civilization's decisions.

ARMAGEDDON
IN THE
MIDDLE EAST

Armageddon in the Middle East

DANA ADAMS SCHMIDT

The John Day Company
AN Intext PUBLISHER / NEW YORK

Library of Congress Cataloging in Pulication Data

Schmidt, Dana Adams, 1915-
  Armageddon in the Middle East.

  (The New York times survey series)
  1. Jewish-Arab relations. 2. Near East—Politics.
I. Title.
DS119.7.S379   327.5694'017'4927   73-7414
ISBN 0-381-98251-3

The John Day Company, 257 Park Avenue South, New York, N.Y. 10010.

Published on the same day in Canada by Longman Canada Limited.

Printed in the United States of America

Contents

"And there were voices, and thunders, and lightnings; and there was a great earthquake, such as was not since men were upon the earth, so mighty an earthquake, and so great."

Revelations 16:18

ARMAGEDDON IN THE MIDDLE EAST

1

A Personal Note

Without my ever intending it, my career as a journalist has been much involved with the problems of the Jews and the Arabs, first in 1938, with the fate of the Jews in Germany, a decade later in 1948, with the conflict between the Jews and the Arabs in Palestine, and finally, two decades later, with the most recent clashes between the Jews of Israel and the Arabs, and their sequels. I am one of the few journalists who, in addition to many short visits, have served as resident correspondents on both sides of the struggle between the Israelis and the Arabs in the Middle East. I was *The New York Times* correspondent in Tel Aviv from September, 1950, until September, 1952. Then, after an eight-year stint in Washington, I returned in April, 1961, to the Middle East on the Arab side, with headquarters in Beirut. I remained there until August, 1970, except for three years in the London Bureau of the *Times,* from July, 1965, to August, 1968, during which I made frequent sorties to the Middle East. The War of 1956 I covered as the *Times* diplomatic correspondent; the fourth Arab war, of October, 1973, as Pentagon correspondent of the *Christian Science Monitor.*

Certain things in these successive episodes stand out with special poignancy. I think they will speak for themselves.

BERLIN, 1938

In my first assignment as a foreign correspondent, I became the "Jewish specialist" in the Berlin bureau of the United Press of America. I fell heir to this task presumably because I was the "junior" member of the staff, and because no one else was eager to come closely to grips with this depressing and frightening subject. A fresh product of Columbia University's School of Journalism, I was in Europe on a Pulitzer Traveling Fellowship, during which I was permitted—and even encouraged—to seek employment.

One bleak day in the winter of 1938–1939, I went to the "Juedische Gemeinderat" (Jewish Community Council) to find out what the Nazis were doing to the Jewish community. At the Jewish Community Council office I discovered a number of gentle, intelligent, delightful, but miserable people who had been obliged by the Nazis to organize their own people to most effectively carry out the German Government's orders. As an American, and neutral, I was able to maintain these contacts with impunity. Especially, I remember Frau Professor Berliner, an elderly woman whose sad privilege it was to know everything that was going on in the affairs of the German Jews. Just before the war, she escaped to Palestine.

From these people I heard in the most objective and restrained terms, which hid their personal agony, many things. I heard of their frustrated attempts to emigrate. Endlessly they pored over prospects in North and South America, Africa, Australia, and western Europe—and finally Palestine. They showed me decrees defining exactly who was a Jew. It was enough to have had one Jewish grandparent to be so regarded under Nazi law. The Jews were required by other decrees to hand over to the Government jewelry and other precious things to pay a collective fine for the murder of a German diplomat in Paris. They were forced to wear arm bands with a yellow Star of David so that they might always be readily identified, and to use only designated benches in the parks. This was only the beginning of the persecution. Later I heard from my friends at the "Gemeinderat" about the first large-scale arrests among Jews and their experiences in the concentration camps, which were just beginning. One of the officials of the Council—I believe his name was Prinz—had been taken to a camp near Berlin for a few weeks and then released. This is a form of intimidation common to all dictatorships. At that time, when the war had just begun, it was largely a matter of poor food or being routed out and paraded in the cold dawn. Extermination was to come later.

I remember carefully studying *Das Schwarze Korps,* the S.S. (Schutzstaffel) organ, in search of clues as to where Nazi racism would lead. The Nazis were lashing themselves into a racist trance, during which they would commit one of the most incredible crimes in history—the murder of six million Jews. I was no longer in Germany when this crime was being committed, but I saw how it started. I walked down Kurfuerstendamm, the great main artery of West Berlin, one morning in June, 1939, just after the storm troopers had, under cover of darkness, smashed the windows of hundreds of Jewish shops, systematically, from one end of the city to the other—but with a special fury in the fashionable Kurfuerstendamm. The windows of Jewish shops were broken, their doors and pavements smeared with such inscriptions in paint or tar as, "Out with the Jews," "Jewish Swine," "Germans Do not Buy from Jews."

I went to the railway station to see off a group of several hundred Jewish children who were being sent to Holland. They were the lucky ones. Later, in 1940, I saw off other trains, packed with whole families headed eastward to a section of Poland where, so the Jews were told, they would be allowed to settle and begin new lives. This was, of course, a deception meant to lure to their doom people who were bound to grasp at any last straw of hope.

Mass tragedy is often beyond comprehension. We did not know the scope or detail of the disaster that was taking shape. I remember going to the apartment of a Jewish woman who was hiding with her son to avoid evacuation. She begged me for help I could not give, and accepted without protest my inability to do anything for her. It is often the role of the journalist to observe so many things which he cannot affect. He can only write about them.

JERUSALEM, 1948

In May, 1948, I was representing *The New York Times* in Jerusalem. In an area known as Zone B, protected by the British Army, the newspapermen lived in a small Arab hotel, the Pantiles, just down the street from the more commodious King David Hotel. We did our work at the British Public Information Office, a tall building opposite the Windmill, a landmark which all old residents of Jerusalem remember. Along with their information services, the British had concentrated in Zone B the Government, army, and security headquarters, from which they attempted vainly to control the warring factions of Jews and Arabs in Palestine.

From Zone B the journalists could contact the Jewish Agency, their main source of information on the Jewish side, and enter the old Arab city of Jerusalem, where the Arab Higher Committee was the main source of information. It was an extraordinary situation in which the force of the British Army enabled the journalists to cover both sides of what was already, in effect, a war.

Every day at the Public Information Office opposite the Windmill the British produced a sheaf of reports—that staple diet of journalists—about incidents that had occurred during the previous 24 hours. The most common type of incident in those early months of 1948 were raids by Haganah or other Jewish paramilitary groups who would raid a village and blow up houses. The inhabitants of the village would then flee. This was the beginning of the flight of the Arabs from Palestine in 1948. They did not understand dynamite. Who does? The panic of one village infected the next, until whole groups of villages were evacuated.

One day, in the P.I.O., someone whispered to me that there would be a rather special story on the Jewish side if I would be game enough for a trip into the suburbs where there was trouble between Jews and Arabs. That is how I came to cover the massacre of Deir Yassin. That night some members of Irgun Zvai Leumi took the journalists by car into the countryside to a point near Deir Yassin. They explained the tactics of the operation, maintaining that the inhabitants of Deir Yassin had been firing at the Jews and that Irgun, with some Haganah support, had been obliged to take matters into its own hands. "Unfortunately" the Irgun spokesman explained, "there were a good many civilian casualties. We had to throw hand grenades into some of the houses." He declined, however, to allow the journalists to go into the village and see for themselves. That was, as I recall, the only explanation we received from the Irgun. They took us back to a house in the Jewish section and served us tea and cookies before we returned to Zone B.

Not until the next morning, when I went to the Arab side to see Dr. Khalid, the spokesman of the Arab Higher Committee, did I discover the horror of Deir Yassin. He charged that about 200 men, women, and children had been killed in the village and their bodies thrown into a well. Survivors had been packed into a truck and paraded through the Jewish section of the city. This, as he told it, had been a systematic act of terrorism, clinical, calculated, methodical, and designed to reinforce the panic of the Palestinian Arabs already set in motion by the dynamiting of their villages.

Another day at the P.I.O., someone told me that I could interview an Irgun leader if I would go to Tel Aviv. I went to the rendezvous, was blindfolded, and taken to a destination where the Irgun spokesman awaited me. The cloak-and-dagger aspects of the occasion are not important. What impressed me most was the seemingly deep sincerity of this man as he explained that his organization was obliged to resort to terror, bombs, and assassination for the sake of his people. "It is the only way," he said. "We have no other weapons that will move the British and frighten the Arabs. But believe me, it is not out of hatred for them—only out of love for our own people."

AMMAN, 1968

I interviewed Yasir Arafat, the leader of the Fatah commando organization, soon after he had emerged from hiding and became the spokesman for the Palestinian guerrilla movement. He had come to symbolize the Palestinian nationalist movement as it had become since the Six Day War of June, 1967. He was almost a legend, and his men were heroes in the Arab world. After the humiliations suffered by the Arab armies, he and his men had succeeded in establishing themselves as an autonomous, strictly Palestinian force, mainly in Jordan, and had succeeded in provoking their Israeli enemy. Arafat sat at a wooden table in a chilly, bare room. His whereabouts was known only to his most intimate collaborators. "Our ideological theory is very simple," he said. "Our country has been occupied. The majority of our people have been kicked out by Zionism and Imperialism from their homes.

"We waited and waited for the justice of the U.N., for the justice of the world and the governments of the world gathering in the U.N. while our people were suffering in tents and caves. But nothing of this was realized. None of our hopes. But our dispersion was aggravated. We believe that the only way to return to our homes and land is the armed struggle.

"We are not against the Jews," he continued. "On the contrary, we are all Semites and we have been living with each other in peace and fraternity, Moslems, Jews, and Christians, for many centuries.

"We welcome with sincerity all the Jews who would like to live with us in sincerity in an Arab state as citizens having equal rights before the law and constitution.

"It's one of the aims of our movement to liberate the Jews themselves from the domination of Zionism, the Zionism which represents neo-Nazism, which is racial and working for the interests of imperialism and monopoly."

I asked whether he distinguished between the Jews who were in the country before 1948 and those who came later, and his reply indicated that this was a problem that worried him.

"Really, such a question is a little bit complicated," he said. "In principle, we don't make any distinction between kinds of Jews. When we achieve victory we will never throw anybody into the sea! This is what we are sure of. But we will do our best to find a solution for all problems, and for every case—a humane solution."

In July, 1970, I visited the town of Irbid in northwestern Jordan, a few days later Beisan in Israel. The two towns were under bombardment from across the border: Beisan by rockets fired by Arab commandos, and Irbid by the Israeli Army firing its artillery in reprisal.

In Irbid I talked to the mother of a twelve-year-old boy killed as he played in the street outside his home; in Beisan with the mother of a seven-year-old girl killed in a schoolhouse hit by a shell. Between the tears of the Arab and Jewish mothers there was no difference. The Arab mother spoke of her son's hope to become a druggist; the Jewish mother spoke of her daughter's beautiful voice. But there was an ironic difference between the two. The Arab mother's home had before 1948 been Beisan; she was a refugee in Irbid. The Jewish mother was a refugee from Rumania who had settled in Beisan after fleeing a place where most of her family had perished at the hands of the Nazis.

In these few paragraphs I have tried to establish my personal relationship to the tragedy of the struggle in the Holy Land between Jews and Arabs, and my desire to be fair and objective.

2

Israel—The Zionist State

The State of Israel was twenty-five years old in 1973—a child among nations. Israel at twenty-five is a difficult child, the product of a complex past. Her fathers were prisoners in Egypt and had conquered the Promised Land. They were exiles in Babylon, scattered from Jerusalem across the face of the earth, harried through the ghettos of Warsaw and Kiev, Casablanca and Baghdad. Israel's fathers were merchants in Leipzig, bankers in London, professors in Vienna. And six million of her people were killed in the Nazi gas chambers.

Israel was rescued, and given new life in Palestine. At twenty-five, she scarcely remembers her fathers in Europe, Asia, and Africa, and is not sure whether she loves or hates them and what they stood for. She is surer of the meaning of her more distant ancestors—David the fighter, Solomon the builder, the Prophets with their harsh justice and glowing visions.

Certainly, Israel resents advice from her contemporary cousins across the Atlantic. She is, indeed, full of complexes, the most stubborn of which is that she wishes to be rid of all complexes, to be what a normal child should be. That is, perhaps, why she runs so fast and sings so loudly, why she is often wild and rude, given to destructive rages feared by all who know her.

Israel is the product of the dispersion of the Jews and the reaction to it by the Zionist movement. After the destruction of the second Temple, by Titus in A.D. 70, the Jews fled, first to Egypt and all the countries now known as the Middle East, and then across North Africa to Spain. They found their way even to Ethiopia, to India and China. But they became most numerous in central and especially in eastern Europe, Poland, and in Russia. While only a slight remnant remained in Palestine, eastern Europe became the new center of Jewish population and culture, remaining so until Hitler exterminated the main body of eastern Europe's Jews. Thereafter the center of Jewish life shifted to North America and to Israel.

Some scholars challenge the whole Diasporic mythology. They reject the idea of a specific tragic incident at a specific time—the destruction of the Temple—and argue that the dispersion was really a natural process, similar to the Lebanese or Norwegian emigrations to the Americas. Specifically, they contend that the majority of Jews voluntarily left Palestine before the destruction of the Temple to live as Roman citizens in the Roman cities. According to some estimates, one out of ten Roman citizens was a Jew. Of those still in Palestine at the time of the destruction—possibly one third of the total—it is said that a majority remained and did not go into exile. The exile, then, was largely urban, and particularly middle and upper class. Abram Leon, in *The Jewish Question,* * adds that the eastern European Jewish community was largely a product of mass conversion to Judaism of a Baltic tribe, the Khazars, in the early medieval period, which offset massive conversions to Christianity and to Islam by the original Jews of the Roman Empire. In my opinion, it does not matter whether we are dealing with myth or history. The story has played, and continues to play, a vital role in Jewish life. It is certainly true that there is hardly a country in the world to which the Jews did not go, carrying with them always the memory of the kingdom of David and Solomon, of Jerusalem, and of the Temple. Mourning became the characteristic of Jewish worship. When the Jews were in Jerusalem, they went to the western wall of the Haram al Sherif, now the site of

*New York: Pathfinder Press, 1971.

the Mosque al Aksa, the third holiest place in Islam, where the Jewish Temple once stood. As they prayed, the Jews wept for their Temple and for Jerusalem, and the western wall became known as the Wailing Wall. "If I forget thee O Jerusalem," the psalmist declared, "let my right hand forget her cunning; if I do not remember thee, let my tongue cleave to the roof of my mouth." At the end of the Passover feast, with its celebration of release from bondage, the last words of the prayer were always: "Next year in Jerusalem."

The life of Jews everywhere alternated between periods of persecution and of toleration. Without opening an international catalogue of acts of ill treatment, abuse, molestation, oppression, pillage, and murder, one must note that the darkest period for the Jews—prior to the time of Hitler—was that of the Middle Ages, roughly one thousand years, reaching its worst in the Inquisition of 1480. Later, the word "pogrom" became inseparably linked with the word "Jew," and was associated especially with Russia. There were always exceptional periods and exceptional places where Jews rose to great distinction. But most Jews lived in ghettos, sometimes wearing distinctive badges or dress, until the French Revolution in 1789 ushered in the Age of Enlightenment in Europe, more precisely in western Europe. During the late eighteenth century, the nineteenth, and the early twentieth centuries, racial and religious intolerance seemed to be dying out. Jews moved in growing numbers from eastern to western Europe, and to America. Many sought and achieved assimilation into the cultures of their host countries. Even in eastern Europe, the Jews began to live outside the ghettos.

Then Hitler. The Nazis committed the most unimaginable, frightful crime against the Jews the world has ever known.

Zionism is Messianic, based partly on fact, partly on fiction. It is life-sustaining, and it leads men to death. To the true believer it provides the answer to all the problems, fears, and hopes raised by the long history of the Jews.

Zionism was born in the fervent intellectual climate of nineteenth-century Europe. The father of the movement was a young Viennese German, Theodor Herzl, who in 1896 wrote *Der Juden-*

staat, the manifesto of political Zionism. Herzl was not the first to articulate such ideas, but he led the movement out of its verbal stage to one of action. With the confidence of a true believer, he wrote: "The Jewish State is essential to the world; it will therefore be created." The philosophy set forth by Herzl has continued to guide Zionist leaders to this day. It is the bedrock of the State of Israel. This program consists fundamentally of a negative and a positive tenet. First, world Jewry can never find security and fulfillment in any nation-state where they are an ethnic minority. Second, world Jewry must combat assimilation and seek development and fruition of Jewish culture and institutions. The interaction of negative threat and the positive goal resulted in creation of a Jewish state which asserted the right to stand as an equal among the nations of the world.

To realize this goal the movement required a program of action. For the Jews concerned this meant fundamental change—of habits, of philosophy, of character. The image of the passive Jew, given to commerce or scholarship, had to give way to the image of the active Jew, the Jew as tiller of the soil and redeemer of the land. There grew up a cult of manual labor, of the intellectual putting social theory into practice in the land of Palestine.

The Zionist pioneers set aside the ledger and the book, symbols of their past, and zealously took to the land. They lived according to the egalitarian and socialistic beliefs which had been incubated in Europe.

The Jewish influx into Palestine, which by the summer of 1973 had brought 3,100,000 Jews into the State of Israel as it is now constituted, began in the late nineteenth century before and after Theodor Herzl published *Der Judenstaat*.

They came in five waves, generally called the *aliyot*. The first two waves brought eastern Europeans, first from Russia, then from Rumania and Poland, some of them passionately religious orthodox and Hassidic Jews, others atheistic social-activist, political radicals. The latter included the political leadership that rules Israel today. They were escaping from persecution by Gentile society, but many were also in revolt against the strictures of the orthodox society in which they had grown up. Later waves brought streams of Jews from Germany, who formed a second-level elite of technicians and professional people. Still later came the Jews of the Middle East and Africa. Altogether they formed an extraordinary melange of peoples united by the Zionist credo.

The cultural character of the state was European, with Russian Jews dominant in government and German Jews dominant in most technical fields. But numerically the so-called Oriental Jews, those who came from Asian and African, particularly Arab countries, formed a majority of inhabitants by the middle 1950s. Less well educated than the Europeans and often ill adjusted in their new surroundings, the Orientals tended to form a lower stratum of the population. While official policy was to maintain absolute equality among all elements, official policy also spoke of "absorption" of immigrants—absorption of the Orientals by the Europeans. In spite of the "melting pot" effect of the schools and military service, light-skinned European Jews still tend to intermarry among their kind, while dark-skinned Orientals do likewise. The different kinds of Europeans and Orientals tend to form social groupings, at least in the first few generations—Russians with Russians, Germans with Germans, Iraqis with Iraqis, Yemenis with Yemenis, and so on.

Even though conscious efforts are made by well-meaning individuals to bridge the gaps, friction and tension are inevitable. I remember the dark-skinned Indian Jews who in 1951 staged a sit-down strike outside the Jewish Agency in Tel Aviv, demanding to be sent "home" because they had encountered discrimination in Israel. The agency finally provided them with transportation. Three months later most of them were trying to get back to Israel. In 1971 a group of Orientals even formed a "Black Panther" organization.

The possibility that the ethnic composition of the state may be substantially modified by a renewed influx of Russian Jews developed in 1971 and 1972. Quite unexpectedly, 15,000 Russian Jews arrived in 1971, compared with only 1,000 in 1970. Forty-five thousand (out of a total 55,900) came in 1972. If this influx continues at the same rate, half a million Russian Jews would arrive in Israel before the end of the decade.

ISRAEL—ECONOMY

The most characteristic feature in the life of these immigrants to Palestine was the kibbutz. The first kibbutz, Degania, was started in 1910 on the banks of the Sea of Galilee. Today, there are more than 200 kibbutzim, varying in size from 120 to 350 families, and accounting for 112,000 Israeli citizens. The kibbutz has always been a small quantitative aspect of the Israeli state—only 3.8 percent of all Israelis live on kibbutzim now, and the figure has never exceeded 10 percent. But it is not the quantitative but the moral effect of the kibbutz on Israeli society that matters.

The kibbutz is often called the purest form of communism now in existence. While there are many variations, extreme forms of communal living have been softened by concessions to demands for some private life. In general the kibbutzim follow the principle of "from each according to his ability, to each according to his need." Those responsible for running the kibbutz are democratically elected and enjoy no special privileges. Decisions are made by all members. There are no class distinctions. Property is held in common, except for the most personal possessions. While children spend part of each day with their families, most of their upbringing takes place collectively, in schools, nurseries, and dormitories.

The character of the kibbutz has been shaped by economic and military necessity as much as by the political philosophy of the founding pioneers. The kibbutz had to be an institution providing basically for the reclamation of the land and the retraining of Jewish labor, for whom manual work was often a new experience. The communal framework helped them to reinforce one another, to stimulate each other's sense of accomplishment and affinity for the land. It enabled them to test political and social theories against reality. It facilitated the absorption of new labor among the immigrants.

The kibbutz also served a paramilitary function. It was an integrated, mobilized outpost far from the Jewish centers of population and laying claim to and defending the land. Recently, during the 1967 War, the kibbutz-man, always prepared to do more than his share in the army, constituted one quarter of all casualties.

The ideas of voluntarism, social idealism, and egalitarianism, so characteristic of the kibbutz, continue to play a profound role in Israeli life. Two hundred-odd kibbutzim are divided into three major federations, each affiliated with a labor party in the legislature.

For politicians it is important to have the credentials of a kibbutz background. In this realm, Ben-Gurion was pre-eminent. Whenever he tired of the intramural wrangling so much a part of Israeli political life, he would rejuvenate himself in his beloved desert kibbutz, Sde Boker, in the central Negev.

The moral stature of the kibbutzim has, however, been somewhat undermined by the development of kibbutz industries. Most of the laborers in these factories are Oriental Jews from the desolate, new-immigrant townships who do not become members of the kibbutz. Arabs from occupied territories are also employed. Kibbutzniks profit collectively from the factories, and are tending to become a new social-economic phenomenon—a rural collective gentry.

Another form of communal farming is the moshav, or smallholders cooperative, in which 136,000 Israelis take part. Here the family unit is much stronger. The children live with their parents, the concept of private property is accepted, and individual initiative is stressed. Together, the kibbutz and the moshav are the spiritual backbone of the Israeli state. Today they face perhaps their greatest danger in changing Israeli attitudes. The lure of the city and the influx of foreign capital have weakened the attraction of this life style and form of economic organization. Indeed, before the 1967 War Israeli writers showed profound concern over the spiritual vitality of the state, as exemplified in the decline of the kibbutz. The war muted this debate, but only temporarily.

Palestine, according to the Bible, is the land "flowing with milk and honey, whose stones are iron and out of whose hills you can dig copper" (Deuteronomy 8:9). At the western edge of the Fertile Crescent, it has in the past supported dense populations by intense exploitation of these resources.

Geographically Israel can be divided into four principal areas.

The coastal plain varies in distance from three to twenty miles, and includes most of Israel's population. Running parallel to the coastal plain is hilly country, encompassing the Hills of Galilee, Judea, and Samaria. Further inland lies the Jordan Valley. To the south is the Negev Desert, comprising about one-half of Israel's prewar land area.

During the period of Ottoman rule, the productivity of the land was eroded by misuse and neglect. The first task of the new State of Israel was to restore those areas of land which were highly productive in the past, and to develop marginal areas into productive ones as well. Herein the new state succeeded. By the first decade of her existence, the rural population trebled, the number of rural villages doubled, areas under cultivation almost trebled, and the area of irrigated land quadrupled. The reclamation of the malaria-infected Huleh swamps in the northeast corner of the country symbolized the revitalization of the land.

The country has become almost self-sustaining in the production of eggs, vegetables, fruit, dairy products, meat and fish. Citrus fruit has become the largest single export item. Only for cereals, grain fodder, oils, and fats does the state depend mainly on imports.

In spite of the emphasis on return to the land, the rapid growth of population made industrial development essential. Industry now employs 25 percent of all workers and produces 46 percent of all exports. For six years since the 1967 War Israel experienced a continuous boom led by defense-oriented industries.

The diamond-processing industry takes pride of place. Israel handles 30 percent of the world's trade in polished diamonds. Exploitation of minerals is rising—slightly more than a million tons of potash from the Dead Sea and a million tons of phosphate rock from Oron and Maktesh are produced annually. Intensive oil exploration has brought in some modest wells, and prospects for larger finds offshore seem good—quite apart from the output of the wells in occupied Sinai. The refineries at Haifa, which once processed oil from the now defunct pipeline from Kirkuk, are fully employed with oil imported from Iran through the Gulf of Aqaba and pipelines laid from Elat to the Mediterranean coast.

With water resources almost fully exploited from the headwaters of the Jordan to the Negev by the so-called all-Israel water carrier, Israel finds her cultivable land only 40 percent exploited. It looks forward in this decade to the construction of large desalination plants jointly with the United States, with possible use of nuclear power. In the summer of 1973 Israel and AID were negotiating a joint research project under which each country would put up 16 to 20 million dollars for research desalination plants at San Diego, California, and Waterport, Texas, and at the Weizmann Institute in Israel.

Israel's economic effort has been organized and directed, especially before statehood, by a unique institution known as the Histadrut, meaning General Federation of Labor, which is much more than a trade union. The Histadrut began in 1920, its primary concern being the creation of jobs for Jewish labor. It put pressure on Jewish entrepreneurs to hire Jewish labor, and subsidized Jewish labor when it had to compete with Arab wage rates. When private enterprises failed, Histadrut took over rather than allow Jews to become idle and Jewish productive resources to be wasted. It went into business on its own when necessary. Today it operates banks, the largest agricultural producers cooperative, known as T'nuva, and the largest building construction firm, called Solel Boneh, with an international clientele extending from Turkey to Central Africa. It administers welfare services, including health insurance, and it publishes an influential newspaper, *Davar*.

Encompassing 80 percent of the country's workers, not including the Arabs in territories captured in 1967, the organization showed signs of becoming something of a state within the state until 1956, when MAPAI, the country's largest socialist party, intervened. It reorganized the Histadrut under a governing board composed of Israeli labor parties.

All this has been achieved not only through Zionist drive and idealism but also as a result of massive investment. Since the founding of the state more than 10 billion dollars in capital has been imported, about 1.5 billion raised by the United Jewish Appeal (UJA) in the United States, and 1.5 billion by the Bond Drive, again mainly in the United States. Restitution and Reparation payments by West Germany and United States Government grants were among other major sources of capital.

Imports still far exceed exports. In 1972, for example, imports amounted to $3,350,000 and exports, including "invisibles," to $2,275,000, leaving a balance of payments' gap of more than a million dollars. Looking back over a decade, it is possible to discern some progress in the growth of exports as a percentage of imports. But balance of payments seems to recede like a mirage. The more exports grow the more demand there is for imports.

Such progress notwithstanding, no one could say that the Jewish state has solved its central economic problem, which consists essentially of finding a way to become self-supporting. As long as the state has to stand off the military might of a large part of the Arab world, this is out of the question.

The military budget for the fiscal year 1971–1972 (April 1 to March 31) was 1.5 billion dollars, four times as much as before the 1967 War. It constituted 40 percent of the national budget and 24 percent of the gross national product. Including repayment of debts incurred for military purposes, the percentage of the national budget devoted to military spending rose to 55 percent. In fiscal year 1974 the military budget is expected to be slightly higher, but the percentage of the gross national product is expected to decline.

It was this burden more than anything else that made Israelis the most highly taxed citizens in the world in 1970, when they paid 41.2 percent of their country's gross national product to the Government in taxes and loans or bonds deducted from paychecks. Comparable figures were 39 percent for Sweden, 32.8 percent for Britain, and 27 percent for the United States. Here the outlook is for modest relief.

Israel's gross national product has been growing at an annual rate averaging 9 percent since 1950. For 1969 it was 4.7 billion dollars, for 1971 5.5 billion dollars. Per capita gross national product rose to 2,200 dollars in 1972.

The progress in development of the civil economy indicates that if her military burden abated Israel could eventually achieve the goal of becoming self-supporting. Compensating for lack of raw materials by developing such labor-intensive industries as diamond polishing and the manufacture of petroleum derivatives, including fertilizers and plastics, Israel can acquire some of the economic advantages of Switzerland.

Friends of Israel had ample opportunity to prove themselves during the 1973 war. The United Jewish Appeal collected 450 million dollars in pledges in six weeks after October 6 and set itself an unprecedented 18 month goal of 1,250 million dollars. Israel Bonds sold 210 million dollars in October alone and planned in 1974 to assume responsibility for the entire Israeli development budget of 642 million dollars. Between them UJA and Israel Bonds left all past fund raising records far behind.

Meanwhile, several thousand volunteers from all over the world, including more than a thousand from the United States, were reported at work in Israel, particularly in the kibbutzim. Money and volunteers were desperately needed to strengthen the Israeli economy, which had been stretched to the limit by the 1973 war. With about 250,000 men under arms the Israelis found it hard to keep essential services, industries, and agriculture moving. A special appeal went out, for instance, for volunteers to help in the orchards where unharvested fruit was rotting. The mail piled up because there were not enough men to distribute letters. Here one could discern a great strength and a weakness of Israel—an ability to mobilize fast and fully, but at the same time an inability to maintain that effort for more than a short time.

According to Israeli government figures the war cost Israel six billion dollars. Israeli officials attribute half of that sum to direct and indirect costs of the war itself, including weapons, ammunition and transport. Of the rest it attributes one billion to lost production; one billion to the cost of the first 30 days of full mobilization, and one billion to the cost during the war of civilian services, widows, orphans, the families of drafted men, and damage to civilian premises.

ISRAEL—POLITICS

Israeli political institutions, like those in the economic sphere, bear the imprint of the Mandate period. In the Knesset, the 120-man parliament, we can see Israeli democracy at work, with all its virtues and limitations. Members are elected by party lists, from the whole country as a unit. That is, there is no personal or local representation as we know it in Israel—members are elected according to the percentage of the national vote their party receives, and how high they stand on their party's list. Any party that can muster the minimum number of votes will elect at least one representative. As a result, political parties multiply, and it is difficult for any one party or even one group of parties to muster a majority of the votes.

Another basic characteristic of Israeli politics is its preoccupation with ideology. This is due in part to its origins in the ideological hotbeds of eastern Europe, the birthplace of most second and third aliya political leaders. Ideological disputes normally fall into two categories: the nature of the economic system (socialist or free enterprise) and the role of religion in the state (secular versus theocratic extremes). Against this background of ideological division, the Arab military threat acts as a unifier. The interaction produces a volatile, dynamic political life—parties in constant motion, splitting and realigning. Since the 1967 War and its unresolved denouement, which briefly united the fractious political clamor, the political divisions have grown more profound than ever.

In this freewheeling atmosphere, a range of parties flourishes that has no parallel in the Arab world except in neighboring Lebanon. Any 750 Israeli voters can submit a list of their political party if they deposit 5,000 Israeli pounds. If they manage to receive only 1 percent of the vote, they gain representation in the Knesset and a return of their deposit.

Israeli political parties may be divided into three main groupings, the most important of which are the labor parties, MAPAI, MAPAM, RAFI, and Ahdut Avodah, which have merged into the Israeli Labor Party since the 1967 War. Of these, MAPAI is clearly the kingpin, the center of political power from Mandate days to the present. MAPAI has always been the largest individual party, the heart of any government coalition. From its ranks have come every prime minister, minister of defense, and foreign minister. The current Defense Minister, Moshe Dayan, was a member of MAPAI until he switched to RAFI with the split from MAPAI in 1965. It is the founder of and dominant party in the Histadrut. Its leaders were the major figures in the War of Independence, and its once titular head, David Ben-Gurion, its guiding source.

David Ben-Gurion was born and grew up in Plonsk, a Polish

town of 12,000 people along the railroad linking Warsaw with the Baltic coast. Within the tightly knit Jewish community, his father, a lawyer, was a political activist and a member of Hoveve Zion (Lovers of Zion). The spirit and drive of the father and the mystique of Theodor Herzl rubbed off on the six children, but particularly on David. While still in his teens, he formed in Plonsk the Society of Ezra, dedicated to spreading the Zionist philosophy and the Hebrew language. He moved to Warsaw around 1902, and was soon in trouble with the Czarist secret police.

In 1906, at the age of twenty, Ben-Gurion left Poland for good on an old Russian cargo boat bound for Jaffa. His early years in Palestine were hard. He suffered from malaria, and made a meager living as a farm laborer. Typically, Ben-Gurion immersed himself in local issues, the most pressing of which was the organization of Jewish labor and Jewish defense on the small, scattered settlements that were beginning to spring up in Palestine. In 1910 Ben-Gurion dropped his family name, Green, and assumed the one by which he is known today. As for countless others, among them Golda Myerson, Moshe Shertock, and Aubrey Eban, the change of name symbolized stripping off past identity and becoming a new person in the new state.

In the years before World War I, Ben-Gurion and other Zionist leaders were looking for Great Power support for the movement. At this time the fading Ottoman Empire seemed the most likely candidate. So, in 1912 Ben-Gurion traveled to Constantinople and prepared to take up a career in law and politics. He worked with the Young Turks, who promised decentralization of the far-flung empire, and through whom he hoped to bring about the creation of a Jewish state. He learned Turkish, adding this language to the Russian, Hebrew, Yiddish, and Arabic he already knew. He would learn English later.

Two years after his arrival, Ben-Gurion left Constantinople, his dreams for Ottoman support crushed by nationalistic Young Turk policies. He returned to Palestine, but only briefly. Along with other "political agitators" he was deported by the Ottoman authorities.

Arriving in the United States in 1915, Ben-Gurion lectured and wrote in an attempt to stimulate immigration to Zion and use of the Hebrew language. Three years later, in 1918, convinced that Great Britain was the potential patron of the Zionist movement, he joined the British Army's Jewish Battalion, and rose to the rank of corporal in Egypt before he was transferred to Palestine.

From this time on, Ben-Gurion's story is one of constant political and labor organizing in the faction-riddled Jewish community. In 1920 he became general secretary of the Histadrut, and when MAPAI was formed in 1927 he became a power in its highest councils. The head of the shadow cabinet before the evacuation of British troops in 1948, it was unthinkable that he should not lead the new state after independence.

Ben-Gurion's early experiences mirror those of other nationalist leaders of the period, whether Arab, Armenian, or Czech. These men wandered about the great capitals of the world seeking benefactors. They were the shadow figures of the glittering peace conferences in Europe. They were men of multiple talents: part journalist, part soldier, part political organizer and activist. Their job was to convince the outside world to support their nationalist cause (and in Ben-Gurion's case, to support immigration) while persuading their own nationals to organize and endure the hardships. The Histadrut, MAPAI, and the State of Israel itself as they exist today testify to Ben-Gurion's success.

The differences between MAPAI and the other labor parties is more a matter of personalities than ideology. When Ben-Gurion left MAPAI in anger over a long-standing domestic political quarrel, he formed his own party, RAFI, and took along such protégés as Moshe Dayan.

Other labor parties differ from MAPAI in that they advocate a more Marxist brand of socialism; MAPAM and, to a lesser extent, Ahdut Avodah fall into this category. Ahdut Avodah, whose origin can be traced back to the elite Palmach force of Yigal Allon, merged with MAPAI in 1965.

A far more important series of mergers occurred after the 1967 War. In January, 1968, Ahdut Avodah and RAFI formally merged with MAPAI to form the Israeli Labor Party. One year later, MAPAM became the fourth member of the partnership, thus providing Israeli political life with a true majority party for the first time in its history.

The trend toward centralization can also be seen in the parties of the political right, the Progressives, General Zionists, and Herut. These parties have traditionally been characterized by their emphasis on free enterprise in the domestic arena, and their militancy toward the Arabs in matters of foreign policy. In 1961 the Progressive and General Zionist parties merged to form the Liberal Party, which in turn merged with Herut in 1965. This new grouping, GAHAL, is the second largest party in the state. Like most Israeli political chieftains, its leader, Menacheim Begin, was a strong personality in the War of Independence. Begin was the leader of the Irgun, the radical Jewish paramilitary organization. GAHAL's platform still reflects many of these old ideas, such as the call for a "greater Israel" on both banks of the Jordan River, including all of the State of Jordan.

A third bloc in Israeli politics is that of the religious parties, consisting of Mizrachi, Hapoel Hamizrachi, Agudat Yisrael, Poelei Agudat Yisrael—all variously merged or split over the years. Together, they consistently poll about 15 percent of the vote. Two of them, the Mizrachi parties (formally merged into the National Religion Party in 1955) have been represented in every Government coalition, where they have traded off their votes on other issues while demanding adherence to their policies on key issues in the secular/theocratic debate.

There are at present two communist parties, one predominantly Jewish and the other predominantly Arab. They are the only legal communist parties in the Middle East. As in the Arab countries, these communist parties are less important than the leftist groups around which a "peace movement" has formed.

The "peace movement" in Israel, with all its diverse elements, shares certain fundamental propositions. Although they have been severely castigated by their Zionist political colleagues, these groups support the Zionist concept of a Jewish refuge with its own national identity. While they differ among themselves as to the specifics of a settlement with the Arabs, they object to what they call the Israeli Government's inflexibility on the Arab-Israeli dispute. All basically agree on the need to withdraw from the occupied territories, to recognize the Palestinians as an ethnic and national entity, to create a binational state or a federated Arab and Jewish state.

The Ihud Association is an older group, founded by Dr. Judah Magnes, the late president of the Hebrew University, and dedicated in the 1940s to Jewish-Arab coexistence in a binational community of equals. Ihud still speaks through its journal, *Ner*.

New Outlook is another Israeli periodical dedicated to Arab-Jewish rapprochement. Its editorial council includes Israeli and Arab intellectuals, most notably Simha Flapan and Nissin Rejwan.

Smaller, less moderate groups have also made their mark in Israel's internal debate. They have unfamiliar names, such as Siah and Matzpeh, and small followings. Matzpeh is said to have met in Europe with representatives of the Popular Democratic Front for the Liberation of Palestine to discuss ways of solving the Palestinian problems—a bold step for any Israeli or Arab group. The thinking behind such meetings is that the only elements among Jews and Arabs who can ever hope to agree are those who share a common faith in Marxism.

Israeli public opinion is particularly sensitive to criticism from worldwide Jewish organizations. Thus, when the fifteenth Congress of the World Union of Jewish Students was held in Jerusalem in July, 1970, and called for a less dogmatic approach to the creation of a Palestinian entity, the Israeli press and public were stunned and angered. Concern has been aroused in a more general way by the anti-Israeli position now assumed by many factions within the "New Left" in the West. Leftist and liberal groups have for so many years almost automatically supported Israel that it comes as a grievous shock to Israelis to discover the left drifting away and themselves more and more identified with the right.

The most popular group within the "dovish" wing of Israeli politics is the Ha'olum Hazeh (This World) Movement, or the New Force, led by Uri Avneri. The movement derives its name from the moribund weekly taken over by Avneri in 1950 and transformed into a popular, rather sensational journal. Avneri's party is active on local issues, but is known primarily for its stand on the Arab-

Israeli conflict. In his book, *Israel Without Zionists,* * Avneri calls for a federated Palestine consisting of Israel and the Republic of Palestine, with Jerusalem as its capital. The Republic of Palestine envisioned under this scheme would include Gaza and the West Bank. Eventually the proposed federated Palestine would take its place in a Semitic Union of all Middle Eastern states.

The New Force is the kingpin among Israeli doves because it has two far-reaching forums from which to gain popular recognition. The first is its widely distributed weekly, and the second is the Knesset itself. Except for the communist members of Rakah and Maki, Ha'olum Hazeh is the only "dovish" movement represented. In the 1965 elections, Avneri's list polled 1.2 percent of the national vote, thereby placing him in the Knesset. In the 1969 election, the New Force garnered 1.23 percent of the vote, enough to seat a second deputy in the Knesset.

The psychology of Israeli politics after the fourth Arab-Israeli war was somewhat different from what it had been after the 1967 war. In the 1967 war many an Israeli felt qualms about overrunning Arab territory. The groups which for a generation had been expressing the Jewish conscience became a political factor in the ensuing years. But in 1973 almost all Israelis felt that their country, even though its armies were standing on occupied lands, had been the victim of a heinous attack. Although there were plenty of thoughtful Israelis who felt that the standoff result of the fighting in Sinai offered a marvelous opportunity to come to terms with the Arabs, the voices of the "peaceniks" were muted during the campaign for the December 31 elections.

Instead, Israelis debated the question, insistently raised by General Ariel Sharon, whether the country's intelligence agencies and the government itself were at fault for not anticipating the Arab attack. General Sharon, heading a new party, maintained that failure to launch a preemptive attack and later tactical errors and delays committed by General Moshe Dayan, the Minister of Defense, and the general staff cost the Israelis both lives and tactical advantage.

*New York: The Macmillan Company, 1968.

ISRAEL—CULTURE

All that this chapter has dealt with—history, ideology, economics, politics—are elements in the background of Israeli culture. In the earliest chapters of Jewish history, what distinguished the Jews from their neighbors was their idea of monotheism. From the beginning religion and culture set them apart, and in the years of dispersion held them together as a people.

In the Israel of today what distinguishes these people from their neighbors is still, more than anything else, a matter of the spirit. The Bible remains the main cultural focus—Israeli schools devote 20 to 30 percent of their time to its study—but its inspiration is by no means exclusive. Indeed, the immigrants from eastern Europe who dominate Israeli society are more secular intellectuals than religious leaders. Their leadership is more nationalist than religious, even though the most agnostic among them show at least a poetic appreciation of the Bible. Ben-Gurion, who never enters a synagogue, nonetheless insists that the Bible is the best guide to Israeli politics and even to economic planning.

At every hand in the Israel of today are men of science, of letters, artists and musicians. There are more Ph.D.s and doctors of medicine per capita in Tel Aviv than in any other city in the world. It sometimes seems that bookstores are as numerous in Tel Aviv as drugstores in New York or pubs in London. There are one thousand libraries with eight million books in Israel. Two thousand titles are published annually, one of the highest rates per capita in the world. Theaters and concerts and the so-called political cabaret, where Israelis make fun of politicians, are perpetually thronged. Subscriptions to the Philharmonic are passed down in families from generation to generation.

The most important institution of learning is the Hebrew University in Jerusalem, with an enrollment of 40,000 students. Another 40,000 attend Tel Aviv University and Bar Ilan University in Tel Aviv and the Technion in Haifa and three smaller institutions. Between them they have links with the most distinguished scholars, scientists, technicians, and artists in the world.

To live in Jerusalem or Tel Aviv is to partake of an intellectual and cultural feast. Each year the greatest names in every sphere of the arts come to this relatively small community.

The parade of great names in recent years has included persons of the stature of Leonard Bernstein, Jascha Heifetz, Yehudi Menuhin, Marian Anderson, David Oistrakh, and Leonid Kogan.

Young Israel, dwarfed by the fantastic panorama of twenty centuries of history, overshadowed by the giants of the Diaspora of today, stands diffidently before the task of expressing herself. Jews have absorbed from their host lands every characteristic and every level of civilization—the songs and dances of Turkey and Afghanistan, the chamber music and symphonies of western Europe, the spiritualism of India and the technical discipline of the most sophisticated American laboratories. Young Israel's problem is to find common denominators in this bewildering complexity, to choose among the conflicting values of the past and the present, to fashion a new Jewish culture and national character.

One can see the first glimmerings of Israel's efforts to solve this problem. Perhaps it is significant, after the long tradition of mourning, to find among the "Sabras," those born in Israel, a certain lightheartedness and humor, a willingness to talk about "Jewish questions" without self-consciousness. The Sabra feels himself very much an Israeli, somehow different from being simply Jewish.

In literature there are such men as Moshe Shamir, who from the vantage point of being an Israeli has tried to write a historical novel that links the present not to the Diaspora but to the ancient past of the Kings of Israel. Others, such as Yariv ben Aharon, relate the values of pioneering to a more recent past in Europe. Chaim Guri reconstructs the experiences of concentration camp survivors and relates them to the problems of the present. And Mordechai Tabib interprets the mind of Yemeni and other Oriental Jews in their new relationship with Israel's Europeanized culture. The musician Paul ben Haims links Sephardi and Yemeni styles to modern forms.

And there are many others in every art form who have tackled the problems of melding past and present cultural resources. Their efforts were illustrated by the East-West Conference sponsored by International Music Councils in 1963 and which surveyed the cavalcade of Jewish music: the eight-stringed lyre of the psalmists, the songs of the Diaspora and the countries of eastern and western Europe, and the Orient, the compositions of Mendelssohn and Schoenberg.

Among the most recent writers and artists, the salient characteristic is doubt. Israeli intellectuals are questioning all that has been handed down to them, including the values of the Zionist movement itself. The questioning had begun before the 1967 War and was reflected in a weakening of youth movements and of that central pillar of Zionism, the kibbutz. After the revivifying effort of the Six Day War, the questioning has been redoubled. Added to the basic doubts about Zionist values are searching questions about Israel's relationship to the defeated Arabs and what to do with the occupied territories.

ISRAEL'S SUPRANATIONAL TIES

The state the Zionist pioneers built was unique among nations. It was a national state based on religion, with supranational ties. Israel is a state based on a worldwide movement. The state is the expression of the Zionist movement. There is a constant interplay between the state and the Jewish people who live outside it. Israel acts as though responsible for Jews everywhere, while world Jewry, or an important segment of it, acts as though it were responsible for the State of Israel.

The organizational arms that reach across national boundaries are the World Zionist Organization (WZO) and the Jewish Agency. Founded in 1897, the WZO has traditionally been charged with fostering immigration, settlement, and mobilization of financial and political support for the Jewish community in Palestine.

The WZO saw the need for a broadly based, all-inclusive Jewish organization to oversee and finance the Jewish nationalist movement in Palestine. To serve this purpose, it adopted the Jewish Agency, which had been legally and publicly recognized by the Mandate Power as the representative of the Palestinian Jewish community. The Fourteenth Zionist Congress, held in 1925, passed a resolution for the enlargement of the Jewish Agency to include non-Zionist Jews who might oppose the creation of a Jewish state but who nevertheless wished to help in the reconstruction of the Palestinian Jewish community. One half of the the members of the Jewish Agency were to come from the World Zionist Organization, and one half from Jewish communities around the world. Actually, the WZO maintained strict control of the Jewish Agency at all times.

Creation of the State of Israel did not lead to dismantlement of either organization. Passage of the Law of Return (1950) by the Israeli Parliament, which guarantees immediate citizenship to any Jew who decides to immigrate, provided the WZO with new tasks to go along with those carried over from prestatehood days.

For Israel the WZO and its executive arm, the Jewish Agency, work as an instrument of state and an arm of diplomacy. The relationship between the two is defined by the Israeli Status Law of November, 1952. The WZO is officially charged with overseeing the immigration, rehabilitation, and resettlement of Jewish immigrants. Since statehood, the WZO has undertaken to combat assimilation in the Diaspora by promoting Jewish education and culture. Even more important, the WZO continues to support Israel by providing financial support and exerting tremendous pressure on Western governments as to foreign policy issues.

The State of Israel is the product of a utopian dream and the workings of practical international politics. The ideology of Zionism was visionary, humanitarian, noble. But in the process of realization, the dream has been confronted with harsh reality. The embodiment of that dream—the State of Israel—is far different from the vision.

The vision of the state is articulated in its Declaration of Independence, "The State of Israel will be based on the principles of liberty, justice, and peace . . . (it) will uphold the social and political equality of all its citizens without distinction of religion, race, or sex. . . ." The transformation from dream to reality is intimately tied to her relationship with the Palestinian Arabs, those who are refugees, and those who have remained in their homes under Israeli rule.

The dream of the Zionist movement was to establish an egalitarian, socialist state which would be the heartland of Jewish culture and the refuge of world Jewry. Zionist leaders, past and present, have had to weigh the absolute necessity of establishing and protecting a Jewish state in Palestine against cold, hard population statistics. In 1948 the land granted to Israel under the United Nations proposal was neither large nor homogeneous enough to be either a refuge or a heartland. Nearly 50 percent of the proposed inhabitants were Arabs. As of April, 1973, official Israeli statistics showed 500,000 non-Jews, mostly Arab Moslems, Christians, and Druze, living in the pre-1967 area. Another million Arabs, including 640,000 on the West Bank and 310,000 in the Gaza Strip, inhabited the occupied territories.

Since the founding of the State of Israel, the Zionist leadership has been faced with irreconcilable conflict between maintenance of security and minority (Arab) rights. In order to survive, the state had to choose, or its leaders thought they had to choose, security. In the process the egalitarian and humanistic aspects of Zionism have been compromised.

In 1948 it was obviously in the interests of the Israeli leadership to convince Palestinian Arabs of the relative merits of living elsewhere. In the interests of the Jewish State, principle had to conform to practical needs. After the fighting subsided, only 150,000 Arabs —18 percent of the new state's inhabitants—remained under Israeli jurisdiction. They were leaderless, disorganized, and confused. Ironically enough, Israelis governed their Arab subjects by the same regulations which Great Britain, as the Mandatory Power, used to control Jewish "terrorists" before the establishment of the state. The Defense Emergency Regulations of 1945 divided the country into three military governorates ruled by military governors charged with maintenance of "public security." The governors could limit individual movement, impose restrictions, issue deportation orders, take over land "in the interest of public safety," declare "closed areas" from which civilians without special permits were barred, and try individuals in special military courts. Trials were conducted in closed session, and the verdicts handed down could be reviewed only by the Israeli Supreme Court sitting as the High Court of Justice. Israeli Arabs found military rule most repressive in matters of freedom of movement and land policy.

Arab citizens had to obtain passes to visit different areas, and were required to take specific routes for specific lengths of time. Especially onerous was the military authority's practice of declaring "closed areas." At the time of the second round of warfare, "closed areas" which Arabs could visit only with passes, or not at all, totaled one-half million acres.

Most Israelis recognized that the system of military rule was a danger to the democratic foundation of the state. In 1951 the Knesset officially recognized it as such by a vote of 53 to 1, with forty abstentions. But lack of a better alternative, and bureaucratic inertia, resulted in the system's remaining in effect. In that year, military rule was pared down to cover 89 percent of the Arab inhabitants. The scope of military rule was gradually trimmed until it was terminated altogether in 1966. With the June War, it was reimposed.

At first, after the 1948 War, the Arab community fared no better in economic matters than in security matters. Assets in Israeli banks belonging to Arab refugees were frozen. Arabs were barred from the Histadrut and all its ancillaries. They were not allowed to market their produce. As for military rule, however, time brought an easing of restraints upon Israeli Arabs. In 1953 the Histadrut accepted Arab participation on a limited basis in the sick fund and mutual aid organizations. Israeli Arabs gained full membership in the Histadrut in 1957; and two years later the government acted to equalize pay rates between Arabs and Jews by nationalizing the labor exchanges.

There can be no doubt that gradually the Arabs in Israel have benefited under Israeli rule in socioeconomic fields. Specifically, this has meant better roads, better sanitary facilities, better pay. Not least in importance has been Arab inclusion in the Compulsory Education Law, requiring nine years of free schooling.

Arabs have benefited less in the sphere of Israeli politics. To be sure, Arabs are represented in the Knesset. Their number—around seven—has not varied much, except after the first election in 1949, when only three Arab representatives were elected. The Arab members of Knesset (MKS) come from lists affiliated with the

Israeli labor parties (mostly MAPAI) and from the two Israeli Communist parties. These deputies are wealthy notables who rationalize their association with Zionist institutions by seeking material and social gains for their constituents. Deputies from the Israeli Communist Party (MAQI before the split of 1965) have the psychological advantage of being free from organizational ties with the Zionists. The Arab splinter of MAQI, called RAQAH, the only party in Israel with an Arab majority, is palatable to Israeli officials for a number of reasons. It provides an outlet for Arab political energy which will never pose a threat to Israeli security because of its limited appeal and non-nationalistic program. Furthermore, a semblance of Arab participation in the political sphere reinforces the democratic, multiparty structure of the state. Communist parties are banned almost everywhere in the Arab world.

Every attempt to form a truly nationalist Arab party has been smothered by the Israeli Government because it would pose a legitimate threat to the state, and by the Communist Party because it would undermine the basis of the communists' support. According to the chief of the MAPAI Department of Arab Affairs, as quoted by Jacob M. Landau in *The Arabs in Israel** just before the June War:

> There is a great danger in the very existence of an Arab party not allied with any Jewish party. Experience in the Middle East shows that extremist elements always get the upper hand within a nationalist party; then they remove the moderates by labeling them 'traitors' . . . A nationalist party which does not identify with the State is liable to bring disaster upon the Arab population in Israel. . . .

If the Arabs found themselves treated in some respects like second- or third-class citizens, it was because Israel is first and foremost a Jewish state. Other religious minorities can be a part of that state, but none can be allowed to cloud this primordial proposition. The proposition is buttressed by two laws, the Law of Re-

*New York: Oxford University Press, 1969.

turn (1950) and the Nationality Law (1952). The conflict between the humanistic doctrine of Zionism and its shortcomings in practice stems from these laws.

The Law of Return fulfills the destiny and the purpose of the State of Israel. It declares that any Jew is a citizen of the state, and may avail himself of that right by entering. The Nationality Law states how one may qualify for Israeli citizenship: either by return, residence, birth, or naturalization. Any Jew gains citizenship by returning. Arab residents of Palestine could become citizens of the new state if they could prove their residence in Palestine before Israeli statehood, either through a Palestinian passport or a Palestinian identity card, and if they were registered by Israeli authorities as of March 1, 1952. Anyone born to an Israeli father or mother would become an Israeli citizen at birth. Anyone else would have to gain citizenship status through naturalization. This entailed living in Israel three out of five years prior to the citizenship request, being settled or intending to do so, having some knowledge of Hebrew, and renouncing prior nationality. First- and second-class citizenship are thus defined in the most fundamental laws of the State of Israel.

Nonetheless, it can be said that until the 1967 War overthrew everything, Israel was making progress toward reconciling the contradictions between her security, her laws, and her highest ideals. But the June, 1967 War created new contradictions, not only between Israel and her Arab inhabitants but also between Israel and the larger community of 40 million Arab neighbors and between Israel's ideals and practices. Israel gained territory which she deemed necessary for her security but at the same time brought a million Arabs into her sphere.

In so doing, Israel may have jeopardized the goal of cultural uniqueness and the humanitarian and democratic quality of Zionism. The old image of Israel has been replaced by the image of a militant state, a new Sparta, perhaps, which unquestionably has the power to realize the worst fears of her neighbors.

As in 1948, Israel faces a "problem of population statistics." The Israelis must either abandon the occupied territories or persuade enough Arabs under their jurisdiction to live elsewhere. On October 27, 1967, C. Hodgkins, the Foreign Editor of *The Times* of London, in a remarkable article written after visiting the occupied territories, reported this familiar cycle:

> (Palestinian Arabs) fear that the occupation is only the preliminary to annexation.
>
> I must confess that when going around on the West Bank I found it difficult to avoid the conclusion that this is Israel's aim. Israelis see the Jordan River as historically and strategically a natural frontier. . . .
>
> The only inconvenience is the presence of a lot of Arabs. . . . As it would be much simpler if these were not there, every effort is being made to persuade them to go. The most important ones to be got rid of are those with education and authority. . . .
>
> There is no need to evacuate the whole million: trimmed to half or even three-quarters of its size, and judiciously split up by new roads, garrisons and settlements, the Arab population would be of little trouble.

Although Egypt and Syria did relatively well in the war of 1973 it remains true that no combination of Arab might now conceivable could defeat Israel in a conventional war. Hardened border defenses and a combination of improved economic conditions and harsher security precautions for Arabs living under Israeli jurisdiction will make guerrilla attacks less of a problem.

Her own preponderance of strength and impenetrability will in the end promote a situation in which extreme leftist Arabs led, if not by today's guerrillas, then by their successors, take over the Arab governments and confront Israel. The Israeli "hard line" and the long-term movement to the left which I anticipate in the Arab world feed on one another in the familiar vicious circle of violence we have witnessed so often in the Middle East.

3

Israel's Neighbors and the Rise of Arab Nationalism

In the next few chapters I shall draw a contemporary picture of the Arab countries with which Israel must contend for the next generation—if the nations last that long—whether a political settlement is achieved or not. I shall examine Egypt, Syria, and Iraq, and the Arabian Peninsula—Saudi Arabia, the two Yemens, the Gulf states, and Oman.

Here, to begin, is a breakdown, based on State Department data, of basic information about these and other countries of the Middle East:

These countries share the memory of Arab greatness, the period between the seventh and tenth centuries when Arab armies overran territories from Spain to Persia, and when the Ommayad and Abbasid dynasties ruled in Damascus and Baghdad and developed a high order of political life and culture.

While most of these countries are Arab and Moslem, there are exceptions. The Egyptians are predominantly Hamitic descendants of the ancient Egyptians, and include more than one million Coptic Christians who, according to their tradition, were converted by St. Mark, to whom a church has recently been dedicated in Cairo. Their name is derived from Coptos, a city in upper Egypt now called Kuft.

Also exceptional are the Lebanese, who trace their origins back to the Phoenicians. Somewhat less than half the Lebanese are Christians of a wide variety of denominations. Most numerous are the Maronites, numbering about 350,000, who belong to the Church of Rome. They are followed by the Greek Orthodox, with more than 100,000, the Armenians, with somewhat less than 100,000, and another 100,000 members of smaller groups.

Except for the Maronites, who are almost all in Lebanon, these Christians spill over into Syria, Jordan, and what was formerly Palestine. In 1947 Albert Hourani, the historian, calculated approximately 2,500,000 Christians in the Levant as follows: 1,000,000 Copts, 300,000 Greek Orthodox, 600,000 Uniate Christians, 250,000 Armenians, and 300,000 other Christians. The minor denominations included Syrian Orthodox (Jacobites), Nestorians (Assyrians), and Chaldaean Catholics, all remnants of the early churches established in the first century after the life of Jesus. Their numbers have of course increased since then, by about 30 percent.

Another historical memory shared by most of the Arabs is Turkish rule. It is difficult to think of many constructive things that the Arabs inherited from 400 years of Turkish rule. Rather, the Arabs inherited a land suffering from economic neglect and widespread deforestation. From the Turks they learned to veil their women and restrict them severely to the home. They acquired the habits of bureaucratic arrogance, delay, and inaction. Perhaps because their own sense of ethnic Arabism is so strong, however, they did not copy the Turkish millet system of administration, by which the Turks accorded most ethnic groups a large measure of autonomy.

The British and French, who were successors to the Turks in the Arab world, were largely responsible for drawing the frequently illogical Middle Eastern borders that we know today. The French were paramount in Morocco, Tunisia, Algeria, Syria, and Lebanon; the British in Egypt, Jordan, Iraq, the Gulf, and South Arabia. In Saudi Arabia and neighboring Persia, too, the British dominated, although these countries, along with the Kingdom of Yemen, clung tenaciously to their independence.

The imprint left by the French and the British is perhaps less profound than that of the Turks, but it is more specific. The Arabs' reaction to the French and British was one of love-hate. They

	Total sq. mi. (000)	Culti-vated (per-cent)	Pasture (per cent)	Popula-tion Mid-1971 (Millions)	Lit-eracy (per-cent)	Religion % Muslim
ISLAMIC-ARAB						
Algeria	920	3	14	14.3	25	98
Bahrain	231	5	*	.2	25	98
Iraq	168	18	26	9.7	14	95
Jordan	37 7[1]	10	*	2.4[2]	32	93
Kuwait	6	1	*	.9	53	98
Lebanon	4	31	*	3.1	86	50
Libya	679	6	*	1.9	27	95
Morocco	158	19	19	16.4	20	99
Oman	82	*	*	.8	low	100
Qatar	6	*	*	.1	25	98
Saudi Arabia	830	1	*	5.7	5-15	99
Sudan	967.5	3	9	16.2	10	73
Syria	71.5	38	31	6.7	39	90
Un. Arab Emirates	32	5	*	.2	low	95
Tunisia	63	29	34	5.3	30	95
Egypt	386	3[3]	*	33.7	30	92
Yemen (Sana)	75	20	*	5.9	15	100
Yemen (Aden)	115	32	*	1.5	10	100
ISLAMIC-NON ARAB						
Iran	636	17	6.1	29.8	20	98
Turkey	305	34	34	36.2	46	98
NON-ISLAMIC						Greek Muslim
Cyprus	3.6	47	10	.7	76	Ortho. 77 18
Greece	50.9	28	35	8.8	80	Greek Ortho. 97
Israel[4]	8	20	40	3.0	84	Jewish 90

*Insignificant
[1] 2.2 in West Jordan
[2] Including West Jordan
[3] Multiple cropping results in 10 million acres total per year
[4] Including East Jerusalem

Ethnic	1971 GNP $ Millions	Per capita GNP Dollars	Main source of revenue	Type	Status of Communist Party
Ar.-Berber	5,300	370	Oil-Agr.	Republic	Illegal
Arab	1,000	470	Oil	Shiekhdom	*
75% Arab-15% Kurd	3,800	393	Oil	Republic	Illegal
97% Arab	575	286	Agr.-Mining	Constitutional Monarchy	Illegal
85% Arab-15% Kurd	3,460	4,170	Oil	Sheikhdom	*
93% Arab	1,770	580	Agr.-Tour.	Republic	Illegal
95% Arab-5% Chris.	3,946	2,036	Oil	Republic	Illegal
98% Arab-2% Jewish	4,011	245	Agr.-Mining	Constitutional Monarchy	Illegal
Arab	266	355	Agr.	Sultanate	*
Arab	2,000	1,700	Oil	Sheikhdom	*
Arab	3,910	708	Oil	Absolute Monarchy	*
66% Arab-33% Neg.	1,900	117	Cotton	Republic	Active
90% Arab-9% Kurd	1,978	307	Agr.	Republic	Illegal
Arab	1,300	5,000	Oil	Shiekhdoms	*
95% Arab-4% Chris.	1,741	331	Agr.-Mining	Republic	Small
92% Hamitic-7% Cop.	6,970	207	Agr.	Republic	Illegal
90% Arab	165	110	Agr.	Republic	Illegal
Arab	472	80	Agr.-Trade	"Peoples Democratic Republic"	*
72% Iran-22% Turk	12,750	428	Oil-Varied	Constitutional Monarchy	Illegal
90% Turk-8% Kurd	13,030	360	Agr.	Republic	Illegal
78% Greek-18% Turk	673	1,053	Agr.-Mining	Constitutional Republic	Active
96% Greek-2% Turk	10,770	1,222	Varied	Constitutional Monarchy	Illegal
86% Jews-14% Arab	5,554	1,823	Varied	Republic	Legal-Small

admired and often copied the French or British way of doing things, but at the same time resented the superiority implied by the foreigners' long presence and power and wealth.

You can tell whether you are in former French or British territory by the school system, and by the way the taxi drivers operate. Beiruti drivers are as wild as any in Paris; those of Amman and Baghdad are less reckless. Wherever the French ruled, in Beirut, Damascus, Tunis, or Casablanca, you can still get good French food and wine. French priests, along with professors employed by the French Government, still doggedly teach the French language and purvey "la culture française" to the generally receptive minds of the Arabs.

Where the British ruled there is less talk of "culture" but the English language is omnipresent. It is the language of commerce. If you dig into any legal question in a government office, you discover that English common law has struck root in these countries and that British notions of civil service exist alongside the most bizarre Turkish-style bureaucracies.

At the southern end of the peninsula, at Aden, the British built one of the great military bases of their empire which determined the fate of the surrounding countries, first by its creation and then, in November, 1967, by its elimination. Similarly, the British for more than a century maintained a Pax Britannica in the Persian Gulf, from which they withdrew at the end of 1971, leaving behind a web of unresolved conflicts among the sheikhdoms and between Arabs and Persians.

The French built the Suez Canal, and the British took control of it. The existence of the Canal proved a vital element in the life of Egypt, and a major cause of war.

The political form and phraseology of constitutions and the shape of cabinets and parliaments in the Arab countries show where the British and French formerly held sway. But these forms are superficial. They are not the things that impart true flavor to political life. They are submerged by the native forces of family and tribal structure intermingled with the new forces of the army and newly rich merchants.

The traditional elites usually consisted of tribal leaders who became the representatives of the Ottomans and later the leaders in the legislatures set up by the British and French. Today the traditional elites still rule in Jordan, Saudi Arabia, the Gulf states, and, in a sense, in Lebanon, where they have managed to dominate the parliamentary structure.

A new military elite mixed with political party ideologists has swept aside the old elites as well as foreign rulers in Egypt, Syria, Iraq, and South and North Yemen. In North Africa the traditional elites still hold sway in Morocco, while they have been overturned in Tunisia, Algeria, Libya, and Sudan.

These revolts were responses to forces that have resulted in military overthrows throughout the underdeveloped "Third World." In these countries, with rare exceptions, civilian elements such as landowners, trade unions, businessmen, intelligentsia—even political parties—lacked numbers, organization, wealth, and tradition. They lacked also the notion so deeply instilled in more advanced nations that there is something immutable and sacred about the supremacy of civilians over the military. They were, on the contrary, totally overshadowed by the military, who were by far the largest organized body of trained men in the country, and whose resources were incomparably greater than those of any other group. Revolutionary leadership in most cases fell into the hands of officers just below the highest rank, men of middle- or lower-middle-class origin who had risen through the military hierarchy but finally found themselves frustrated by a coterie of officers drawn from the traditional elite of wealthy landowning families who monopolized the highest places. These ambitious officers sublimated their personal frustrations by making themselves the leaders of social revolutionary forces in their own countries.

The coups were stimulated first by the defeat of the Palestinians in 1948, and then by the continuing conflict between Israel and the Arabs. The young officers fed on the notion that they had been betrayed by the "politicians" and, more generally, by the old elites. First in the series of revolutions was that of Husni Zaim, whose coup d'état in Damascus in 1949 received an extraordinary assist from American intelligence agents who imagined that they would be able to control or at least influence the new regime. But history and the circumstances of the Middle East were against the Americans, and the revolutionaries, as though preordained, assumed anti-Western, anti-American positions. The Nasser coup took place in 1952; Abdel Kerim Kassem's in 1958 in Iraq; Abdullah Sallal's in Yemen in 1962. The South Arabian Federation overthrew its seventeen Sheikhs in 1967; Muammar el Qaddafi deposed King Idris in 1969.

The first coups d'état seemed designed mainly to overthrow the traditional regimes or to put an end to British or French influence. Nasser and Kassem instituted land reform, but it was not until Nasser began in 1961 to apply the doctrine of Arab Socialism that the cult of Marxism got a firm foothold in the Arab world.

Since then, every military takeover has insisted on calling itself a "revolution." In fact they are military coups with social overtones. In Egypt there is the Arab Socialist Union and in Syria and Iraq the Baath Party, but the officers make the decisions. The officers all subscribe to Arab Nationalism of one kind or another.

Before discussing individual countries, it would be useful to consider how ideas of Arab nationalism have developed.

Nationalism—like subsequent infusions of liberalism and Marxism—came to the Arabs from Europe.

The Arabs had lived for centuries within the Turkish Empire, which was ruled by a Caliph in Constantinople who acted as supreme temporal as well as spiritual chief while more immediate concerns were dealt with within the framework of provincial administrations, tribe, and family.

Napoleon's arrival in Egypt in 1798 shook the Arab World out of its lethargy and opened new channels of communication with Europe. There were some stirrings in the years that followed among Arabs demanding, not independence, but autonomy. Among the earliest were Nasif Yazeji and Butrus Bustani, Christian Lebanese, born early in the nineteenth century. Both were well-to-do, conservative intellectuals and in no sense either social or political revolutionaries. It was too early for them to think in terms of Palestine, much less Lebanon, for that entire region, including the area that is now Jordan, then formed the Turkish province of Syria. Their activities inevitably led to the formation of secret societies, whose ideas moved step-by-step toward more radical conceptions.

Arab nationalism developed also in reaction to the nationalism of the young Turks, who set about in the decade before World War I repudiating the traditional ethnic and linguistic tolerance of the cosmopolitan Ottoman Empire.

The Arabs learned something as they mingled with the earliest Zionist immigrants in Palestine, with a large variety of Christian missionaries, and with the British, first in Egypt and later in other parts of the Middle East. The American University of Beirut unquestionably played a role in inculcating the ideas of self-determination and the rights of man.

The subsequent development of Arab nationalism can conveniently be divided into four phases:

First, religious renewal and national awakening during the last third of the nineteenth century and the first thirty years of the twentieth.

Second, a semisecular phase beginning in the thirties, led, as during the first phase, by the traditional elite which sought in vain to lead the Arabs, and in particular the Palestinians, under the stresses of European imperialist domination, of revolt and war.

Third, after the 1948 War, there was a period of military coup d'état in the life of the new Arab states and, slightly later, after the 1967 War, a liberal moderate phase in the Palestinian resistance movement.

A fourth phase, now beginning, and discussed in Chapter 14, takes the form of a politically much more radical Pan-Arab Marxist resistance movement more interested in subversion than military operations.

In the first phase, the father of Arab nationalism is generally considered to have been Jamal Addin al Afghani, a charismatic leader of the period from 1870 to 1890. This was just before Theodor Herzl wrote *Der Judenstaat.* But whereas Herzl was interested in building a secular state for the Jews, Afghani rejected secularism and sought to reform and renew Islam—to awaken the Arabs as a nation.

One of his disciples was Mohamed Abdu, a writer who in turn

influenced Rashid Rida, an editor of the review *al Manar,* one of the influential journals in the first third of the twentieth century. This kind of thinking, seeking to combine Islam with Pan-Arab nationalism, spanned a considerable period of time well into the twentieth century.

More religious emphasis was given to this movement by the writers Mustaphal Kamel and Kawakebi in Egypt in the last quarter of the nineteenth century and first decade of the twentieth. Their approach, which led eventually to the formation of the Moslem Brothers, has more recently found expression in the attitudes of Muammar el Qaddafi, the President of Libya.

Although aware of issues raised by the arrival of Jewish immigrants, these early writers were only incidentally concerned with the problem of Palestine. It was not until after the Balfour Declaration in 1917 that the Arabs began to awaken fitfully to the challenge. The second phase pitted the traditional leadership of Palestine—landed families such as the Nashashibis, the Khalidis, and the Husseinis—against the wiles and resources of the Zionist movement, the Jewish Agency, and the various paramilitary Jewish forces. Their hopeless endeavors may be considered to have begun with deluded young Prince Feisal who traveled to London to make a deal with the British Government and Zionist leaders. He agreed to terms on behalf of the Arabs for which he was later severely criticized.

Because of its unique bearing on the whole subsequent evolution of Arab nationalism in the Middle East, the British-fostered Arab revolt against the Turks, in which T. E. Lawrence played a romantic part, I examine this oft-told tale once again.

In a letter of July 14, 1915, Sherif Hussein of the Hejaz, obviously looking for postwar gains, asked that Britain recognize the independence of all Arab countries south of Turkey with the exception of Aden. He did not mention Egypt.

In reply on October 24, 1915, Sir Henry McMahon, High Commissioner for Egypt and the Sudan, wrote Sherif Hussein that he was authorized by the British Government to pledge that Britain was prepared "to recognize and uphold the independence of the Arabs" in all the regions lying within the frontiers proposed by the Sherif.

In his letter, McMahon made the reservation that "the districts of Mersin and Alexandretta, and portions of Syria lying west of the districts of Damascus, Homs, Hamma, and Aleppo cannot be said to be purely Arab, and must on that account be excepted from the proposed delimitation."

Unbeknown to Sherif Hussein, soon after this correspondence Britain entered into negotiations with France, as a result of which F. Georges Picot and Sir Mark Sykes concluded a secret agreement in the spring of 1916 dividing the Middle East into spheres of influence which ignored the commitments to the Sherif. A later agreement between the two countries at San Remo in 1920 recognized French control in areas known as Syria and Lebanon and British control in regions now known as Palestine, Jordan, and Iraq.

Sherif Hussein learned of the agreement when its existence was disclosed by the new Bolshevik Government in Russia, which had found it in the Tsarist archives. In the ensuing confusion Britain and France issued a statement assuring the Arabs that their goal was the complete and final liberation of the peoples who had for so long been oppressed by the Turks, and the setting up of national governments and administrations that would derive their authority from free exercise of initiative and choice by the indigenous populations.

"In pursuit of those intentions, France and Great Britain agree to further and assist the setting up of indigenous governments and administrations in Syria and Mesopotamia. . . ."

In November, 1918, Emir Feisal, Sherif Hussein's son, who had never gone abroad before traveled to London and Paris, but was unable to persuade the Allies to carry out the pledges that had been given his father.

One year before Feisal reached London, the British Foreign Secretary, Arthur Balfour, had further undermined the McMahon pledges by issuing on November 2, 1917, the famous Balfour Declaration.

> His Majesty's Government view with favor the establishment in Palestine of a national home for the Jewish people and will use their best endeavors to facilitate the achievement of this object, it

being clearly understood that nothing shall be done which may
prejudice the civil and religious rights of existing non-Jewish communities in Palestine, or the rights and political status enjoyed by
Jews in any other country.

This document, the fruit of long and intensive lobbying by Dr.
Chaim Weizmann, who later became the first President of Israel,
served as the foundation for all Zionist development that followed.

In his effort to obtain British support, Feisal went far toward
recognizing Zionist aspirations in a document dated January 3,
1919, signed by himself and by Chaim Weizmann, representing the
World Zionist Movement. It recognized "national aspirations" of
the Jewish people as well as of the Arabs, and agreed to establish
definite boundaries "between the Arab State and Palestine." Further, the signatories agreed "to encourage and stimulate immigration of Jews into Palestine on a large scale," while "Arab peasant
and tenant farmers would be protected in their rights."

Feisal covered himself in a concluding statement that he would
not be bound "by a single word" of the agreement unless the Arabs
obtained their independence within the borders demanded by his
father. Yet it seems unlikely that he would have signed this document had he been more experienced in international diplomacy and
had been able to anticipate the criticism it aroused in the Arab
world.

Feisal returned from Europe in May, 1919, to find pressures from
Arab nationalists more insistent than ever. A movement to elect a
National Congress from all parts of the Syrian provinces (Syria,
Lebanon, and Palestine) was under way, and Feisal gave it his
blessing. The deliberations of the Congress resulted, in July, 1919,
in a series of resolutions calling for the complete independence of
the area. The delegates to the Congress saw their only hope of
gaining independence and freedom and avoiding the French control envisioned in the Sykes-Picot agreement in the good will and
continued presence of the British troops garrisoned in the area. But
the French were exerting mounting pressure for removal of British
troops. Lloyd George consequently once more invited Feisal to
Europe to negotiate an acceptable compromise.

After discussions with Lloyd George and Clemenceau, Feisal agreed to withdrawal of British troops and their replacement by French garrisons in the area west of the Homs, Hamma, and Aleppo line, leaving the Arabs in control of the eastern province.

On Feisal's return in January, 1920, he found nationalist feeling higher than ever, and a general unwillingness to chop off part of the great independent Arab state promised in the Hussein-McMahon correspondence. While relatively receptive to the British, the nationalists strongly objected to a French military presence. They were convinced it would lead to French control.

On March 8, 1920, the National Congress, reacting against French pressures and Feisal's willingness to compromise, formally declared the region of Syria, Lebanon, and Palestine an independent, sovereign state and a constitutional monarchy, with Feisal as King. It recognized a special autonomous status for Mount Lebanon. A similar meeting in Iraq proclaimed Abdullah, Feisal's younger brother, as King.

The Allies responded at the meeting at San Remo in April. Taking a hard line, they declared a formal division into British and French Mandates of the Arab territories comprising the "Greater Syria" envisioned by the nationalists in Damascus and Baghdad. News of the San Remo decisions, made public in May, swept aside with crushing finality whatever illusions the nationalists may have had about the intentions of the Great Powers.

In June, General Gouraud, commander of French forces in the Middle East, issued Feisal an ultimatum demanding that he accept the French Mandate on both sides of the ephemeral line joining Homs, Hamma, and Aleppo. Feisal, a realist among romantics, capitulated, but the people of Damascus fought against the advancing forces. In a matter of weeks, the French, after bombarding Damascus, took complete control. Without much delay, they invited Feisal to leave. On July 28, the son of the proud Sherif Hussein left Syria for the Italian Riviera. He had ruled less than five months.

Arabs throughout the old Turkish province of Syria were obviously embittered by these events. Meanwhile, immigrants were flowing into Palestine. The story of the ensuing friction is described in Chapter 10, along with some discussion of the political devices the Arab notables sought to develop before and after the revolt of 1936 and up to the disastrous war of 1948. The war of 1948 is also described separately as the "first round" of conventional warfare.

Among the traditional leaders who sought during this period to cope with the influx of Zionists, perhaps the most notable were Abdullah of Jordan and Haj Amin el-Husseini, Grand Mufti of Jerusalem. King Abdullah was notable in that he was one of the few who sought not only to oppose the Jews but also to find some way to come to terms with them.

Exactly what he had in mind, whether a federation, a binational state, or an economic union, is not clear. There are still secrets about the meetings (to which Golda Meir traveled in disguise) at his palace at Shuneh in the Jordan Valley just after the 1948 War. In any event, they cost him his life at the hands of a fanatical nationalist assassin. They formed, also, the background for willingness shown by his grandson, King Hussein, to come to terms with the Israelis.

Haj Amin el-Husseini was the chairman of the Arab Higher Committee, and sought for years after the 1948 War to preserve his role as principal leader of the Palestinians. Somewhat compromised by his wartime dalliance with the Nazis, he was unable to establish a popular following, nor were the other traditional leaders able to inspire the Palestinians. They were hopelessly outclassed by the Jewish Agency before, during, and after the 1948 War. They were charming gentlemen but could not lead, nor generate the ideas their people needed.

Just before the 1967 War a third phase begins, one marked by a new leadership. A word, to begin, about the roles of Nasser and of the Baath Party in the intellectual development of the third period following the war of 1948.

Nasser was the first and the greatest of the "Colonels" who seized power by coup d'état. Ideologically, his leadership was equivocal. It shifted uncertainly between the rival attractions of nationalism, socialism, and Islam. It was his own personality that held the equivocations together, an element he was not able to pass on to his successor, Anwar Sadat. He could not make up his mind whether to follow the course of "unity of ranks," which implied cooperation with the traditional regimes of Saudi Arabia, the Gulf, and Morocco, as well as with the so-called liberated regimes, such as Syria, Iraq, and Algeria, or whether to adopt the rival slogan of "Unity of Purpose," which implied cooperation only with other "liberated" regimes. One might say that in the Fedayeen movement Fatah follows the first of these two slogans, and the PFLP the second.

As I have indicated in Chapter 7, the Baath Party operating in those countries exerted great ideological influence in the Arab world, and may exert more. But now the party's principles are overshadowed by the personal power of the military men who run the two countries in the name of the Baath.

Liberal-moderate nationalists in the guise of guerrillas or "commandos" undertook during this third phase to organize the liberation of Palestine from the Israelis by force of arms. The dominant figure here is Yasir Arafat, described at length in Chapter 11.

Arafat's movement, Fatah, is Palestinian nationalist. He preached the unification of all elements among the Palestinians and other Arabs, whether leftist or rightist, for the liberation of the homeland. He is not a Pan-Arabist.

Nonideological by inclination, he has nonetheless, along with a number of similar leaders, adopted the liberal, humanistic concept of the distinction between Jews and Zionists in Palestine. Although somewhat vague about what he would do with the Jews if he scored a military victory, he holds that Jews and Arabs could live together in a single unified, nonsectarian and democratic state.

Fatah does not neglect Islam. It receives the greatest part of its financial support from intensely Islamic Saudi Arabia. Arafat himself was once a Moslem Brother. These facts are reflected in Fatah's use of the word "nonsectarian" rather than "secular."

Perhaps because it lacked a firm ideology of its own, Fatah has been shaped by circumstances and external pressures. Although opposed in principle to terrorism, Fatah found itself under pressure from such smaller organizations as the Popular Front for the Liberation of Palestine (PFLP) and the Popular Democratic Front for the Liberation of Palestine (PDFLP) to participate in ruthless and sometimes rash operations. Their relationship reminded me of that which I had observed before and during the 1948 War between Haganah, the Jewish paramilitary secret army, and the radical groups, Irgun Zvai Leumi, and the Stern gang.

Since the commandos, mainly Fatah, were driven out of Jordan by King Hussein, Arafat has clung to the leadership of the entire movement, including Fatah. But he has grown increasingly isolated in terms of real power, which has shifted to those members of Fatah who are identified with the phrase "Black September." They represent not a separate organization but a state of mind.

Paradoxically, about the time Fatah, under the rubric "Black September" was engaging in some of the boldest and most ruthless operations of its entire existence—at Munich, where the Israeli Olympic Team was attacked, and at Khartoum, where two American diplomats and a Belgian were murdered—the PFLP, under the leadership of George Habash, was gradually changing its tactics. This group, which had carried out the most sensational of the skyjackings when four airliners were forced to an improvised landing field in Jordan in the fall of 1970, had decided to give up skyjacking and drop terrorism in favor of political action. It founded a new Socialist Workers Party, similar in principle to, but more radical than, the Arab Nationalist Movement.

The PFLP and the PDFLP, led by Hawatmeh, a Christian Transjordanian, are still cooperating with Fatah in greatly reduced operations in and out of Lebanon and elsewhere, but the formation of the Socialist Workers Party suggests that a new fourth phase, in which the Pan-Arab Marxist groups will take the lead in subversive political activity throughout the Arab world, lies ahead. From their point of view, overthrowing King Hussein is on the same level as overthrowing Dayan. Jordan is occupied territory. Furthermore, they see subversion of Israeli society in the same terms as subversion of Arab society. Just as they see Arabs willing to overthrow their own regimes, they also see potential allies in Israel. Theirs is a classical Marxist-Leninist approach within the framework of what Habash calls the Red Front. In *Al Horriah,* the daily newspaper, and *Hadaf,* the weekly, both of Beirut, they dispose of the most sophisticated leftist publications in the Arab World.

But the apparatus of the PFLP, the commando organization, and of the Socialist Workers Party, along with their top leader, George Habash, has gone underground. This is what Kanafani, the former editor of *Hadaf,* told me to expect the last time I saw him in Beirut, the summer of 1970, about two years before he was assassinated.

In pursuing their subversive objectives, it is unlikely that the Pan-Arab Marxist-Fedayeen movements and their new Socialist Workers Party or "Red Front" will pay much more respect to the regimes of Syria, Iraq, and Egypt—whose Marxism the Fedayeen consider largely fraudulent—than they do to those of Jordan and Saudi Arabia. They will find the economic and political disruption caused by the fourth Arab-Israeli war favors their cause in all the Arab states.

4

Egypt

Egypt after Nasser is still Egypt—the nucleus, in relative terms, of the Arab world—bound to be the leader because of its size and location, even when it attempts to turn away from the terrible problem of Palestine. President Nasser had sensed this in his "Philosophy of the Revolution" when he alluded to Egypt's role of leadership.

Egypt, with its population of more than 30 million—and still growing rapidly—is an anthill society toiling on the fertile shores of the mighty Nile, that unique and majestic river which sweeps out of Central Africa, a giant that has succored six thousand years or more of civilization, and whose strength has now been harnessed by the Russian-built dam at Aswan.

When you walk through Cairo you feel, as in few other cities of the world, the presence of the city, seething with human beings, scurrying down the broad avenues and through the labyrinthine sidestreets in sandals and long, white djellaba, the nightgown-like dress of the Nile Valley, eating, trading, sleeping, indeed living very much in the streets. Cairo is also a city sparkling with great hotels, lush apartment houses, splendid skyscrapers, adorned with monuments of past and present—ancient mosques, museums, and universities—all in the shadow, as it were, of the pyramids.

A special reason for Egypt's influence in the 1970s is that it bears the legacy of Nasserism. Nasser was a dictator whose considerable stature prevented other strong political personalities from developing in his shadow. He tried to build a collective leadership, a system that would be both a "guided democracy" and one capable of continuously regenerating itself. But he was not very successful. Although Nasserites would like the Egyptian experience to be a guide to the rest of the Arab world, Nasser did not succeed in creating a popular base for his regime. In 1953 he set up the Liberation Rally, followed by the National Union, and in 1962 by the Arab Socialist Union, the only legal political party. Other "liberated" Arab states, as those that have thrown off traditional forms of government are sometimes called, have adopted similar one-party systems. But these parties have little life of their own; they stir nobody's enthusiasm; everyone knows they have no power of their own but are mere reflections of the power of the president, the "Revolutionary Command Council" or whatever the top military authority chooses to call itself.

Nasser's National Charter, proclaimed in 1962, embodies the principles of his ideology and established representative organizations in which half of the seats were allocated to the peasants and workers. Similar systems were adopted in Syria and Iraq. If they did not result in anything Westerners would recognize as democracy, it was perhaps because they issued from the single party system.

Nasser introduced socialism to the Arab world. His land reform program of 1954 was copied throughout the Arab world. He led the way also in nationalization of banks, insurance companies, and industry. He often emphasized, however, that his socialism was "Arab" and not Marxist. He called it "believers' socialism," in contrast to atheistic communism. He did not believe in the class struggle, much less the dictatorship of the proletariat. His approach was significant because it sought change while preserving traditionalist feeling based on Islam. He realized that Arab society, even during its transition to modernism, remains profoundly religious. He was unable, for instance, to separate church and state or to abolish polygamy, because it is sanctioned by Islam. In short, he was no Ataturk, nor has his

"Arab socialism" proved a panacea for the ills of the Arab Middle East.

In pursuit of his objectives, Nasser vacillated between the slogan of "unity of purpose" which aligned him with the so-called revolutionary states, Syria, Iraq, and Algeria, and "unity of ranks" which broadened the concept to include the so-called reactionary states such as Saudi Arabia and Jordan.

He tried to strike a balance between the United States and the Soviet Union, playing off one against the other so as not to fall too far under the sway of one. But here again he was not to be entirely successful. By the time Nasser died on September 28, 1970, Egypt had slipped far off balance. It had become heavily dependent on Soviet military and economic assistance, most of which had to be paid for. By defying the Western powers and obtaining military aid from the Russians, he had nonetheless achieved unparalleled popularity in the Arab world. His external feats and internal reforms restored to the Egyptians a sense of dignity and importance, purposefulness, and direction which they had not known for many generations, and certainly at no time since the British arrived to quell the nationalist revolt of 1882.

Nasser's extraordinary popularity throughout the Arab world was based on a series of triumphs: He forced the British to agree to withdraw their army of 80,000 men from the Suez Canal Zone in 1954; he acquired Soviet arms in 1955; he nationalized the Suez Canal in defiance of Western interests. Most dramatic of all, he succeeded in surviving an invasion of Israeli, British, and French forces in 1956. Nasser's magic seemed irresistible when the United Nations—with U.S. backing—obliged the Israelis to withdraw from Sinai.

But from then on a long series of miscalculations slowly tarnished his image. In 1957 Nasserite revolutionaries failed to overthrow King Hussein in Amman. In 1958 a Lebanese civil war ended, in spite of large-scale covert Nasserite intervention. A revolution in Iraq installed in Baghdad a new regime which soon turned against Nasser. In 1962 he allowed himself to be drawn into war in defense of a revolutionary regime in Yemen, and for the next five years Yemeni royalists played havoc with an Egyptian army numbering up to 80,000.

Nasser's climactic error was the war of 1967. He could probably have avoided it, but thought he could go to the brink and come back with diplomatic gains. Instead he came back with disaster.

Even after that, Egyptians and other Arabs remained captivated by Nasser's personal mystique. His threat to resign was met by hysterical demonstrations all over the Arab world. But Nasser was deeply shaken in the months before his death on September 28, 1970. Nasserites disappeared from Yemen and the Persian Gulf.

On the economic side, too, Nasser's achievements were great, but, in important aspects, equivocal.

He kept Egypt in funds, basically by playing off East against West. That is, he obtained credit from the Soviet Union and bloc countries on the one hand and the U.S., the World Bank and private Western institutions on the other. Boldly he launched agricultural projects, huge hydrological and irrigation schemes which are vital if Egypt is to feed its burgeoning population. His industrial schemes, the most ambitious Egypt has ever known, were the very essence of the ultimate solution of Egypt's economic problems—if there is a solution. And his social projects included apartment houses for the poor of the cities and new villages for the fellahin.

No one who has known the Egypt of King Farouk's day as well as the Egypt of Nasser can doubt that the poor of the cities and countryside—the lowest economic bracket—have benefited. Not much, but enough to make Nasser a patron of the poor. Many who were barefoot now wear shoes. Many have moved from hovels to new dwellings.

But in so doing, Nasser also made costly errors. One was overinvesting, given the limitations of capital and of the skills to use it. Another was concentration on showpieces, such as a steelworks and an automobile assembly plant. The great Aswan Dam may eventually prove to have been the costliest blunder of all. There are signs that the ecological damage that is being caused by the damming of the Nile flood may outweigh the benefits of increased electric power and irrigated lands. By cutting off the annual flood of the Nile the dam has also cut off the mud and sand rich in phosphates and nitrogen that used to roll over Egyptian agricultural land and eventually into the sea. Not only have farmers been forced to depend on artificial fertilizers but the fish population of the Eastern Mediterranean has begun to decline, according to studies made by the American University of Beirut. The university's measurements showed also that the Eastern Mediterranean was getting saltier and warmer, creating conditions unfavorable to some fish because less of the Nile's relatively cool fresh water reaches the sea.

Whatever the errors, they have been magnified by the size, ineptitude, and corruption of the Egyptian bureaucracy. Whether for these or other reasons, in the last year before the 1967 War, the cost of living, which had been rising steadily, soared by 25 percent, the deficit in the balance of payments reached half a billion dollars, and the country's external debt rose to 1.3 billion dollars. Toward the end of the year, Egypt sold one-third of its gold cover and defaulted on its payments to the International Monetary Fund.

The war made matters much worse. Egypt lost the canal tolls which had reached 227 million dollars in 1967 and were covering nearly half the deficit in the balance of payments. She lost 96 million dollars per year from Sinai oil. She lost, for a while at least, much of the tourist trade, which had been worth 100 million dollars per year before the war.

On the plus side, to compensate Egypt for her losses, and enable her to continue her military effort, Kuwait, Saudi Arabia, and Libya agreed at Khartoum in August, 1967, to subsidize Egypt, compensating for her war losses to an amount equivalent in sterling to 228 million dollars per year. Withdrawal from Yemen, which was the unspoken, or at least unwritten, condition of Saudi aid, doubtless saved a great deal. Estimates of the annual costs of the Yemen campaign, which lasted from September, 1962, until January, 1968, varied from 40 to 250 million dollars, depending on whether you figure only the foreign currency costs or all costs.

The Egyptian economy benefited some from the growing exploitation of oil in the Gulf of Suez, totaling about 300,000 barrels a day. Oil fields in the Western desert have, thus far, proved disappointing.

It looked, in mid-1973, as though the French, British, and Italian backers of a project to build an oil pipeline paralleling the Suez

Canal had, after years of argument, about worked out their financial problems and would soon get the work started. Forty-two inches in diameter, the same as the existing Israeli Elat to Haifa pipe, it will connect Ain Soknam 50 kilometers south of Suez with a terminal 20 kilometers west of Alexandria, will cost about 200 million dollars, and will put Egypt back into the profitable oil-transit business even if the Suez Canal is not reopened.

President Sadat, although lacking Nasser's charisma and mystique, has succeeded much better than most observers expected in following in Nasser's footsteps. In the eyes of many Westerners, Sadat's bombastic belligerency has made him an object of ridicule. In particular, the proclamation of 1971 as the "year of decision" and talk about resuming the "war of attrition" seemed irresponsible as well as unrealistic. But Arab tolerance for this kind of talk is high, and in other respects Sadat has emerged as a forceful, pragmatic leader capable of keeping opposition leftist students and radical officers well in hand while striking out on new lines of policy.

While the Egyptian economy has continued threadbare and strained, Sadat has largely shelved socialistic principles and given private enterprise a little more freedom. His policies have somewhat eased the pressures on the urban middle class, who are the first to suffer from restrictions on imported consumer goods and high prices (the rich use the "black market"; the poor do not use much in the way of imported goods and benefit, in any case, from subsidized food prices).

A so-called new class of prosperous bureaucrats and state-employed technocrats has meanwhile given rise to allegations of favoritism and corruption. This is the inevitable fate of a revolution grown middle-aged.

Nonetheless, Sadat has shown himself to be a more than ordinary Egyptian politician, one capable of striking out on original and courageous lines of policy. These include the following:

Sadat stated clearly on February 15, 1971, that he was willing to consider a peace agreement with Israel. In spite of subsequent belligerent talk, he has not repudiated this stand, which is a notable advance on the position Nasser took.

On May 13, 1971, Sadat purged his regime of pro-Soviet elements, notably of Aly Sabry whom he accused of plotting against him. Following up this move, on July 18, 1972, he expelled from Egypt most of the 14,000 or more Soviet technicians and advisors on the grounds that the Soviet Union had declined to supply Egypt with the sophisticated weapons she needed.

This dramatic move was a declaration of independence, a correction of a balance which Nasser had allowed to become lopsided. It altered profoundly the whole position of the Soviet Union in the Middle East. At a single stroke, Russia was deprived of her main base in the Middle East; and subsequent emphasis on Syria and Iraq was no substitute. Their population was too small and their economic and cultural weight too slight. The Soviet Union in the Middle East had been profoundly weakened.

Again Sadat showed his ability to orchestrate Arab politics by managing his relations with Muammar Qaddafi, the headstrong President of Libya, while at the same time, in preparation for his 1973 war against Israel, gaining the political and financial support of King Faisal of Saudi Arabia.

In September, 1971 a "merger" of Egypt with Libya and Syria was proclaimed, and Sadat, who saw union as a purely political gesture to be realized in some entirely indeterminate future, had his hands full heading off demagogic attempts by Qaddafi to force immediate union. At the same time, Sadat carefully protected Egyptian access to Libyan oil revenues which could eventually make Egypt financially independent and more powerful than ever before.

Sadat's most memorable role came with the fourth Arab-Israeli war, which he personally planned and for which he must take the credit or blame. During the war, Sadat gained immensely in stature. Although it is probably true that he could never attain anything like the charisma of Nasser, the success of the Egyptian Army in crossing the Suez Canal in the first days of the war made Sadat for the first time a truly popular leader. Much of this popularity he has managed to retain in spite of the subsequent Israeli crossing of the Canal from east to west which cut off the Egyptian Third Army. The idea that Arabs can stand up to and even defeat the Israelis, a certain renewal of Arab self-confidence, has stuck in the Arabs' mind and will be associated forever with Sadat's bold initiative.

Unlike Israel, Egypt did not suffer greatly from the economic impact of the war. The mobilization of manpower was not such a heavy burden on populous Egypt. Industry and agriculture went on functioning without severe problems while the army was fighting.

Should the war eventually result in the reopening of the Suez Canal, Egypt will regain a major source of income. Combining income from a widened and deepened canal with oil discoveries in the western desert and Soviet-financed industries with possible new credit from the West and a partial return to private enterprise, Sadat might move the threadbare Egypt he inherited from Nasser into a new period of prosperity.

The Egyptian Government began even before the fighting ended to plan clearing the Canal and to discuss the possibility of dredging on a dramatic scale to accommodate the giant oil tankers that now carry most of the Persian Gulf's oil around the Cape of Good Hope. It was understandably indignant when the Israelis, toward the end of November, 1973, built an earth-fill causeway right over the central part of the canal which they controlled.

5

Jordan

It has been well said of Jordan that if it did not exist, it would have to be invented, and Winston Churchill, with more prescience than he realized, did invent it to suit British foreign policy after World War I. To provide an appropriate realm for the Emir Abdullah, second son of the Sherif Hussein of the Hejaz who had supported the British against Turkey, he carved this country out of the part of the Turkish province of Syria which had been awarded by the League of Nations to Britain as a mandate.

The original state of Transjordan was enlarged to become "Jordan" when King Abdullah, its first ruler, occupied the part of Palestine on the River Jordan that had not been taken over by the new State of Israel in 1948. But it lost this West Bank to Israel in the war of 1967. Into the part of Jordan known since the 1948 War as the East Bank and again after the war of 1967 have poured the largest portion of the Palestinian refugees so that today the East Bank is the home of approximately two million Arabs, of whom slightly more than one million are of Palestinian or West Bank origin.

This dual nature of the State of Jordan is the reason for the internal turmoil from which it has suffered since 1967. The Palestinian element served as a base for the powerful Palestinian commando organizations which for a few years formed within Jordan something approaching a state within a state. The commandos sometimes found the Jordanian state and its King a compliant host. It was said that El Fatah, the largest commando group, did not seek to overthrow the monarchy because it could not ask for a better base of operations. Yet, commandos and the Jordanian state repeatedly clashed.

In 1948 I wrote in *The New York Times* that there wasn't much of note in the desert kingdom of Transjordan except the king and his army. Before I come to this extraordinary monarch, I will describe the role of his army and give some account of the economic development which has transformed this country since 1948.

The army, originally known as the Arab Legion, is above all a Bedouin army, a force first recruited by a remarkable Englishman, John Bagott Glubb Pasha, among selected Bedouin tribesmen. Today great numbers of Palestinians, more than half of the army's 55,000 men, have been added to its ranks. But the Bedouin element remains dominant among its senior officers and in key units, and they determine its character.

The Arab Legion served both as an internal security force and as a means of subsidizing about thirty Bedouin tribes, most of which were in the process of settling on farms or in towns. The army became the link between the Crown and the Bedouin.

When the Bedouin-oriented Transjordanian army moved into the West Bank during and after the 1948 War, they were received by the Palestinians on the West Bank with mixed feelings. Some of the tribes overlapped the River so that it would be hard to say exactly where Jordanians leave off and Palestinians begin. Nonetheless, there was a difference, a trace of the ancient conflict between the desert and the town. The Palestinians, who represent the town, felt themselves culturally superior. They resented the rough authority exerted by the Bedouin Legion. The West Bank elite, landowners and big merchants, however, overcame its feeling of resentment sufficiently to accept office in the new Jordanian state administration. Thereby they lost the sympathy of the rank and file and prepared their eventual replacement in the hearts of the Palestinians by a more radical leadership.

One member of the Palestinian elite who did not readily accept

Jordan's hegemony was the Mufti of Jerusalem, Haj Amin el-Husseini, who in 1948 and for some years thereafter headed the only existing Palestinian political organization, the Arab Higher Committee for Palestine. He regarded King Hussein as an enemy of Palestinian nationalism, and for many years King Hussein in fact barred the Mufti from his realm. He was allowed to return only after the formation in 1964 by an Arab Summit Conference of the Palestine Liberation Organization (PLO), an overall organization of Fedayeen, also known as the commandos, who are dedicated to continuing the struggle against Israel in an attempt to regain their homeland. In view of the sanction given the PLO by the Arab states, King Hussein felt obliged to allow it and its Chief, Ahmed Shukairy, to function on the West Bank and in Jerusalem, but only after it had averred in writing that it had no territorial claims on Jordan. The King presumably hoped that the Mufti would serve as a counterweight to offset Ahmed Shukairy, first chairman of the PLO, whom he heartily detested.

Jordanians and Palestinians crowded now on the East Bank, competing for its limited resources. By no means all the Palestinians who poured across the Jordan River were indigent refugees. The wealthier and better educated among them, to the chagrin of those on the East Bank, quickly established themselves in business and in the professions, and moved into civil service posts. They even assumed prominence in the officers' corps of some units, and some gravitated after 1967 to the Fedayeen.

This Transjordanian, later Jordanian, state has always depended on external subsidies. First, it was the British who paid because of the necessity to ensure the existence of the British-officered Arab Legion. After the expulsion of Glubb Pasha, the British Commander, Egypt and Saudi Arabia undertook to support Jordan, but soon defaulted. It was the United States that took up the burden and provided Jordan with something close to fifty million dollars a year in budgetary and general economic support during the decade preceding the 1967 War.

Just before the war, the United States was beginning to cut down its assistance to Jordan because the Jordanians were doing phenomenally well. In real terms, the Jordanian gross national product grew between 1957–1958 and 1965–1966 at an annual rate of 8.5 percent, or 5.7 percent per capita—a very high rate of increase by any standard.

The 1967 War completely changed that picture. Jordan lost to Israeli occupation the agriculturally rich West Bank of the Jordan River. The state lost the tourist trade centered on Jerusalem, which had attracted more than half a million visitors annually before 1967. At the Khartoum conference of August, 1967, Kuwait, Saudi Arabia, and Libya undertook to help the Jordanians overcome the economic loss of the West Bank and to maintain their armed strength with annual subsidies (as already stated in this chapter). Since September, 1970, the Libyans have withdrawn their contribution, allegedly in protest against the monarchy's brutal suppression of the commando movement. And the United States has once again become a vital contributor to the maintenance of the Jordanian state. While avoiding any admission that it is picking up the Libyan tab, the United States in the year after the September, 1970, showdown gave the Jordanians 40 million dollars in economic and military grants (5 million dollars in budgetary support, 5 million dollars in a Presidential reconstruction grant, and 30 million dollars in a military aid program grant), plus a credit for 30 million dollars from foreign military sales.

Since then, American aid to Jordan has been running at the rate of about 50 million dollars a year in economic support and continuing contributions toward the modernization of the Jordanian army and air force. During King Hussein's visit to Washington in January, 1973, the United States agreed to supply Jordan with two squadrons of F-5 jet fighters. These fighters are very appropriate to Jordanian conditions because they were designed for use by less-developed countries lacking in highly sophisticated maintenance and short of highly trained pilots. The F-104 Starfighters the United States had previously supplied to Jordan were probably too difficult for the Jordanians to handle.

The economic damage to Jordan from the loss of the West Bank was less than might be supposed, and in any case proportionately less than the damages suffered by Egypt from the loss of Sinai. The Jordanians were deprived of 20 to 25 percent of their grain production, 40 percent of their vegetables, and 70 percent of their fruit, not to mention the profitable Jerusalem tourist trade, which had earned thirty-four million dollars for Jordan in 1966 and was growing fast. In addition, Jordan was burdened by another 300,000 refugees, bringing the total to well over 1,000,000.

However, the fastest growing, most promising industries of Jordan are on the East Bank, notably phosphates, cement, the refinery, electric power production, and the Aqaba Port. One should also mention the East Ghor agricultural development in the Jordan valley, which produced most of the country's exportable agricultural surplus in the form of citrus and early vegetables, which was severely damaged in 1969 and 1970 by Israeli attacks against the Canal, but subsequently restored.

In spite of the buffetings resulting from Israeli and commando operations, the Jordanian economy remains astonishingly vigorous. West Germany financed an extension of the railroad system from Maan to Aqaba, while French companies doubled the road between the Dead Sea and Aqaba. A Yugoslav concern is exploring for oil. An international airport has been built at Aqaba, along with deep berths for ocean-going ships and ambitious hotel and beach development for tourists. If Jordanian development seems to focus on the town of Aqaba, it is probably because this port, tucked between Saudi Arabia and Israel, and just across the bay from Egyptian territory, is King Hussein's favorite. This is where he goes for water-skiing and to relax with his friends at a beach cottage only a few hundred yards from the Israeli border.

Prolonged external subsidies have resulted in a somewhat artificial prosperity in Amman, which contrasts painfully with the hard lives of many of the Palestinian refugees. The constructors of lavish villas in the suburbs of Amman in the midst of all the tensions of commando-army confrontations and the overriding confrontations with Israel constitute flagrant evidence of corruption in high places. This remains a grave weakness of the Hashemite Kingdom and a source of endless indignation among some of its citizens.

During and after the September, 1970, showdown with the Fedayeen, King Hussein removed several of his top aides friendly to Nasser. In spite of this, President Nasser, on September 27, the day before he died, presided at yet another reconciliation between the King and Yasir Arafat, the Fedayeen leader. The death of President Nasser removed the man on whom the King had long relied to restrain the Palestinians. But the King no longer needed him. His army had just scored a decisive victory over the Palestinians. He no longer needed Bahjat Talhouny, the perennial Premier, one of whose political virtues was that he was acceptable to Nasser.

Along with Talhouny, King Hussein swept out a crowd of political hacks who, while serving the crown, had served themselves too well.

The King turned—as those who knew him well were sure he would—to his old favorite, Wasfi Tal, an incorruptible, tough-minded, outspoken anti-Nasserite. Once before, a decade earlier, Tal had served as Premier and carried out a program of financial and administrative reform until the King had found it necessary to remove him in order to appease Nasser. Wasfi Tal had been waiting in the wings ever since, commuting daily from his house, situated only a few hundred yards from King Hussein's personal residence at Suweillah, to the lobby of the Intercontinental Hotel in Amman, where he met his political contacts and kept his fingers on the political pulse of the country.

Wasfi Tal had the quality, rare among Arabs, of calling a spade a spade, and sometimes even a shovel. It made him widely respected but also intensely disliked by many, including the Fedayeen, who considered him their particular enemy. On November 18, 1971, he was assassinated in Cairo by members of a group previously unknown—Black September. It was the first of a series of acts of violence of this most extreme element among the Fedayeen, who are actually high-ranking members of Fatah.

I will now turn to King Hussein. The ruler of Jordan, once known as a "boy king," and who has often in the past been written off by the most astute observers, has now become the dean among Arab rulers and seems destined to play one of the key Middle East roles in the wake of the 1967 War. To understand his role, one should know something of his character, which is an amalgam of two elements: his British education and the influence exerted by his grandfather, King Abdullah.

Hussein was educated at Harrow, the famous British public school, and at Sandhurst, the British military academy. From these he acquired some very British notions of fair play and propriety and a taste for the company of English people and vigorous sports. Hussein likes driving fast cars, water-skiing, and go-carting. When a back injury sustained in an automobile accident, combined with his political preoccupations, prevented him from continuing his more active diversions, he became an avid "ham" radio operator, and maintained enthusiastic communications with a host of "friends" around the world. Some of these he has sometimes gathered together for parties during his nearly annual pilgrimages to Washington.

He is the only Arab ruler who flies to London and goes to tea with the Queen as naturally as a desert sheikh sits down to mutton and rice in his tent. He loves to stay at Claridge's in London and spend short holidays very quietly with English friends.

After divorcing his first wife, Dina, who was a very beautiful, very intellectual great grandniece of Sherif Hussein, who had studied at Oxford, he married a rather plain English girl, the daughter of a Colonel Gardiner who had been a member of the British aid mission in Jordan.

In his autobiography, *Uneasy Lies the Head,** he reveals one of the reasons he chose his English bride, whom he gave the name of Muna, meaning "desire or hope," and the title of Princess—but not Queen. He said he had always wanted to live and be treated like an "ordinary person," a condition most difficult for a ruling monarch to attain. He decided that Toni, as she was then called and who was employed as a telephone operator and later announcer at the Jordanian broadcasting station, cared for him as a man more than a King. He invited her to make some tape recordings for him at the palace. He was charmed by such simple things as the way Muna's mother fixed him a cup of tea when he came to call at their house.

After they were married in 1962, Hussein built Muna a villa on a hilltop at Suweillah, ten miles west of Amman, where it is said

*London: William Heinemann Ltd., 1962.

he delighted in taking turns with his wife at preparing breakfast. They had four children, two boys and twin girls. The two boys, after first acquiring a basic knowledge of Arabic, were sent to school in England. An older girl, Aliyah, sixteen, the daughter by the King's first marriage, lives with the family in Amman.

Probably no one will ever really know why King Hussein decided to divorce Princess Muna. A rather plain and simple girl when he married her, she had developed in social grace as the years went on. Given to overweight, nonetheless she managed to remain slim. And there were signs from time to time—in spite of reports of royal dalliance with this or that beauty—that King Hussein was very fond of his English family. Some say that after a visit to Teheran, where he met Queen Farida, King Hussein realized what an asset the right sort of queen could be. Or, having already made it clear publicly that the sons of his English wife could never inherit the throne, he may have sought an Arab heir. Or perhaps he was tired of his second wife.

Queen Aliam, twenty-four, is a handsome, intelligent, upper-middle-class girl whose father, Baha Eddin Touqan, a former ambassador to the United Nations and to London, was born in Nablus and whose mother is a Damascene. She studied in Rome and at Hunter College, and speaks perfect English. The wedding took place on December 25, 1972, and the King extended his official visit to Washington in January into a Florida honeymoon.

Princess Muna was given a fine villa in Amman but has chosen to spend much of her time since the divorce in the United States, where she has enrolled her children in small New England schools, the names of which have deliberately been kept secret to preserve their security.

King Hussein's father, Tallal, ruled for only a few months. When his son, Hussein, was seventeen years old, attending Harrow, it became apparent that King Tallal was mentally unbalanced and he was persuaded to abdicate. He has lived ever since in a sanitarium in Istanbul. Old King Abdullah, Hussein's grandfather, had obviously foreseen for many years that Hussein would eventually become his heir. Aware of his son's inadequacies, he set about educating Hussein. He used to take the young prince with him on his various missions around the Kingdom, visiting the tribes and consulting with politicians and the British. He saw to it that, in addition to his British education, young Hussein got a good foundation in the lore of the Koran and of the Arab classics and in the traditions of the Hashemites. The Hashemites consider themselves direct descendants of the Prophet and as such they automatically have great prestige among tradition-minded Arabs. From his grandfather, Hussein acquired a profound sense of family honor, a sense of *noblesse oblige.* To him it is inconceivable that he would ever exchange his perilous duties as a ruler for retirement in some safe haven in Europe.

At the age of sixteen Hussein was with his grandfather at the Mosque of al Aksa in Jerusalem when the King was assassinated. It is said that Hussein himself escaped death only because a medal he was wearing deflected a bullet. King Abdullah was shot by a Palestinian who believed that the King was preparing to make peace with Israel. It is true that Abdullah had engaged in secret consultations with Golda Meir and other Israelis at his palace at Shuneh in the Jordan Valley. Ever since those days, Hussein too had had reason to fear assassination, and often for reasons very similar to those that led to his grandfather's death. Over the years there have been not only several attempts to overthrow the monarchy, but at least a dozen attempts to assassinate King Hussein directly. On several occasions his car has been fired at. He exposed another plot by noticing some dead cats on the palace grounds. An assistant cook had been experimenting with poison intended for the King. Another time he noticed the nose drops he was taking had been tampered with. He had them analyzed and discovered that they had been contaminated with deadly poison.

One of the King's security devices is always to keep secret the details of his daily movements. No one ever knows exactly when or where he will go, and appointments with him are almost never kept exactly on time. Indeed, while punctuality may be the courtesy of kings, this king finds that security makes it desirable for him to keep visitors waiting anything from fifteen minutes to four hours. But he never hesitates to expose himself to crowds. His most remarkable triumph over a crowd occurred during the attempted coup d'état of 1957. Informed that a brigade was moving on the capital, the King declared that he would "see for himself." He jumped into a palace Chevrolet next to the driver with his faithful uncle, Sherif Hussein, in the back seat and roared through the night to Zerqa, base of the rebellious units. According to his own account in his autobiography, *Uneasy Lies the Head,* he strode into the camp: "Officers pointed submachine guns unknowingly at their supreme commander, not recognizing me until I jumped out and shouted: 'I am Hussein. I am all right. My life is yours. All is well. Back to your camps. I will be there shortly.' " His sudden appearance had a magical effect. The soldiers were astonished. Some cheered, others wept. They rallied to their king, and the rebellion collapsed.

Although the Hashemite monarchy was imposed on this region by the British, King Hussein has undoubtedly won the hearts of many of those on the East Bank, and at least the grudging respect of many Palestinians. The King is not a great intellect, but his political instincts have thus far rarely misled him.

He has shown that he has the courage to adopt unpopular and sometimes dangerous policies because he is convinced that they are right.

His decision to suppress the Fedayeen in 1970 is a notable example. Of equal importance is his unswerving insistence that he is willing to make peace with Israel if the Israelis will first return the occupied territory. I will have more to say about this in Chapter 16, "Solutions."

Thanks to King Hussein's clever leadership, Jordan managed to come through the fourth Arab-Israeli war unscathed. Although he was under great pressure from his Arab neighbors, including King Faisal, to go to war immediately after President Sadat's attack on October 6, King Hussein hesitated. He knew that he had neither the aircraft nor the ground-to-air missiles necessary to defend against an Israeli air attack. Once before, in 1967, he had gone to war, relying upon an Egyptian promise to provide air cover, and had been cruelly deceived. Now he was determined not to lead his army to the slaughter once again.

Just a week after the fighting had begun, as the tide was turning against the Arabs, King Hussein found the way out of his dilemma. He sent his best tank unit, known as Armored Brigade 40, numbering 3,000 men, into Syria to help stem the Israeli advance from the Golan Heights toward Damascus. The Jordanian brigade fought well, losing one third of its equipment, which included British-built Centurion tanks. Most Arabs felt the King had chosen a difficult but adequate and honorable course.

6

Lebanon

This small country of only two and a half million people plays many roles which lend it an importance out of all proportion to its size in the Middle East.

I believe that I experienced the essential qualities of this country as I traveled back and forth for nearly a decade between Beirut and the various points of interest in the region. Beirut was my secure base, and setting off from Beirut was like plunging into a dark sea. The rest of the Middle East seemed blanketed by the clouds of various forms of dictatorship, the Baath in Damascus and Baghdad, the theocratic autocracy of Saudi Arabia, the military monarchist authority of Jordan, the police state socialism of Aden. But here in Beirut was a working democracy. Not at all perfect, to be sure, but a place where an American newspaperman could work with reasonable freedom without worrying too much about censorship.

To appreciate the meaning of Lebanon you must know its beginnings. The French, who took charge of the League of Nations mandate in Lebanon and Syria after World War I, found in the region known as Mount Lebanon a Christian community, basically Christians who had taken refuge in these mountains over a period of centuries. French Catholic missions had made a profound impression on these people beginning during the time of the Crusades. The French confirmed and expanded their cultural imprint on the new state of Lebanon.

In 1943 Lebanese politicians, on the threshold of independence, drew up what became known as the National Covenant, a "gentlemen's agreement" in which there is no text but which has served the Lebanese systems as an effective foundation. The National Covenant provided that Christians and Moslems should always remain in balance, with neither element attempting to dominate the other. It provided that Lebanon would never align itself with the West, nor would it join any union with any Arab state. In deference to these principles, Lebanon joined the Arab League only on condition that the League's constitution state that its decisions would be binding only when adopted unanimously. It succeeded in imposing the same condition on the Arab Boycott Office, whose decisions are not binding until approved by each Arab government separately. Rather than submit to the possibility of majority decisions that could infringe upon the principle of the Covenant, Lebanon has declined to join an Arab Common Market. In accordance with the principles of the Covenant, it was agreed that the President should always be a Maronite Christian, the Premier a Sunni Moslem, the Speaker of the Chamber of Deputies a Shia Moslem, and the Deputy Speaker a Greek Orthodox.

The rest of the government was based on the formula of six Christians to five Moslems so that parliamentary committees normally have eleven members and the total number of seats in Parliament—now ninety-nine—is always divisible by eleven.

The electoral system was so devised that constituencies were shaped according to religious concentrations. Candidates run not on a general political platform, but for seats labeled for the Sunni, the Shia, the Armenian Catholics, the Greek Catholics, the Maronites, the Greek Orthodox, the Armenian Orthodox, and one for minorities, meant to represent the Jews (but there has never been a Jewish candidate).

This system was founded on the assumption that Christians are still in the slight majority. But Moslem leaders point out that the higher birth rate among Moslems has in recent years undoubtedly given them a majority. The Christians counter by insisting that a true estimate of the population of Lebanon should include two million Lebanese emigrants, about 80 percent of whom are Christians. They have succeeded in maintaining the principle that all emigrants have the right not only of return, but also of voting. Because of these complications, and a reluctance among responsible leaders to upset the system, demands for a new census are always deferred. The census of 1935 remains the operative basis of the state.

In this political setting many things became possible. Lebanon served the whole Arab Middle East as a land of refuge where exiled political leaders of interminable series of coups and revolutions in Arab countries could live in safety until, perhaps, they found an opportunity to repair their fortunes. Here was a system of political and economic *laissez-faire* which permitted private enterprise to flourish as nowhere else in all of the Middle East. It resulted in some remarkable successes, and also in many less admirable developments. In this environment Lebanon could become the banker and broker of the Middle East—although one of its largest banks, the Intrabank, crashed in 1966 and the Lebanese economy was shaken but not broken. Investment in the tourist industry—hotels, beaches, and a glittering casino—also flourished until the 1967 War cut off the flow of Christian tourists bound for the Holy Land. But Moslem Arab visitors continued to crowd Lebanon's mountain and beach resorts, and Western tourists return gradually after every disturbance—civil war between the Lebanese army in October, 1969, and again in April and May, 1973—in spite of such major deterrents as the Israeli raid to assassinate Black September leaders in April, 1973.

Sheikhs from the oil-rich countries of the Gulf and Saudi Arabia flock to Beirut as a playground where all kinds of pleasures can be found and where they can also invest in real estate. Their investments produced a decade of boom, broken finally by the Intrabank crash and the War of 1967, but the unsuppressible Lebanese are flourishing again in the seventies, at least insofar as their financial and trading community is concerned. Investments in construction produced also an architectural nightmare. Where there were once streets lined with villas and trees, now there are traffic canyons lined with high-rise apartment houses and office buildings. Jet aircraft roar overhead to an international airfield situated within minutes of the center of town. Beirut has become synonymous with noise.

Lebanon is Middle East headquarters for all kinds of Western business represented by twelve American banks and an astonishingly large community of 15,000 Americans, and somewhat smaller communities of British, French, and other Westerners. The political East is represented as well, by such as the Soviet Union's Narodny Bank. Also Lebanon is a center for international organizations representing, among others, the United Nations, and for political movements that cover the entire spectrum of political activity.

The Lebanese maintain a rather subtle principle according to which the state bars international political parties whose direction comes from outside the state, such as the Communist Party, the Party of the Baath, and the Arab Nationalist Movement (ANM), but has no objections to the expression of political ideas of whatever kind. In fact—and this again is characteristically Lebanese— all these parties are organizationally represented in Lebanon under slightly different names. The Communist Party and the ANM even manage to maintain Middle East headquarters in Beirut. But because their status is equivocal and they could be closed down at any time, they keep activity in Lebanon at a minimum—which is just what the state wants.

The Lebanese press represents all of the political trends of the Middle East and nearly all of its governments. For example, Syria, Iraq, Saudi Arabia, Jordan, and Kuwait each have one newspaper reporting their points of view, and Egypt has at least ten. The major commando movements are also represented. While the system sounds venal by American standards of journalistic ethics, it results in everybody's stories being on record. An observer in Beirut can watch them all. Their views and activities are marshaled daily in an English-language review called *The Arab World*.

Most of the major newspapers of the world now make their

Middle East headquarters in Beirut because correspondents can work there with a minimum of interference and censorship. Censorship exists but is concerned only with internal Lebanese affairs and is, in any case, easily evaded. Correspondents from all over the world have for more than two decades gathered in the bar of the Hotel St. George in Beirut and made it one of the world's notable clearing houses for information both publishable and unpublishable.

One of the stories they tell is about a certain Lebanese journalist who was once summoned to visit King Saud, then in exile in Athens. The King informed the Lebanese that he had decided to regain his throne and wished to launch a press campaign. An aide handed the journalist an envelope containing no less than 300 one thousand dollar notes. Startled by the sight of so much money, the Lebanese returned rapidly to his hotel, wrapped the payment around his waist, and took the first plane back to Beirut. King Saud waited a week, two weeks, a month, but there were no signs of a campaign for his return in the Beirut press. At length he sent one of his sons to Beirut to find out what had happened. Guilelessly the Prince called on the President of the Lebanese Press Association and told him all about the affair. Horrified, though not quite for the reasons the Prince had in mind, the President called in the journalist in question. The journalist admitted that he had received money but not how much. His defense was merely to say: "The King did not tell me to share it. . . . He gave it to me. You have nothing to do with it." There appeared to be nothing that anyone could do about it. The campaign never took place and the journalist lived happily ever after.

Beyond the expensive apartments rented by trading and international enterprises, Beirut is a city of tenements and vast slums. The French St. Joseph University and the American University of Beirut, with its magnificent new medical research center, stand out like jewels for the use of the whole Middle East. But Lebanon almost alone in the Middle East lacks a working free educational system. It maintains only the most rudimentary system of social security and welfare.

Most serious of the negative by-products of Lebanon's system of freedom is the narcotics trade. There isn't much that can't be had for money in Beirut. Here narcotics from half the world are collected and transshipped. Lebanon itself is a major producer of hashish. Drugs reach Beirut even from the secret French and German laboratories where Turkish opium is refined into heroin. They are then redistributed to a world-wide market under the surveillance of big-time drug traffickers.

Against foreigners the Lebanese authorities enforce their strict laws against the use of and traffic in hashish. Since 1969 there have always been at least two dozen young Americans and Europeans in jail in Beirut, some serving sentences as high as four years for trying to export hashish. But everyone knows that while American and European travelers are often stopped at the airport for having a few pounds of hashish in their baggage, big-time operators export vast quantities—some of it grown in fields that belong to high political personalities. The export of hashish, though unrecorded, is in fact a significant source of Lebanese wealth. Compared with the official hypocrisy concerning drugs, the rest of Lebanon's vice —although considerable—fades into insignificance.

The Lebanese system is founded on balance. Whenever one element has tried to upset that balance, the system has faltered. In 1958, when President Shamoun attempted to succeed himself in office, thereby shifting the balance in favor of the right-wing Christian element, and when Nasser sought to take advantage of the situation to shift the balance in the other direction in favor of a left-wing Moslem combination, the resulting civil war almost destroyed the system. Again in October, 1969, the Palestinian commandos, in alliance with leftist political parties, almost upset the system by attempting to carry on a mini-war with Israel in defiance of official Lebanese noninvolvement.

In May, 1973, the Lebanese army and the commandos clashed again, but this time it was not the Palestinians but the Army that took the initiative in an effort to establish Lebanese government control over the refugee camps which had, in effect, been ruled by the commandos since October, 1969. What the Jordanian army did, or began to do to the Palestinian commandos in September, 1970, the Lebanese army would have liked to do in May, 1973. But it is not the Lebanese way to go to extremes, so the further rounds to be expected between the army and the Palestinians are unlikely to be so decisive. In any case, the Lebanese, numbering only 15,000 men, only half of whom are actually combat troops, do not at all enjoy the kind of physical superiority over the commandos enjoyed by the 50,000-man Jordanian army. As for the commandos, they are likely to make far-reaching compromises in order to save at least a little freedom of action in their last major base, in Lebanon.

Official Lebanon pays lip service to the Arab cause in general, and the cause of the Palestinian "resistance" in particular, but in fact maintains, insofar as it dares, a de facto neutrality. The dominant Christian conservatives like to think of themselves as Phoenicians rather than Arabs. A growing number of Moslems, too, have become conscious of Lebanon's advantage as a spectator rather than participant in the struggle with Israel. Both Christians and Moslems have grown weary of Palestinian disruption of Lebanese life.

With all that can be said of good and evil, with all that is beautiful and ugly about Lebanon, I believe that this country is essential to the well-being of the Arab Middle East. Without it, the Arabs would suffer from infinite frustrations. They would be deprived of a way of expressing themselves, of letting off steam, and of having a good time. They would suffocate politically and morally.

7

Syria and Iraq

Syria and Iraq are ruled by rival factions of the Baath Party, and this is the reason for dealing with these two countries together. While Egypt and Jordan have done most of the fighting against Israel, Syria, and Iraq—even before the advent of the Baath—exceeded all other countries in the virulence of their hostility toward Zionism.

Apart from this very recent history, the two countries have some important things in common. Damascus and Baghdad are proud and ancient cities whose histories go back to the seventh to the tenth centuries A.D., when the Ommayad and Abbasid dynasties ruled in the region know as the Fertile Crescent—the lands that extend from the plains north of the Sinai Desert through what is now Israel and Jordan, Lebanon, and Syria, into the Valley of the Tigris and Euphrates. The leaders of these countries, especially of Syria, have always considered themselves to be at the center of the Arab world, with a special claim to authentic "Arabism." Egypt became the center of Arab affairs, as they see it, only because of the role of Gamal Abdel Nasser. Syria and Iraq fought against the Turks and against European rule, and the leaders of each had a lot to do with the origins of the idea of Arab nationalism.

But the historic differences between Syria and Iraq are more significant than the similarities, and they are worth examining before we return to the contemporary question of the Baath.

Damascus, the capital of Syria, built in an oasis set in a semidesert, communicates naturally with the habitat of all the old Arab tribes in the heart of the Arabian Peninsula. From Damascus the caravan routes extended eastward to the Persian Gulf, India, and the Far East, southward to the deserts of Saudi Arabia, northward to Turkey, and westward across the mountains to Beirut and the sea.

The bazaars of Damascus became one of the greatest commercial centers of the Arab world. Here were not only traders but also craftsmen, famed for the making of Damascene swords in ancient times, and more recently for brocades and copperware. Yet, with all the opulence of their capital, the Damascenes remained relatively austere in their way of life, scorning the venality of Levantine Beirut, the seaport across the mountains. Nor has the socialism of the current regime affected the social conservatism of Damascus.

Damascus, which lays claim to the title "oldest continuously inhabited city in the world," became the seat of the Ommayad Dynasty after Muawiyah, the fifth successor to Mohammed, founder of the Islamic religion, shifted the seat of the caliphate from the Hejaz. A visual sense of the city's history is conveyed by such splendors as the Ommayad Mosque and such relics as the Biblical "Street Called Straight," whose Roman columns and arches have been excavated to a depth of fifteen to twenty feet below the level of the streets of the bazaar.

Syria itself was rarely the center of empire, but more often part of and ruled by larger empires of Egyptians, Assyrians, Hittites, Persians, Greeks, Romans, Byzantines, Turks, Crusaders, and finally of the French.

The Iraqis, whose capital is Baghdad, are very different. By comparison with the voluble but physically gentle Syrians, the Iraqis are dour and violent. Whereas casualties have been rare occurrences in the long succession of coups in Damascus, the changes of regime in Iraq have often been bloody. The Damascus mob shouts; the mob in Baghdad kills.

Baghdad derives its character from its role as a true center of empires founded on the rich irrigated agricultural lands between the Tigris and Euphrates rivers known as Mesopotamia, empires which lived in perpetual conflict with the barbarians who swept down periodically from the mountains of the north.

The history of civilization in Iraq is as old as that of Egypt. Here, where the Garden of Eden of Adam and Eve is said to have been situated, the Kings of Sumer and Akkad reigned prior to 3000 B.C. Hammurabi devised one of the first codes of law around 1800 B.C. The Jews who had been exiled to Babylon by Nebuchadnezzar were still captives when Daniel, in 550 B.C., read the doom of the dynasty at the hands of Cyrus of Persia in the words written by the moving fingers on the wall of Belshazzar's Palace beginning: "Mene, Mene, Tekel, Upharsin," meaning "God hath numbered thy kingdom. Thou art weighed in the balance and art found wanting. Thy kingdom is divided and given to the Medes and the Persians."

In this center of ancient civilization, the Abbasid Dynasty, after destroying the Ommayads, established itself in A.D. 750. It rose to its greatest glory as the center of an empire whose wealth was gathered from and whose power extended to the whole region from the Atlantic Ocean to the gateway to India. During subsequent centuries of progressive decentralization and decline, the empire fell under Persian, Mongol, and eventually Turkish domination.

After World War I, the British, who had occupied Mesopotamia during the war, established a new kingdom in Baghdad with Feisal, whom the French had expelled from Damascus, on the throne. The weakness of the new kingdom (1970 population, 9 million) was that it was composed of a volatile mixture of three elements. In the center of the country lies a plain populated by Sunni Arabs, adherents of the largest orthodox branch of Islam, and who have long dominated Mesopotamia. The south, however, is inhabited by Arabs of the Shia branch of Islam, who make up about one-third of the country's population, and who are slightly more numerous, though less educated, developed, and influential than the Sunnis of the center. Excluded from most places of power, the Shia sometimes turned for support to neighboring Persia, where the Shia are dominant. The Shia believe that Ali, the son-in-law of Mohammed, was the legitimate successor to the Prophet. Most do not recognize the legitimacy of the three caliphs who preceded him, and none recognize the caliphs who came later.

The north of Iraq is inhabited by one and one half to two million Kurds. The Kurds are a non-Arab people of Indo-European origin related to the Persians. They are spread across Eastern Turkey (five million), Western Iran (three million), as well as northeastern Iraq. A fringe of Kurds also live in northeastern Syria (300,000) and the southern Caucasus of the U.S.S.R. (175,000). These estimates are guesswork because all the host countries feel that it is in their interest to minimize the numbers of these people. But Kurdish nationalists estimate the total number of Kurds at twelve million or even more.

From the time of the earliest Mesopotamian empires, the Kurds and their ancestors have fought against Arabs, Persians, and Turks, but have never, except briefly at Mehabad in 1946, succeeded in establishing more than autonomous principalities.

The Baath—the party of Arab Renaissance—is the political organization which, with the iron-fisted backing of Arab armies, first established itself in Iraq in February, 1963, and in Syria in February, 1964. Now that Nasser is gone, its importance looms greater than ever.

The Baath was founded in the 1930s by two Syrian students attending the Sorbonne in Paris. One was Michel Aflaq, a Christian student of literature, the other Salah Bitar, a Moslem student of law. At the time, World War II was impending, and Arab liberation movements were stirring in the Middle East. The Arab movement against the British and French lacked formulated ideas as to the future, and only the communists offered an ideological anticolonial movement. But communism was too international to appeal to the Arab nationalists. Aflaq and Bitar saw this.

In his later writings, Aflaq acknowledged the influence on his thinking of André Gide and Romain Rolland, whom he called "noble souls, far above communist factionalism." He acknowledged also his debt to Marxism and to the romantic and idealistic German theories of nationalism expounded by Herder and Hegel.

"We learned from the German philosophers that there is something deeper than external events or economic relations in explaining the march of history or the growth of society." Describing what he regarded as the mystical marriage of nationalism and socialism, Aflaq wrote that "Socialism is the body, national unity the spirit."

Upon their return home in 1940, Aflaq and Bitar began teaching school in Damascus but soon shifted their political headquarters to the fringes of the American University of Beirut. In Feisal's cafe across the streetcar tracks from the university, Aflaq spent many hours smoking cigarettes and sipping tea and coffee with students from all over the Arab world. These students became, in due course, the founders of the international network of the Baath Party. Aflaq was the theoretician, a somewhat mystical man whom the *Times* of London once called "the Gandhi of Arab nationalism, a pale, slight man of painful shyness, deep sincerity and debilitatingly frugal habits." Bitar backed him up with reason, legal interpretations, and administrative ability.

The Party appealed mainly to intellectuals. Organized on the basis of party cells of seven men each, on the communist model, it spread a semiclandestine network across the Arab world, except Egypt. The Baathists' emphasis on Ethnic Arabism did not appeal to the Egyptians.

After the defeat of 1948, many disillusioned Arab intellectuals were drawn to the Baath, and Syria's first dictator, Brigadier General Husni Zaim, in 1949 sought cooperation with Aflaq. After first assenting, Aflaq tried to withdraw. Zaim had him arrested and tortured until he signed a declaration endorsing the regime. Deeply humiliated, Aflaq sought solace in exile in Brazil.

In 1957 Aflaq, who had returned from exile, and Bitar led the parade of Syrian politicians to Cairo to beg Nasser to save Syria from the communists. They had hopes then that the Baathists, as the older movement, could dominate Nasserism and "polish and crystallize Nasser's thoughts." They agreed to dissolve their own party. But by 1959 the Baathists fell out of favor with Nasser. The present split in the party dates from that time. Akram Hawrani, leader of a small Arab Socialist Party which had merged with the Baath in 1949, decided to revert to an independent role. A second group of Baathists living in exile in Egypt formed their own inner circle under the leadership of Salah Jadid. The third group were Aflaq, Bitar, and their followers.

When the coup d'état of May, 1963, took place in Damascus, the Jadid group and the Nasserites cooperated with Aflaq and Bitar. The Nasserites were purged a few months later, leaving the Jadid and Aflaq groups together. But these two elements never really reintegrated, and in February, 1966, the Jadid group succeeded in ousting Bitar as Premier. It condemned Aflaq, and even expelled him from the party. But Aflaq retained the Pan-Arab following of the party, and it was his followers who seized power in Baghdad in July, 1968.

The confusing history of shifts in Baathist power may be summarized as follows:

Baghdad: February 8, 1963, secret Baathist revolutionary command overthrows Premier Abdel Karim Kassem.

September, 1963, army led by Major General Abdel Salaam Aref overthrows the Baathist regime; he is killed in helicopter accident April 13, 1966, and succeeded by his brother, Lieutenant General Abdel Rahman Aref.

July, 1968, Baathists led by Major General Hassan al Bakr overthrow President Abdel Rahman Aref.

Sidam Hussein Takriti, assistant secretary general of the party, becomes dominant personality beginning early 1970.

Damascus: March 8, 1963, Baathists led by Aflaq and Bitar seize power.

June, 1966, Salah Jadid faction takes over, ousting Aflaq and Bitar. Aflaq goes to Baghdad.

September, 1970, General Hafez al Assad takes over bloodlessly.

In both countries it was Baathist officers, or officers sympathetic to the Baath, who made it possible for the party to take power and who are the ultimate sanction of the party's power. They have often talked about establishing a democratic system with an elected parliament. But the regimes have remained in fact dictatorships working behind the mask of what the Baathists call "collective leadership."

Within its own ranks the party does maintain a system of election in which card-carrying members of the basic cells elect the leaders of city blocks, districts, the town itself, and the country. The heads of these units form the National Congress, which meets annually and elects the leadership inside a particular country. The Pan-Arab system of the party is based on a congress of representatives from all the Arab countries which elects the Pan-Arab leadership, the highest party authority, at least in theory.

The 1966 split in Damascus occurred because the Syrian national leadership would not submit to the Pan-Arab leadership. But the general public remains unaffected by these forms of intraparty democracy. What the regimes in the two capitals insist on calling a "collective leadership" appeared until recently to the Syrian people and to the world to be a rather faceless dictatorship.

After the split of the Baathist movement into two parts, one in Damascus and the other in Baghdad, the factions devoted much of their energy to attempts to overthrow each other, each claiming the rights of legitimacy. Yet they are much alike. Both use the slogans "Unity, Freedom and Socialism" and "One Arab nation with an immortal mission." Without denying the existence of a hard core of idealism, in practice the slogans are a mask for very practical politics and ethnic pride, if not racialism. Both parties lack popular following and depend on the discipline of their tightly organized membership of petty intellectuals, schoolteachers, white-collar workers, technicians, and bureaucrats, backed by some of the military and a ubiquitous secret police. While the former party has purged nearly all possible military opposition, the latter has rooted out the old moderate political parties. So efficient has been this process that only the communists and the Kurdish Democratic Party maintain an effective existence outside the framework of the official Baath party structure.

Police-state methods have gone farthest in Iraq, where in 1969 and 1970 approximately 100 persons, including fourteen Jews, were executed on charges of conspiracy to overthrow the government or espionage on behalf of the United States or Israel. During this period life in Baghdad was in many ways reminiscent of life in eastern European capitals in the first few years after World War II, when the communists were breaking the back of the middle class. In Baghdad in 1970, as in Prague in 1950, the ring of the doorbell anytime after midnight was likely to signify a visit from the police, and people disappeared mysteriously from their homes. Western foreigners were always under surveillance and the secret police questioned and sometimes arrested Iraqis who associated with foreigners.

The state's determination to survive at any cost also led to intrigue and deception. The Baathists cooperated with conservative officers to bring about the coup of 1968, only to purge them thirteen days later. Many of those purged were accused of being CIA agents and were imprisoned. Abdel Razzak el Nayef, who had been Premier for only a few days, had the good fortune to be bundled onto an airplane and flown to exile in Rabat.

The Kurds will never forget that in June of 1963, while they were negotiating with the Baathist government in Baghdad, the regime suddenly arrested the negotiators and launched a military offensive against the Kurds.

In terms of socialism, the regime in Syria has gone considerably farther than the one in Iraq. The Syrian Baath began in 1963 by restoring the measures of socialization which had been introduced by the Nasserites and watered down by the secessionist regime which expelled the Egyptians in 1961. This meant agrarian reform, state control of banks, and nationalization of the main industries. The Baathists poured 82 percent of foreign trade into state enterprises. They attempted to spread socialist ideas. All Baathists had to go into the fields during the harvest season and hold sessions explaining the meaning of socialism and agrarian reform to the peasants. They assigned commissars to each factory to indoctrinate the workers at weekly meetings.

Public statements emphasized the regime's success in producing and selling oil from the fields in the northeastern corners of the country. They boasted that Syria was the first Arab country that has managed to get along without the big oil companies. Yet the economic significance of the oil remains slight. Of far greater importance economically is the Euphrates Dam which, in relation to the size of the Syrian economy, will in the 1970s loom as large as the Aswan High Dam in Egypt. It will bring a vast new acreage into agricultural production and provide the country with almost unlimited electric power without raising the kind of ecological problems that have been noted in the case of the Nile.

Even before the advent of the Baath, Syrian revolutionaries had showed themselves eager to export their revolutions, and especially to Lebanon. This was the case in 1958 during the Lebanese civil war, when the Nasserites made Syria their base. The Baathists have the additional excuse that they consider themselves a Pan-Arab movement.

In October, 1969, the Syrian Baathists tried to back the Fatah insurgents in Lebanon, but did not reach the point of sending the regular Syrian army into action. Only units of Saiqa, the commando group, made use of Syrian army trucks and other equipment, thereby causing much consternation among the Lebanese, who thought they were being invaded by the Syrian army.

In September, 1970, the Syrians turned their proclivity for exporting revolution against Jordan, and sent 250 tanks across the border to reinforce the commandos against King Hussein. It took the combined pressure of the United States and the Soviet Union and the threat of Israeli intervention—not to mention some pressure from the Jordanian armed forces—to turn them back.

Again, in May, 1973, the Syrians allowed a few units of the Palestine Liberation Army and of Saiqa, the Syrian Government sponsored commandos, to cross briefly into Lebanon in a show of support for the Fedayeen against the Lebanese army. But pressures much like those that turned back the Syrian tanks from Jordan prevented the incursion from becoming an invasion.

The rise to power on November 15, 1970, of Major General Hafez al Assad in a bloodless coup d'état (which some statisticians figured to be the twentieth since that of Husni el Zaim in 1949) turned Syria in a new, more moderate direction. He called it "a correctional movement." General Assad is a reluctant strong man who could have taken power several years before he did, but was restrained by loyalty to his colleagues in the Baath Party. He was jolted into action, however, by the rashness of his principal political rival, Salah Jadid, who sent tanks into Jordan. As commander of the air force, as well as Minister of Defense, he refused not only to give the tanks air cover but also placed Jadid and Jadid's front man, Nureddin Attasi, the Chief of State, under house arrest.

Having made himself President, Hafez al Assad introduced a new style in Syrian politics. Now foreigners are welcomed at the borders instead of being harassed by the secret police. Instead of the furtive, impersonal leadership exercised behind the scenes in which Jadid had specialized as Assistant Secretary General of the party, Assad addressed his people directly on radio and television, and distributed pictures of himself with his five children (but without his wife). He relaxed political police surveillance, brought a number of political police officers to trial for abuse of authority, relaxed the system of exit permits so that Syrians could get relief from the austerity of their economy, encouraged a revival of private business, and decreed a reduction in the prices of tea, coffee, flour, and kerosene. Far from interfering in neighboring Jordanese affairs, he offered to mediate the next squabble between the guerrillas and King Hussein. A man who has shown that he has the courage to talk back to the Russians, he has succeeded in getting from them more modern tanks and aircraft. The new strong man of Syria also came to terms with King Faisal. Damascus as a center for revolutionary groups and their broadcasts has consequently been muted.

Iraq, which never went as far in its socialism as Syria, also embarked on a more moderate course in 1971 under the leadership of its strong man, Sidam Hussein el Takriti, whose methods recall those employed by Jadid in Syria until he was shunted aside by Assad. Sidam Hussein, as he is usually called, exercises his powers from behind the scenes as Assistant Secretary General of the party. He is a frustrated lawyer whose studies were interrupted by political arrests. Now, it is said, he will never complete his law studies because he is so busy making law.

Sidam Hussein shapes Iraq's new policies much more than the

Council of Fifteen, who are nominally the collective leadership and highest authority. Here are some major points in what he has done.

(a) He has brought home Iraqi army units which had been stationed in Syria and Jordan much of the time since the 1967 War and which had at one time numbered 12,000.

(b) Although rhetorically still centered on Palestine, the real focus of Iraqi policy has gradually shifted to the Persian Gulf— much to the alarm of the Kuwaitis and of the Shah of Iran. Ostensibly the Iraqis had abandoned their claim to Kuwait after the Baathists overthrew Abdel Karim Kassem in February, 1963. Kuwait sealed this renunciation with a substantial loan. But the Kuwaitis are necessarily disturbed by Baathist sponsorship of revolutionary movements in the Gulf. Revolution and subversion is Iraq's weapon also against Iran's claim to have succeeded Britain as dominant power and keeper of the peace in the Gulf.

(c) After eight-and-a-half years of futile fighting, Sidam Hussein insisted on making peace with the Kurds. Understanding that Iraq would never subdue these people, he obliged the Iraqi army on March 11, 1970, to swallow its pride in a recognition of Kurdish autonomy.

His policy required a personal settlement with another strong personality of Iraq, Mullah Mustafa Barzani, the Kurdish leader, one of the most remarkable men of the modern Middle East. Mullah Mustafa's father and grandfather fought and were killed by the Turks, and he himself grew up fighting the British. Toward the end of World War II he led his own tribe on a remarkable trek through the mountains from Iraq into the area of the Mehabad Republic, which for a brief period in 1946 enjoyed something very close to independence in the zone between British and Russian forces in Persia. Suppressed at last by the Persians, Mullah Mustafa, with a few hundred followers, fled in 1947 to Moscow. The Russians, hoping no doubt that he and his men would become communists, treated them well. Many of them learned trades or engaged in higher studies, and some took Russian wives. Then, in 1958, Abdel Kerim Kassem overthrew King Faisal and invited

Mullah Mustafa and his men to come home. The Russians let them go and they returned with the understanding, which was written into the new Constitution, that the Kurds would be equal partners with the Arabs in the new Republic.

The honeymoon between the Kurds and the Arabs did not last. Kassem could not resist the nationalists who wished to Arabize the Kurds. The Kurdish War began in September, 1961—a war which has been of great significance to Israel because it has continuously occupied at least two divisions on the Northern Front. The struggle enabled Mullah Mustafa to unite the Kurds, mostly by consent, but also by force, and established him clearly as the leading anticommunist among the Kurds—which must have disappointed the Russians.

In word and deed Mullah Mustafa has been careful never to involve the Kurds of Turkey or of Iran in his insurgency. He even went so far as to send back to Turkey Kurdish Turks who tried to volunteer to serve him. In Iran the situation was different in that the Shah showed sympathy for the Kurds, whom he recognized as fellow Aryans, and whom he used to put pressure on Baghdad. Beginning in 1963, therefore, the Persians allowed a trickle of arms and other supplies across the border and permitted wounded Kurds to obtain medical care in Iran.

The March 11, 1970, settlement between Mullah Mustafa and Sidam Hussein distressed the Shah. But he may take comfort in the knowledge that it could break down at any time. The Kurds were supposed, according to the agreement, to receive five posts as ministers, a post as vice president, far-reaching economic assistance, and help in restoring a Kurdish educational system. Thus far, they have obtained only the posts as ministers. Other measures have been stalled in disagreement over the future of the town of Kirkuk, at the center of the richest oil fields. The Kurds claim Kirkuk on the grounds that the population of the district is overwhelmingly Kurdish. A census planned in the autumn of 1970 to establish the facts was postponed indefinitely because of disagreement about the regulations under which the census should operate. An eventual renewal of violence seems likely.

After President Sadat had, in 1972, expelled Soviet technicians from Egypt, the Soviet Union shifted its attention to Syria and Iraq to the extent possible. The Russians tried to get Syria to sign a Treaty of Friendship similar to that previously concluded with Iraq but found President Assad unwilling to do so. They have, however, stepped up military and economic aid to both countries. In April, 1973, Syria was reported to have received forty MIG jet fighters, including thirty MIG 21s.

Among the achievements of the Baath in Syria and Iraq, one must note that they have given their countries a kind of stability, albeit oppressive. It is easy for Europeans to deride their ideologies as "half-baked socialism," yet they have introduced to the Arab world, which previously had scarcely thought in such terms, the rudiments of ideology. The Baathists were first among the Arabs in the 1920s to marry radical ideas of social justice and reform to the half-century-old dream of Arab unity. They anticipated the revolutionary ideology of the Arab Nationalist Movement and its PFLP in holding that the ideals of "unity, freedom and socialism" (the trinity of the Baath Party) must be used against "reaction" at home as well as against "imperialists" from abroad. For the first time in Arab experience, loyalty to a party is observed to transcend loyalties to family, tribe, and religion.

8

The Arabian Peninsula, Persian Gulf, and Oil

The Arabian Peninsula and the Gulf are called the backdoor of the Middle East—but what a backdoor!

Here is, above all, oil, which has been translated into great wealth, some very conspicuous consumption, and some remarkable welfare states. A new, educated, progressive middle class has arisen in these countries, although there are plenty of areas in them where there is no oil or where its benefits have not trickled down to the people. Here is great poverty. A few of the inhabitants of these countries live almost exactly as their ancestors did five hundred years ago in medieval towns with ancient customs, unspeakable hygiene, barbarous penology, or in the desert with camels, tents, tribal raids, disease, superstitions—and sometimes great dignity.

Here are the traditional regimes of the Arab world—a king, a sultan, a dozen sheikhs—and, across the Gulf, on its eastern shore, the Shah-in-Shah of Iran. But the region also includes several republics, two of which are ruled by the most radical political parties in the Arab world, and who make it their business to foment civil war and revolution in the rest of the region.

Here is a large slice of the "romance" of the Middle East, a region which some might imagine to be happily removed from the turmoil and vexation of the Arab-Israeli struggle. But it is not. For the oil which finances the sheikhly palaces and the welfare states also finances the Arab effort against Israel. In 1948, when the Israelis won their first victory over the Arabs, the Arab cornucopia was just beginning to pour out its bounty, and no one could have predicted that the financial resources available to the Arabs would proliferate so enormously as they had by the 1970s.

Let us see just how rich the Arabs have become, and are likely to become in the future.

U.S. STATE DEPARTMENT ESTIMATES OF PRODUCTION AND REVENUE, 1975

(Stated in thousands of barrels per day, billions of dollars annually)

MIDDLE EAST	*Production*	*Revenue*
Iran	7,300	4.7
Saudi Arabia	8,500	5.4
Kuwait	3,500	2.2
Iraq	1,900	1.2
Abu Dhabi	2,300	1.5
Other Persian Gulf	1,800	1.0
Subtotal	25,300	16.0
NORTH AFRICA		
Libya	2,200	2.0
Algeria	1,200	1.1
Subtotal	3,400	3.1
TOTAL	28,700	19.1

From insignificant beginnings in the first years after World War II, oil production and revenues have soared. The latest figures available show an impressive picture.

In an arc around the Gulf lie about 75 percent of this earth's oil reserves, one of mankind's basic resources and prime source of energy. In 1968, in a paper written for The Center for Strategic Studies of Georgetown University, Christopher Tugendhat, a noted British authority on oil, has called it "the most important area in the world" because, "if the world was a united economic

PRODUCTION*

Countries	Reserves (billions of barrels)	1961 to 1965 (in thousands of barrels)	1966	1967	1968	1969	1970	1971	1972
Saudi Arabia	143,000	9,011	2,393	2,600	2,830	2,995	3,550	4,771	5,700
Kuwait	78,198	7,269	2,275	2,292	2,421	2,575	2,735	3,198	3,000
Iran	65,500	7,380	2,017	2,595	2,850	3,375	3,830	4,540	4,900
Libya	30,400	—	458	1,745	2,600	3,110	3,320	2,760	2,230
Iraq	29,000	5,709	1,383	1,222	1,503	1,521	1,518	1,693	455
Abu Dhabi	21,000	3,371	362	384	499	599	591	933	1,000
Qatar	7,000	—	289	324	340	356	361	429	450
Oman	5,200	—	—	57	240	328	333	287	280
Dubai	2,000	—	—	—	18	—	—	125	130
Syria	7,300	—	—	—		48	81	130	120
USSR	75,000	17,260	5,335	5,795	6,190	6,585	7,130	7,470	7,900
U.S.	37,250	36,290	8,292	8,810	9,095	9,240	9,630	9,530	9,500
Venezuela	3,700	13,395	3,405	3,595	3,640	3,630	3,740	3,610	3,200

*Oil & Gas Journal Estimates.

unit its oil production would be centered in the Gulf. The littoral countries would dominate the international market to the same extent as Britain dominated the market for industrial manufactures in the late eighteenth and early nineteenth centuries."

Oil is important for reasons of finance and economics and as a factor in world strategy. Let me begin with the financial picture as it existed up to the great cutbacks and embargoes of the fourth Arab-Israeli war.

The largest American interests were represented in Saudi Arabia by the Arabian-American Oil Company—ARAMCO—combining Standard Oil of New Jersey, Standard of California, Texaco, and Mobil Oil. In Kuwait, Gulf Oil became a half partner along with British Petroleum in the Kuwait Oil Company.

United States companies, which control about 60 percent of the company interests in the Gulf, reported annual profits of one and a half billion dollars a year. If you capitalize that at 10 percent you could estimate the value of the investment at 15 billion dollars. On the other hand, if you talk about replacement costs it comes to something like 60 billion dollars.

Actual remittances to the United States were about one to one and a half billion dollars a year. Remittances to Britain were somewhat less. The British have an interest in about 30 percent of the oil in and around the Gulf, but it represents for them a much larger proportionate share in overseas investment and in contributions to their balance of payments than in the case of the United States.

These earnings were proportionally reduced by an agreement with the companies which gave the host countries a 25 percent "participation" in the companies as of January 1, 1973. This will gradually rise to 51 percent by January 1, 1982.

Earnings of host countries in 1973 were in the order of four to five billion dollars per year for Saudi Arabia and Iran and one and two billion dollars for Kuwait. Since the Teheran Conference early in 1971, the revenues of oil-producing countries have increased something like 20 to 100 percent across the board, depending on the resources of the country. Quite enormous sums are involved: big for the companies, big for the American and British balance of payments, and big for the host governments. OPEC has estimated that the cumulative incomes of all Arab countries from 1973 to 1980 will be over 210 billion dollars. If their cumulative expenditures during the period were 100 billion dollars, they would thus be left capital of 100 billion dollars or more.

But far and away more important than the money was the fact that about 65 percent of western Europe's oil, and 80 percent or more of Japan's, comes from the Gulf. These vital statistics signify the dependence of Europe and of Japan on the Gulf. To the United States this is a matter of great concern because the safety of western Europe and of Japan is of great concern to the United States. Any hostile force that gained control of this oil would have its hands on Europe's and Japan's jugular.

To these considerations, some new ones had recently been added. The United States, which hitherto had taken very little Gulf oil for its own consumption, was beginning to buy it in quantity. According to some eminent students of world energy patterns, the United States was likely by 1985 to be obtaining 57 percent of its oil from abroad, most of it from the Gulf and other parts of the Middle East. There were signs that the Russians, too, were becoming interested in this fabulous source of energy. As their economy expanded and their exportable surplus declined, they were directing their East European satellites to the Gulf for their oil, and the Soviet Union itself might well be in the market before long. Already the Russians had acquired an interest in the great Rumeili oil field of southern Iraq. The United States, on top of the considerations already listed, had acquired a direct interest in the Gulf and the Soviet Union was acquiring a substantial indirect interest at least. Obviously, the oil of the Gulf represents power for whoever controls it. Arab recourse to the "oil weapon" in October, 1973, may drastically change the picture as we will see in the section on oil in Chapter 14. The use of oil as a weapon in the Arab-Israeli war may well turn out to have been its most significant feature.

One thing seems certain. Quite apart from the effects of the application of the Arabs' "oil weapon," Saudi Arabia will emerge in the next few years as one of the great financial centers, perhaps the "banker of the world." It has been calculated that within three years Saudi Arabia will have greater financial reserves than the United States, Western Europe, and Japan combined. By the end of the decade, the Saudis may have accumulated 100 billion dollars in reserves. This is assuming that King Faisal will eventually agree to expand his country's daily production from 8.2 million barrels in the latter part of 1973 to 20 million barrels in 1980. While some may boggle at the prospect of Saudi financial power, close observers maintain that Arab financial dealings have thus far been responsible. More precisely, Saudis and Kuwaitis were not the cause of the runs on the dollar in 1973.

The British presence in the Gulf dates back to the days when it was deemed necessary to protect British access to India and the Far East. But after the empire had begun to decline the British never had any doubt about why they were still in the Gulf. It was to defend the oil. They forcefully demonstrated their purposefulness on several occasions in recent times. In the 1950s they intervened several times to save the Sultan of Oman by preventing Saudi Arabia from gaining control of the strategic bases at Buraimi and from installing a rebel regime in the interior of Oman. Again in 1961 the British landed amphibious forces in Kuwait to forestall the threat of Iraqi invasion of Kuwait, at that time the richest oil sheikhdom of all. This was the last occasion when the British used force on any scale in the Gulf, and was the last great gesture of the British raj. Meanwhile, the British economy was faltering, and in November, 1967, Britain withdrew from the great naval base at Aden from which British power once radiated throughout South Arabia, East Africa, and the Indian Ocean, as well as the Gulf. As the burden of empire became more and more unbearable, Prime Minister Harold Wilson announced in the House of Commons on January 16, 1968, that Britain must "come to terms with our role in the World." It must not be asked in the name of foreign policy to undertake commitments beyond its capabilities. "We have accordingly," he said, "decided to accelerate the withdrawal of our forces from their stations in the Far East, which was announced in the Supplementary Statement of Defense Policy of July 1967, and to withdraw them by the end of 1971. We have also decided to withdraw our forces from the Persian Gulf by the same date."

The British in fact withdrew at the end of November, 1971. They took with them the political apparatus of the British Resident, based in Bahrain and the agents who represented him in the Sheikhdoms, as well as about 3,000 ground troops and 3,000 airmen who had been stationed in Bahrain Island and at Sharjah.

Preoccupied as it has been with Vietnam, the United States has given no clear indication of its policies in the Gulf or in the Indian Ocean, into which the Gulf opens, following the departure of the British. One possible direction of that policy is suggested by the decision made early in 1971 to develop the British-owned island of Diego Garcia in the central Indian Ocean as an Anglo-American communications center. Probably the navies of both countries would like to develop the island, an almost uninhabited coral atoll curving around a lagoon, into a naval and air base. Meanwhile, after the withdrawal of British forces from the island of Bahrain and the Sheikhdom of Sharjah, the United States remains alone in the Gulf at Bahrain, with two destroyers and an LSD (Landing Ship Dock). This is, however, a ready-made excuse for the Russians to set up a similar base.

Since the British withdrawal there has been no significant Western defense force primarily assigned to the Gulf. The nearest effective force is the U.S. Sixth Fleet in the Mediterranean whose aircraft might be deployed all the way to the Gulf. In addition, patrols of the U.S. Pacific fleet occasionally carry out sweeps in the Indian Ocean. The Pentagon said early in 1972 that such sweeps would be made frequently—presumably to offset the steadily growing Soviet presence, which includes periodic Soviet naval visits to the Gulf. In October, 1973, at the height of the U.S.-Soviet confrontation during the fourth Arab-Israeli war, the USS *Hancock,* one of the U.S. Navy's smaller carriers, was detached from the 7th Fleet in Far Eastern waters and sent into the Indian Ocean.

Now that the British no longer stand guard in the Gulf, the United States must replace them as best it may. But the United States cannot reproduce the political and military system the British built up over centuries. American methods must be different but could achieve similar results. Whatever methods are adopted, it seems obvious to me that the first and basic consideration must be to maintain good relations with the Arabs and the Persians in the Gulf. This presents grave problems insofar as the Arabs are concerned, for two reasons. The first is the United States' commitment to Israel. This commitment will raise infinitely graver problems for the United States if and when the traditional regimes of the Gulf are replaced by revolutionary regimes who would be anti-American even if there were no Israel. The second is that the United States appears to be relying on Iran, which had differences with a number of Arab states, to replace the British as keeper of the peace in the Gulf.

To this end the United States in May, 1973, concluded a two-and-one-half billion dollar, five-year arms deal with Iran, including the very latest weapons in every field. The United States has tried to soften the impact of this very real power relationship for its Arab friends, Saudi Arabia and Kuwait, by expressing willingness to sell Phantoms to them too.

In June, 1973, it became known that the Saudis were spending more than one billion dollars on American weapons, probably including an unspecified number of Phantoms. Although the Israelis have had Phantoms for several years, the Saudis would be the first Arab country to acquire them. In addition, the Saudis were negotiating for 600 million dollars worth of ships for their navy.

The Kuwaiti arms package is for about 500 million dollars, and will probably also include Phantoms.

Ostensibly, all three countries are buying these arms because of the influx of Soviet military supplies into Iraq. Joseph J. Sisco, the Assistant Secretary of State for the Near East, also gave credence to Saudi Arabia's feeling of insecurity resulting from threats from the People's Republic of South Yemen (Aden). The South Yemenis have in fact been quarreling with the relatively defenseless Republic of North Yemen (Sana) and supporting the insurgents of Dhofar in Oman. In April they also bombed the Saudi border post at Wadeiya.

So, the Saudis really do have something to worry about, including the long-term threat of internal subversion.

Unfortunately, the real reason these three countries want Phantoms and other expensive weapons is because of their rivalry with one another. Iran and Saudi Arabia are two powers who should maintain the stability of the Gulf, but they are also deep-seated rivals. As for little Kuwait, it is especially afraid of Iraq, but it is afraid of all its neighbors.

The Shah of Iran has left no doubt that he regards himself as the heir to the British mantle in the Gulf. With a population of 30 million, a rapidly expanding economy, a well-equipped army, a growing navy, and Phantom aircraft from the United States, the Iranians dominate; they represent a force no Arab nation, and probably no combination of Arab nations, can equal. Yet the Arabs decline to regard the Gulf as in any sense a "Persian Lake" in the way it has been for centuries a "British Lake." Their attitude is symbolized by their insistence on the name "Arab Gulf" rather than the traditional "Persian Gulf."

Iraq and Iran have quarreled over their border for centuries. In recent years friction between them and more generally between Iran and the Arab states has centered on Persian demands that Iraq revise a 1937 treaty concluded under British influence which gives Iraq control of the whole of the Shatt al Arab, the watercourse formed by the confluence of the Tigris and the Euphrates. Early in 1970 the Shah sent Iranian naval units to escort Iranian ships up the river to the Iranian port of Abadan rather than submit to Iraqi controls. The Iraqis have since desisted from enforcing their treaty rights.

Iraq on many occasions since 1962 has accused Iran of assisting the Kurdish insurgents in northern Iraq, and has accused Iran of backing an unsuccessful attempt to overthrow the Iraqi government in January, 1970.

The day before Britain ended her treaty obligations with the Trucial States, Iran occupied three small islands—Abu Musa, owned by Sharjah, and the Greater and Lesser Thumbs, owned by Ras al Khaimah, all near the straits of Hormuz. The Shah said he had to control the islands to protect Iranian and other oil tankers that file through the straits in endless procession.

Iranian troops landed on Abu Musa by agreement with the Sheikh of Sharjah. They are now confined to a part of the island, and the Sheikh's flag still flies over the fishermen's village of about

300 persons. The agreement is working. But several Arabs were killed in the defense of the Greater Thumb, whose 150 inhabitants fled to the mainland. Iraq led the resulting Arab outcry against "imperialist" Iran.

Even Saudi Arabia had to join in the outcry, although King Faisal and the Shah had in November, 1969, agreed to cooperate against subversive leftist forces in the Gulf, which of course meant the Baathist regime of Iraq as well as the leftist regime of Aden.

The oldest conflict between Iran and the Arab states, Iran's claim to the island of Bahrain, was resolved by a United Nations Commission which, in 1968, ruled that the island's people wished to be independent. The Shah's willingness to accept the U.N. Commission's ruling was widely interpreted as a gesture of conciliation toward Iran, which should be rewarded by Arab concessions on Abu Musa and the Thumbs.

Although papered over with loans and speeches of good will, the conflict between Kuwait and Iraq remains fundamental. Iraq has some basis for a historical claim to Kuwait as a district of the province of Basra, which it was in Ottoman days. The separate identity of the Sheikh of Kuwait was established by British fiat, not in response to any Arab needs, but to make it easier for the British to keep out the Turks. As already mentioned, the British defended Kuwait against an Iraqi threat in 1961. After the Baathists came to power in Baghdad in 1963, Kuwait bought security for herself by extending large loans to Baghdad. This is a fundamental tactic of Kuwaiti foreign policy—in other circumstances it is called "buying protection." The Kuwaitis have used this tactic also in dealing with Cairo and Damascus. But it is unlikely that it will work with all governments and at all times.

In April, 1972, the Iraqis quite suddenly occupied a border post and bombarded another, demanding that the Kuwaitis give them long-term leases to two islands opposite the new Iraqi oil port of Umm Qasr. Only after Iran had made threatening noises did the Iraqis withdraw.

Saudi Arabia has never given up its claim to the oases of Buraimi from which it was driven by the British-officered Trucial Oman Scouts in 1952. Seven of the ten oases are in the hands of Abu

Dhabi, while Oman controls the rest. The Saudis have maintained this claim not so much because they are interested in the oases but because they hope to use the claim as a bargaining counter to obtain territory leading to the Gulf between Abu Dhabi and Qatar.

Long before the British intention to withdraw from the Gulf became known, the need for some sort of federation or union of the weak sheikhdoms along the shores of the Gulf was apparent. The British encouraged some cooperation in the framework of a Development Council of the Trucial States. These are the seven sheikhdoms that in the eighteenth and nineteenth centuries concluded a treaty with the British promising to abandon piracy and the slave trade in return for a British promise of protection from all forms of sea-borne aggression. Once the British were gone, how could such "states" as Ras Al Khaimah or Sharjah, each with only a few thousand population, or even the stronger sheikhdoms such as Dubai and Abu Dhabi, maintain their identities against outside pressures? In February, 1968, Sheikh Zaid and Sheikh Rashid of Dubai set aside their mutual rivalries, proclaimed a federation, and invited seven other sheikhdoms to join. These were the five other Trucial sheikhdoms (Sharjah, Ras Al Khaimah, Fujaira, Ajman, and Umm Al-Qaiwain), the Island of Bahrain, and the sheikhdom of Qatar. On July 17, 1971, it was announced in Dubai that six of the nine had at last agreed to federate, with Abu Dhabi as capital and Sheikh Zaid of Abu Dhabi as president. The population of the new state is between 120,000 and 150,000. Bahrain, the most populous, and Qatar, which is under Saudi influence, declined to join, along with Ras Al Khaimah, which demanded greater representation in a proposed assembly of states. Abu Dhabi and Dubai, the richest of the six, agreed to devote 10 percent of their oil revenues to the others.

In the Sultanate of Oman, a civil war epitomizes the struggle that may eventually overwhelm the entire Gulf. This conflict grew out of a revolt against the oppressive rule of the former Sultan, Said Bin Taimur, who attempted to insulate his country from the outside world and from the twentieth century. He succeeded, but at the same time gave revolutionaries ample ground for action. Beginning as the Dhofar Liberation Movement, in the mountains of

Dhofar, the southernmost province of the Sultanate, the revolutionaries have expanded their movement into an organization for the liberation of the Arab Gulf. There is evidence that the Baathists have supported isolated guerrilla operations in northern Oman, but the Dhofari revolutionaries receive support mainly from Aden and secondarily from the Soviet Union and Communist China.

In 1972 the Sultan's British-officered army, newly strengthened with helicopters, carried the fighting into the mountains and established itself permanently on high ground identified as Simba. The Sultan's men intercepted some guerrilla supply convoys passing through the mountains and interior deserts close to the South Yemen border. Other guerrillas were forced to pull back into South Yemen.

In 1973 the guerrillas have come back with new Russian and Chinese automotive weapons, mortars and rocket launchers, but the Sultan, too, is stronger. Iran is now openly providing helicopters and crews for logistical support. Saudi Arabia has begun to ease the Sultan's economic burdens with support for schools and hospitals. Abu Dhabi is considering economic aid, as is Libya. Meanwhile the Sultan, whose oil wells have proved disappointing, continues to devote 40 percent of his revenues to the war.

Most remarkable here is that China has found it worthwhile to establish a tiny military and political foothold in one of the most remote corners of Arabia—presumably with the hope of expanding eventually into the richest parts of the Peninsula. The Marxist-Leninist-Maoist radicals of Aden have succeeded in enlisting primitive tribesmen in a cause they can scarcely understand.

The new Sultan of Oman, who overthrew his father in August of 1970, adopted a progressive policy, giving his people personal freedom and beginning the construction of hospitals, schools, and roads. He succeeded in luring some of the rebels out of the mountains, but the hard core, convinced that it will inherit the future, remained unresponsive. In 1973 both sides were building up.

The heart of the revolutionary forces not only in Oman but in all of Arabia is in Aden. The sparks of revolution were struck here in the conflict between the British, who had made Aden one of their great military bases, and several movements that sought to oust them. The movement that won the upper hand and formed a successor government, when the British at last departed in November, 1967, was the National Liberation Front. The Front had its ideological roots mainly in the Arab Nationalist Movement, ANM, founded by George Habash after the 1948 War in Palestine. The most extreme of all Arab political movements, the ANM and its guerrilla offshoot, the Popular Front for the Liberation of Palestine (PFLP), are ideologically closer to the Communist Chinese than to the Soviet Union.

I became acquainted with the Adeni revolutionaries during the weeks after the British had withdrawn from Aden, and they left me with no doubt that their first objective was to overthrow the Sultan of Oman and then "liberate" the entire Gulf.

Meanwhile, the Aden regime, which has adopted the name "People's Democratic Republic of Yemen," has become embroiled in a quarrel with its sister republic of Yemen, which emerged from the overthrow, in September, 1962, of the thousand-year-old Hamad Ed Din dynasty. After a long struggle, the republic has not only suppressed the royalist tribesmen of the north but has also expelled the Marxists from its midst, establishing itself as the first truly conservative republic in the Arab world. An agreement to merge the two Yemens concluded in September, 1972, seems unlikely to last, given the fundamental differences separating the two regimes.

It is possible to think of all these states on the periphery of the Arabian Peninsula, Kuwait to Yemen, as a necklace composed of beads of greatly varying size and value hung around Saudi Arabia.

The Saudi state, now the largest, richest, and most important in the Peninsula, was formed early in this century by Abdel Aziz Ibn Saud, who led the fierce tribes of the Nejd, from the arid interior, in the conquest of their neighbors, extending his rule from the Red Sea to the Gulf. The strength that Ibn Saud imparted to the Saudi Arabian state was an amalgam of varied elements. His tribesmen belonged to a fanatical, puritanical religious movement known as Wahabism, which still pervades the kingdom. Their abhorrence of alcohol, disapproval of smoking, objections to photography, including moving pictures, adherence to a cruel, Koranic penal code, and the restrictions they place upon their women, make Saudi Arabia appear to the outsider like a backward, theocratic anachronism. The visitor from the West may overlook the changes that have brought relative liberalization to Saudi life since the early sixties, and may not realize the extent to which adherence to religious law imparts to Saudi life a toughness of moral fiber lacking elsewhere in the Arab world.

Ibn Saud conferred on his country yet another element of strength by marrying into all the important tribes of his kingdom. As a consequence, he fathered more than fifty sons and knit the kingdom together in his own family. Perhaps because he chose his marriage partners carefully, his sons have proved competent as administrators of the kingdom, and remain today at the top of the Saudi ruling hierarchy.

The biological prowess of King Ibn Saud thus endowed the Saudi kingdom with one of its prime elements of security. Others are the great size of the country, which would make it difficult for any revolutionary group to gain simultaneous control of all key points, the dispersal of the regular armed forces over this vast territory, and the existence of an alternative internal security force, which could offset the regular forces should the latter ever fall into the hands of revolutionary officers. The alternative is the White Army, a Bedouin force composed of the descendants of the army of Wahabi fanatics with which Ibn Saud united his country. It has been uniformed, and trained by a British officer in the use of modern arms. Unquestionably loyal to the Royal Family, the White Army had to make a choice when Crown Prince Faisal, in 1964, dethroned his brother Saud. Perhaps because they disapproved of Saud's self-indulgence, they chose Faisal.

It has been said that the kingdom's basic stability was proven by its ability to survive a decade of misrule by King Saud, who succeeded his father at the end of 1953. Saud's failing was that he had no conception of the limits of his growing wealth. Not only did he lavish unnecessarily large sums on his own tribes, but he also attempted, unavailingly, to shape Arab political affairs outside his kingdom by means of bribery and subsidy. He imported an army of Egyptian artisans to build handsome ministries in Ryadh. He constructed a railway from Dammam on the Persian Gulf to the capital, and had built for himself a pink-plastered palace so vast that its air-conditioning system consumed more electricity than all the rest of the town. The palace symbolized his own and his family's massive extravagance. By the late 1950s the royal treasury was empty, internal and external debts were out of hand, the value of Saudi currency was dwindling, and the Saudi economy was in the grip of inflation.

In 1958 Crown Prince Faisal became Premier and began to draw the fiscal reins. He gradually brought the government's internal and external indebtedness under control, and halted the runaway decline in the value of the Saudi currency, the Riyal, on international markets. After prolonged friction between Faisal and his free-spending brother, who spent longer and longer periods under the care of physicians in foreign countries, the highest authority in the land, composed of the elders of the royal family sitting with the chief religious teachers, and known as Ulema, decided to dethrone Saud. In November, 1964, Faisal was proclaimed King. With full authority in his hands, he developed the reforms which he as Premier had begun in 1962 to offset Nasserite subversion. These reforms included the promise of greater personal freedom to his people by reduction of arbitrary powers exercised by the religious police and by authorization of "harmless pleasures." He also promised more rapid economic development and steps toward introduction of constitutional rule.

In most of these spheres, the King made progress. But always within careful limits. He was willing to curb the religious police, who had a habit of invading homes to check on what people were drinking, and of using bamboo staves to encourage reluctant worshipers on their way to the mosque—but only to an extent that would not anger the old school of religious leaders. He wanted economic development, but within the limits of a balanced budget. He approved "harmless pleasures" in the form of rigidly censored television programs, but could not bring himself to authorize movies. As for constitutional reform, he simply forgot about it.

Although King Faisal was popular with the young intellectuals and businessmen in the early part of his rule, he lost ground with them as the limitations of his reforms became apparent. In the summer of 1969 the Saudi secret police uncovered evidence that revolutionary plots were in the making in several different sectors of society—the armed forces, the bureaucracy, among businessmen, and especially among the immigrants from the Hadramauth, who provide a large part of Saudi Arabia's skilled labor force. Several hundred persons were arrested, and the government has been on the alert ever since. A sense of tension pervades the kingdom. While King Faisal can probably keep control during his lifetime, everyone wonders what will happen when he dies.

The answer may be determined not only inside Saudi Arabia but also in the countries on its periphery, likened before to a necklace. This is a necklace that could become a noose if the revolutionaries in Aden and Baghdad succeed in overthrowing the traditional rulers in the Gulf.

9

A Family Divided Against Itself

The struggle between the Jews and the Arabs goes back to the time of Abraham. Nearly four thousand years ago, Abraham with his flocks and his tents migrated from Mesopotamia to the land of Canaan. Abraham was a Semite, one of those who were known in ancient times as "sand dwellers." The detailed paintings that have been found on walls of tombs of that time indicate that Abraham probably had a pointed beard and wore a blanket drawn over one shoulder and sandals on his feet. He carried a long shepherd's crook and rode on a donkey, for this was before the domestication of the camel. Some members of his party undoubtedly carried eight-stringed lyres.

Some passages in the Bible say that Abraham came from Ur, a well-developed town in southern Mesopotamia, others that his home was Haran in the north. Archaeological investigation makes the latter seem the more likely. He traveled, probably by way of Damascus to the land of the Canaanites, to Egypt, to Sodom, to Hebron, and to Beersheba. According to Arab tradition, Abraham reached as far south as Mecca, with his two sons Ishmael and Isaac. In a later visit he established a center of prayer and worship; this center remains today, and the Arabs celebrate the return of Abraham to Mecca each year.

Here, in the form of biblical quotations and summaries supplemented by a little history and archaeology, are the elements in the story of Abraham and his family that bear on the history of the Jews and Arabs.

Abraham, who came out of a heathen land, appears as the champion of monotheism. He set out in response to divine command. Three times God appeared to Abraham promising him the land of Canaan and more for his descendants. On the most dramatic of these occasions, when a "dread and great darkness fell, . . . the Lord made a covenant with Abraham, saying, 'To your descendants I give this land, from the river of Egypt to the great river, the River Euphrates, the land of the Kenites, the Kenizzites, the Kadmonites, the Hittites, the Perizzites, the Rephaim, the Amorites, the Canaanites, the Girgashites and the Jebusites'" (Genesis XVI: 18, 19, 20).

At the suggestion of his wife, Sarah, who despaired of conceiving, Abraham took as his concubine Hagar, his wife's Egyptian maid, who bore him a son, Ishmael. But God appeared again to Abraham and promised him that his wife, Sarah, would nonetheless bear a son so that "she shall be a mother of nations, kings of peoples shall come from her."

Abraham pleaded that Ishmael might instead find favor in God's sight, but God replied that Sarah would indeed bear a son, who should be named Isaac and "I will establish my covenant with him as an everlasting covenant for his descendants after him.

"As for Ishmael, I have heard you, behold, I will bless him and make him fruitful and multiply him exceedingly; he shall be the father of twelve princes and I will make him a great nation" (Genesis XXVII: 20, 21).

Isaac was born, and Sarah expressed the jealousy she had doubtless felt since the birth of Ishmael. She demanded that Abraham cast Ishmael and his mother out into the desert. Abraham hesitated, but God told him: "Whatever Sarah says to you, do as she tells you, for through Isaac shall your descendants be named, and I will make a nation of the son of the slave woman also, because he is your offspring" (Genesis XX: 12).

Of Ishmael God had told Hagar that "He shall be a wild ass

of a man, his hand against every man and every man's hand against him; and he shall dwell over against all his kinsmen" (Genesis XVI: 12).

Abraham turned Hagar and Ishmael out into the desert, but when they were near death from thirst God made a well appear before them and they were saved.

According to both Jewish and Moslem tradition, the Jews are descended from Isaac and the Arabs from Ishmael. The biblical story is of course the Hebrew version, which emphasizes that Isaac and not Ishmael is the inheritor of both the temporal and spiritual blessing, and it is with Isaac that God renews the "covenant" he had made with Abraham. The Moslem accounts, however, make no distinction between the two sons. According to Islamic scholars, it is inconceivable that God would favor one over the other.

While the Jews regard Abraham, his son Isaac, and grandson Jacob as the three Patriarchs of the Jewish people, the Moslems recognize them all as prophets, and consider Abraham as the original expounder of monotheism.

Jacob's son, Joseph, was sold by his jealous brothers into slavery and was carried off into Egypt, where he rose to eminence through his ability to interpret dreams. His influence with the Pharaoh enabled his tribe, who were called the Children of Israel, to migrate during a period of famine from their home in Palestine into Egypt, where they remained 400 years, until the time of Moses, but this time the Hebrew tribes had fallen into disfavor and had been enslaved. Moses was inspired by God to lead them out of Egypt to the "Promised Land."

The journey through the Red Sea, across the Sinai Desert, and into the mountains of Moab overlooking the Jordan River is said to have taken forty years, during which God delivered to Moses the Ten Commandments and finally appeared to him on Mount Nebo. As Moses looked across the river toward Jericho, God said to him: "You shall see the land before you but you shall not go there, into the land which I give to the people of Israel" (Deuteronomy XXXII: 52).

The movement of the Hebrews led by Moses from Egypt through Sinai into Jordan has been traced archaeologically. Hebrew camping places can be recognized, and the ashes and ruins of towns they destroyed on the way have been found. Religious inspiration aside, the migration is doubtless comparable to that of other peoples who have fled from persecution or in search of sustenance. Their entrance into the "Promised Land" marks the first violent conflict between the Hebrews and the indigenous peoples of the region. The five dominant tribes who then inhabited Palestine and the eastern shore of the Mediterranean were the Canaanites, Philistines, Amorites, Edomites, and Moabites. All are among the forefathers of the Palestinian Arabs as they exist today, together with some of the Jews who were either converted first to Christianity and then to Islam or who remained in the country as Jews even after the "exile" and then went directly to Islam in the seventh and eighth centuries when the Arab invasion from inner Arabia took place. In addition, there was some admixture of Greek, Persian, Roman, Turk, and finally British and French invaders. This view of the mixing of peoples does not suit either Israeli or Arab mythologies, but it is the serious conclusion of ethnologists.

The first period of Jewish domination of Palestine begins with Joshua, who had been chosen leader of the Jews after the death of Moses. Joshua fought the battle of Jericho in which the walls are said to have so memorably come tumbling down in 1447 B.C. Joshua subjugated most, but not all, of Palestine, and divided it among his sons. Palestine was at this time under the sovereignty of the Pharaohs, but Joshua and the successive rulers after him succeeded in maintaining autonomous status.

After a period of 350 years, during which the Jews were ruled by leaders known as Judges, Saul was chosen in 1025 B.C. to be the first King of a fully independent Jewish Kingdom. It was under Saul's successor, David, that the Jews captured Jerusalem from the Jebusites, and David's son, Solomon, built the first temple in Jerusalem, in 962 B.C. This lavish structure of huge blocks of stone and carved cedarwood overlaid with gold was the supreme symbol of the Jewish faith in Jerusalem.

After Solomon, the Kingdom broke up into a Northern Kingdom known as Israel situated in Samaria north of Jerusalem, straddling the Jordan River and including the region known as Samaria, and a Southern Kingdom which included Jerusalem and the region of Hebron. The Northern Kingdom lasted two centuries and the Southern Kingdom three-and-one-half centuries.

The Northern Kingdom was destroyed by the Assyrians, the Southern by the Chaldeans, whose ruler, Nebuchadnezzar, destroyed the temple and exiled the Jewish community to Babylon in 586 B.C. This Babylonian captivity is sometimes called the first Diaspora, although the Jews of the Northern Kingdom, except for a small remnant who became known as the Samaritans, had already been dispersed or had intermarried with their conquerors. In the Babylonian captivity this people, who had once despised the Canaanites as shopkeepers, themselves learned to be traders because they were barred from other occupations.

A century later, as miraculously as in their exodus from Egypt, the Jews were allowed to return to Jerusalem by Cyrus the Great of Persia. In a first wave, 42,000 returned, followed by further waves, who after some delay, in the time of the scribe Ezra, succeeded in 445 B.C. in refortifying Jerusalem. Later, obliged to pay tribute to their neighbors, the Ptolemies and Seleucids, they were unable to regain their independence totally except for a little more than a century under the Hasmoneans.

In A.D. 70 the Romans destroyed Jerusalem totally and barred the Jews from returning on pain of death. At this time many of the Jews fled back to Babylon or to other parts of the Levant, including the Hejaz, where they came into contact with the founder of Islam. Jews date the final dispersion from this time.

The precise dates of the various periods of and during which the Children of Israel ruled in Palestine are controversial. But one may calculate that it was about 650 years from the time Joshua entered the Promised Land until the Southern Kingdom of Judah was extinguished. Thereafter there was another revival, some hundreds of years later in the Second Kingdom, the Hasmoneans, who held sway from 167 B.C. to 63 B.C.

In the time of Mohammed, the seventh-century founder of Islam, large numbers of Jews lived in Medina and in other parts of the Red Sea coast known as the Hejaz and further south in Yemen.

At first, Mohammed found them useful allies, and according to some Jewish sources he issued a letter of protection to the Jews after they had come to his rescue during a critical battle with the heathen.

There is some evidence that Mohammed at first sought from the Jews in Medina recognition of his teachings as a purification of the older Jewish faith and reconciliation on both civic and ideological levels. Like the Jews, his followers turned toward Jerusalem while praying and fasted on the day of Tisha b'Av, which marks the destruction of the Temple in Jerusalem. But as time went on and hostility developed between Mohammed and the four Jewish tribes of Medina, he abandoned these superficial marks of identity, turned his followers toward Mecca in prayer, and introduced the month-long fast of Ramadan.

This local situation had much to do with the subsequent relationship between Jews and Moslems generally. There were undoubtedly more profound reasons for the deterioration of relations between Mohammed and the Jews. Mohammed may have resented theological criticism of his movement by Jews, and his followers may have coveted the wealth of the Jews in Medina. On the other hand, the Jews may have grown jealous of Mohammed's growing influence in religious and civic affairs. The actual break began, as many other Middle Eastern conflicts have begun at other times, in a squabble in the marketplace. Mohammed gathered his supporters and succeeded in having one of the Jewish tribes expelled from Medina. Somewhat later he succeeded in expelling a second tribe after alleging that it had plotted an attack upon him during a parley. A third tribe of Jews appears to have been destroyed—the men killed and women and children sold as slaves. The fate of the fourth is obscure, but it is possible that they adopted Islam.

Mohammed's conflict with the Jews of Medina undoubtedly colored the attitude of Moslems toward Jews in subsequent centuries, but with less friction than has characterized the relations of Jews and Gentiles in Europe. While the Jews have been segregated and required to wear distinguishing dress in some parts of the Arab world, and while there have over the centuries been many serious outbursts of violence, such as the Baghdad Pogrom of 1940, hostility did not become constant until the emergence of the Palestine issue. Indeed, the Golden Age of Jewry occurred in Moslem Spain. Until the rise of Zionism Jews always fled European persecution to the east—Spanish Jews to North Africa and Palestine, Russian Jews to Turkish territory. The Moslem East was made to pay for the crimes of the Christian West.

Jews and Moslems everywhere have in common their belief in the oneness of God. They share the memory of numerous religious figures as well as similar dietary rules, such as the requirement that meat must be slaughtered in a particular way and that pork is forbidden.

There are striking similarities in the traditional law of the Jews, known as Halakha, and that of the Moslems, known as Sharia. Both are considered God-given, and were developed over the centuries on the basis of Biblical and Koranic texts reflecting God's will. Apart from dietary laws, the two systems originally prohibited interest on loans, and laid down similar marriage laws. While Halakha continues to play an important role in the lives of practicing Jews, and Sharia law in the lives of the Moslem faithful, the latter is also the law of the land in Saudi Arabia. In other Arab countries it still determines or influences such matters as marriage, divorce, and inheritance.

Having lived among both Arabs and Jews in the Middle East, I would say that they still share something of the ancient traditions of the desert, of peoples who for centuries gathered in tents during long, hot afternoons or told stories around campfires at night. Among both peoples "the word" is esteemed, although with cultural variations. Among the Arabs the fondness for words runs to poetry and special regard for the man who can speak eloquently. The Arab sometimes regards a good story as preferable to, or even a substitute for, the facts. Among the Jews it is perhaps especially the written word that has been cultivated. Their penchant is reflected in the arduous study of the Torah by orthodox Jews and in the success others have met in the learned professions.

Following the emergence of Islam in the seventh century, the Arabs surged out of the Arabian Peninsula. Palestine was then an administrative subdivision of the Byzantine Empire, sparsely populated by Cannaanites and other indigenous tribes among whom only a small number were Jews who had survived the dispersion of A.D. 70. Most of the population were Christians.

While they were driven economically by the lure of conquest, the Arabs' proclaimed motive as they spread across northern Arabia, including Palestine and beyond, was to spread Islam. They did not impose their faith by force, but their military prowess was undoubtedly persuasive. Along with the new religion went the Arabic language, which readily displaced most of the local languages. Those who adopted Islam became a privileged caste over those who retained the old faith. Conversions took place on a vast scale among pagans and among the Christians who then predominated throughout the regions ruled by Byzantium.

The Arabs became custodians of Greek culture during Europe's Dark Ages, roughly from the seventh until the fourteenth or fifteenth centuries, thus preserving it for Renaissance Europe. They made their own contributions to the development of mathematics and astronomy. They developed the system of numerals which we still use. They excelled in medicine and the decorative arts.

In the twelfth and thirteenth centuries came the Crusades. These European warriors who came to the East to liberate Jerusalem from the infidels encountered a culture more highly developed than their own, and much of what they found they copied and took back to Europe. The Arab elite at the time of the Crusades lived in considerable luxury. They esteemed scholarship and works of art. They used perfumes and spices. The Crusaders left their mark on the Levant architecturally in splendid castles and biologically in the blond and blue-eyed children who can still be seen in the villages around those castles.

United by their greatest military hero, Saladin, the Arabs in 1187 regained Jerusalem after it had for eighty-eight years been a Christian stronghold. By 1291 they had broken the hold of the Crusaders on the Levant. The Arabs like to remember their final victory after centuries of struggle as a precedent for the ultimate victory which they anticipate over the Jews who now rule Palestine.

Saladin's leadership notwithstanding, the unity which existed under the early caliphs and the Ommayad Dynasty when the Arab empire extended from Spain through North Africa to Persia had disappeared. By the time the Abbasid Dynasty rose in Baghdad in the middle of the eighth century power had been decentralized into the hands of provincial governors. Fragmentation followed the rise of regional dynasties. Arab weakness began with disunity—and disunity remains the mark of Arab weakness.

In the sixteenth century the Ottoman Turks captured Constantinople and then spread their dominion over most of what had been the Arab Empire. They remained dominant until the end of World War I, when the victorious Western powers fragmented their empire, dividing it into British and French spheres and promising the Jews a homeland in Palestine.

Against this background, subsequent chapters will examine various aspects of the history of the Jews and Arabs—how they have fought one another, the rise of Zionism, the creation of the modern State of Israel, and the rise of Palestinian nationalism and the commando movement.

10

The Struggle: Guerrilla and Conventional Warfare

T. E. Lawrence, the "Lawrence of Arabia" of World War I who mobilized the desert Arabs against the Turks, understood Arab strengths and weaknesses as warriors. He wrote that they were like "an influence, an idea, a thing intangible, invulnerable, without front or back, drifting about like a gas . . . a vapour, blowing where we listed. . . . Our cards were speed and time, not hitting power."

Lawrence saw the possibilities of utilizing the Arab characteristics in war against the Turks. In his *Revolt in the Desert* he wrote: "Our largest resources, the Bedouin on whom our war must be built, were unused to formal operations, but had assets of mobility, toughness, self-assurance, knowledge of the country, intelligent courage. With them, dispersal was strength."

Arab strengths and weaknesses have not changed much since Lawrence's day.

Arab guerrillas made their appearance in Palestine in the riots of April, 1920, and May, 1921, and again in 1929 in a dispute concerning the Wailing Wall in Jerusalem. The latter resulted in the death of 133 Jews and 116 Arabs. This was the first large-scale violence in the struggle between Arabs and Jewish settlers that is still going on today.

The 1936 Arab uprising against the British and the Jewish settlers began as a spontaneous peasant revolt led by poor village sheikhs. Once it was under way the traditional elite of Arab landowning families, the Husseinis and the Nashashibis, took over and achieved a peak of unity, so far as Palestinians were concerned, in the Arab Higher Committee. The committee directed a general strike against the British, a boycott of the Jewish community, and guerrilla operations in the countryside.

The nature of the factions combined in this committee is apparent. The two most important were the Palestinian Arab Party and the National Defense Party, which represented respectively the Husseini and the Nashashibi families. The other four were the Reform Party, representing the Khalidi family; the National Bloc, composed of a group of Nablus leaders; the Congress Executive of National Youth, led by a Ramallah family; and the Istiqlal, led by a Jerusalem lawyer. The Nashashibis were identified with the business and professional men, and considered moderates who wished to come to terms with the British. But the Mufti, Haj Amin el-Husseini, then young and ambitious, insisted on continuing the fight, and won support from Pan-Arab leaders in Iraq, Syria, and Egypt. He was able, upon Nashashibi's withdrawal, to dominate the Arab Higher Committee, which demanded that immigration of Jews and land transfers to Jews be halted. It called for establishment of a Palestinian national state.

The first guerrilla leader was Sheikh Izz al-Din al-Oasim, a religious and nationalist figure in the hills of Galilee. Later he was overshadowed by an ex-Iraqi officer, Fawzi al-Din al Kawukji.

Guerrilla tactics concentrated on hampering communications by mining and barricading roads, sniping, setting fire to crops, and cutting the oil pipeline from Iraq to Haifa. At first, operations were restricted to Galilee because of its nearness to Syria, the base of Arab support and cover. Guerrillas managed to destroy thirteen Jewish-owned factories whose estimated value was around half a million dollars. Slowly, guerrilla activity spread southward into Samaria. It developed a pattern of sustained and coordinated attacks against Jews and the mandatory government.

It was during this phase of the Palestinian resistance that the

Arab headdress—the Kefieh—became the symbol of the guerrillas, as it did later of the post-1967 guerrillas. The General Command of the Headquarters of the Arab Revolution in Palestine even asked all townsmen to wear the headdress instead of the fez to allow the rebels to circulate more easily without drawing British attention. Among Palestinians this headdress—a simple piece of cloth held in place by a circle of rope on the top of the head—is usually all white or black-and-white checkered. East Bank Jordanians prefer the red-and-white checkered style.

The rebellion—greater in scope and intensity than any previous one—lasted six months. At its height around five thousand guerrillas roamed the hill country of Palestine. Officially the British reported casualties of 89 Jews, 195 Arabs, and 37 Britons. Actually, casualties may have been twice as great.

The British finally moved to suppress the rebels with harsh penalties such as collective punishment and by bringing in troops from Britain. Opposed by the superior force of 20,000 British soldiers in the land, their own resources low and casualties high, the guerrillas' spirits sagged. They and their political arm, the Arab Higher Committee, decided to accept the respite provided by the Royal Commission of Inquiry of 1937. The British troops allowed non-Palestinian Arabs to recross the borders into neighboring countries, and a brief period of uneasy quiet descended upon Palestine.

But Arab guerrilla activity resumed later in 1937, in November, on a far more extensive scale. Rebel numbers rose to 15,000, including volunteers from neighboring countries. Rebel units consisting of professional guerrillas called Mujaheddin (Holy Warriors), and supplemented by part-time auxiliaries, attacked Britons, Jews, and Arabs who opposed the Mufti's control of the nationalist movement. The peak of guerrilla strength came in October, 1938, when, for a short time, they controlled communications to and from Jaffa, the Old City of Jerusalem, Gaza, Beersheba, and Hebron, as well as most of southern Palestine. At that point, the British military cracked down vigorously. World War II was threatening and Britain could not permit such disorders. The White Paper of 1939, which accepted most Arab nationalist demands, also went far toward calming the situation in Palestine. The White Paper severely limited immigration and land transfers to Jews. The cost in terms of casualties was far higher than in 1936. According to British figures, 1,138 guerrillas, 486 other Arabs, 292 Jews, and 69 British were killed in the fighting.

During World War II Palestinian guerrilla activity was relatively slight. In the shadow of the greater world conflict a tacit truce developed between Jews, Arabs, and the British. The country was in any case packed with British troops. Economically, Palestine prospered as a supply base for allied forces.

Meanwhile, Jewish settlers in Palestine were building up their armed strength in preparation for future clashes with the Arabs. They knew they could not rely on British protection.

Jewish paramilitary organization is actually rooted in Eastern Europe where Jews used to organize their communities against the hostile local populations. Two such organizations were the Hashomer (Watchmen) in Russia and the Betar in Poland. In Palestine, these two movements became the backbone of the Haganah and the Irgun Zvai Leumi.

The policy of the Jewish Agency was to work with the British in return for official authorization of gradual increases in Jewish defense forces, which would later become the core of the Israeli military effort. The Haganah, meaning "self-defense," was the paramilitary arm of the Jewish Agency in Palestine. An illegal organization, it was tolerated by British authorities, and began in 1920 to defend Jewish settlements against attacks from Arab guerrillas. In the early years of the Mandate, the Haganah did not practice offensive operations as they feared a repressive British reaction and adverse world public opinion. Thus, the Jewish community depended for protection on the Haganah and local Jewish police during the disturbances of 1920, 1921, 1929, and 1936–1939.

The British allowed both forces to grow during this time span, as both seemed to accept nominal British control. By 1936 the Haganah had around 10,000 members, and 2,000 more belonged to its elite fighting unit, the Palmach. In addition, Jewish members of the regular police force doubled, while the numbers of Jewish "supernumerary" police reached 2,700. In these cases, the Jewish

Agency would nominate members of the community it desired to place on police duties. These men would be valuable sources of information regarding Mandatory policy, and would later form an integral part of the Jewish and eventually Israeli military effort.

Not all parts of the Jewish community were willing to accept the gradualist policies of the Jewish Agency. There were always ripostes in the form of scattered Jewish guerrilla forays when Arab guerrilla violence occurred. But the first organized Jewish guerrilla forces worth noting began in 1935, when Vladimir Jabotinsky formed his revisionist Zionist followers into military units.

From the beginning, Jewish guerrilla activity assumed an urban setting and style, as opposed to the rural environment of Arab forces. The first substantial Jewish paramilitary actions began in 1938 in response to the unprecedented level of Arab guerrilla successes of that year. The organization which directed the attacks was the Irgun Zvai Leumi (National Military Organization), an extension of the Revisionists under the leadership of David Raziel. One Irgun operation in Haifa killed seventy-four people.

In order to arm the Jewish community, the Jewish Agency redoubled its efforts through the Mandatory authorities to expand the Jewish police force. But Jewish Agency leaders criticized Jewish guerrilla activities. Chaim Weizmann, in his book *Trial and Error,** deplored "the tragic, futile, un-Jewish resort to terrorism, a perversion of the purely defensive function of Haganah."

The British were receptive to the Jewish Agency's demands, and actually agreed to train some Jewish volunteers for antiguerrilla raids during the height of the Arab paramilitary successes. "Special Night Squads" were formed under the command of Captain Orde Charles Wingate. Naturally, the Jewish trainees were members of the Haganah and later became the backbone of Jewish guerrilla activities aimed at the British and the Arabs.

The British concessions to Arab demands in the White Paper of 1939 exposed the inadequacy of the Haganah's policy of self-restraint and self-defense in the eyes of many Zionists. Cooperation between the Haganah and the more militant groups increased, and

*Westport, Connecticut: Greenwood Press, 1949.

the Haganah began illegal broadcasts over its radio, The Voice of Israel. The Irgun attacked government buildings in Jerusalem and Tel Aviv.

The outbreak of World War II, however, changed everything. The Haganah stopped its broadcasts and agreed to hold its grievances against the British in abeyance. The Irgun also tacitly agreed to halt its activities in return for the freeing of political prisoners from Mandatory jails. This shift in policy by Irgun caused a split in the parent body. Dissidents known as the Stern Group, after their leader, Abraham Stern, continued operations against the British. They reached their climax with the assassination in Cairo of Lord Moyne, Secretary of State in the Middle East.

During the war, the Jewish Agency concentrated its efforts on the formation of a distinct Jewish fighting force to participate in the war against the Axis. After much equivocation, Britain agreed to the formation of a Jewish Battalion. The goal of the Jewish Agency was to enlarge and legitimize the Haganah and to have it trained in the techniques of modern warfare.

By 1942, 18,800 Palestinian Jews were already in the British armed forces. In addition, the numbers of the Jewish police had risen to 24,000. More importantly, members of the Haganah were given special training in the art of guerrilla warfare by Britain in 1941. The "Jewish Rural Special Police" were trained, in case of an Axis victory in the Middle East, to serve as a potential fifth column in Palestine. Thus, by 1943 there were under arms 43,000 British-trained Jews who would serve as the backbone of the Israeli Army in 1948.

With the war drawing to a close, Jewish leaders began to challenge the White Paper of 1939 and the direction of British policy. The extremist groups, the Irgun and the Fighters for Israeli Freedom (successor to the Stern Group), headed by Nathan Friedman Yellin, were the first to break the truce with the British. Under the leadership of Menacheim Begin, the Irgun made this public call for revolt in January, 1944: "There is no longer any armistice between the Jewish people and the British Administration in Eretz Israel which hands our brothers over to Hitler. . . . This, then, is our demand: Immediate transfer of power in Eretz Israel to a Provisional Hebrew Government." The members of Irgun, no less than the followers of the Mufti, were inspired by religious fervor. Menacheim Begin declaimed: "We shall fight, every Jew in the Homeland will fight. The God of Israel, the Lord of Hosts, will aid us."

The Jewish Agency and its military arm, the Haganah, were faced with difficult decisions in 1944. At first they repudiated Jewish guerrilla activity, but with the British immigration policy fixed against the Jewish community the Haganah eventually began to cooperate with the Irgun. The Haganah's Voice of Israel broadcasts were resumed in March, 1945, with daily broadcasts in English, Hebrew, and Arabic. Operations were concentrated against British immigration facilities and government installations. The British, in turn, cracked down on the Jewish Agency in June, 1946. One month later, the Irgun carried out an attack against British offices in the King David Hotel in Jerusalem. In this, one of the most famous of Jewish terror operations, eighty British, Arab, and Jewish civil servants were killed and another seventy wounded.

In the decade 1936–1946, British authorities in Palestine had faced the gamut of guerrilla operations. In the first part of the decade, they confronted Arab guerrillas in the hills of Palestine; in the latter part, Jewish guerrillas in the cities. Both Arab and Jewish guerrillas conducted operations against one another, but both reserved their hardest blows for the British. The object for both groups was the removal of the Mandatory power. After this was accomplished, they would confront one another for the spoils of the land. The Jews could rely on the Jewish forces trained and partially equipped by the British. By the end of the Mandate, the Haganah was estimated at 45,000 to 60,000 men, including 300 British-trained officers.

As for the Arabs, they could rely on the hard core of guerrillas in northern and central Palestine, and neighboring forces commanded by the veterans of the 1936–1938 battles. In addition, in response to the paramilitary activities in Jewish settlements, two new secret societies had developed in Arab Palestine, el-Futuwwah and el-Najjadah.

The confrontation was fueled by widespread arms smuggling to both sides. The main sources of supply were Axis and British stocks abandoned in Egypt's western desert, equipment stolen from Allied camps, and European surpluses. The agents were local Arabs or European dealers, but the buyers were predominantly Zionists. Both sides were preparing for the inevitable confrontation which would follow the pullout of Great Britain.

Assured in the late forties that the British would give up the Mandate, Arab and Jewish guerrillas increasingly aimed their commando activity at one another. The growing cycle of violence was capped by the attack on Deir Yassin, an Arab village near Jerusalem, by members of the Irgun and Stern. According to British figures, 254 people died in the village, although the actual number of deaths may have been as many as 350. The Arabs replied in kind by attacking a convoy going to the Hadassah Hospital on Mount Scopus, killing seventy-seven Jews.

THE FIRST ROUND

The irregular violence by Arabs and Jews against the British and against one another merged imperceptibly during the first half of 1948 into the first of the three confrontations between a regular Israeli army and the regular armies of the surrounding Arab states.

The British had had enough in Palestine. They could no longer stand the expense of the Mandate; they could no longer stomach the fratricidal Arab-Jewish killings which they were unable to control, and the murder of British soldiers and civilians by terrorists. On May 15, 1948, they quit Jerusalem and returned to the United Nations the Mandate they had received from the League of Nations in 1918. A few months earlier the United Nations, on November 29, 1947, had devised the partition plan as a possible solution. Partition would have divided Palestine into Jewish and Arab states linked in an economic union. The Jewish area would consist of the coastal plains, eastern Galilee, and most of the Negev. The Arab area would consist of most of the West Bank of the Jordan, the western coastal part of Galilee, the Gaza Strip, and its extension into the Negev. Both areas were militarily indefensible.

While the Jews reluctantly accepted the plan, it was rejected throughout the Arab world, and Arab violence spontaneously flared up against the Jews as well as the departing British to prevent its implementation. This was, in effect, the beginning of the 1948 War. During the first few months of the year (1948), Arabs loosely organized by the Arab Higher Committee and inspired by the Mufti Haj Amin el-Husseini, carried out a series of bombings and attacks on Jewish convoys in and around the three main population centers, Jerusalem, Tel Aviv, and Haifa. The Jews replied in kind. This was the period during which Jewish convoys to the Kfar Etzion settlement were ambushed, the Jews bombed the Semiramis Hotel in Jerusalem, and the Arabs blew up the *Palestine Post* building in Jerusalem, as well as exploding a string of trucks filled with explosives in Ben Yehudah Street and dynamiting a wing of the Jewish Agency in Jerusalem. Hundreds of people were killed on both sides and passions flared.

The first Arab incursion of the 1948 War into Palestine was carried out by a force of irregulars, once again headed by Fawzi al-Kawukji, already familiar as the guerrilla leader of the 1936–1939 disturbances. From recruiting centers in Damascus, Cairo, Baghdad, and Beirut he had accumulated an army that by the month of March numbered 5,000 men, with headquarters in Nablus. He crossed the border from Syria and, beginning on January 9, attempted a series of unsuccessful assaults on Jewish settlements. He failed, perhaps because he attempted to operate like a regular army instead of using the guerrilla tactics which he and his men understood best.

The Arab regular armies followed up immediately upon the official termination of the British Mandate on May 15. The well-trained Arab Legion, commanded by Brigadier General John Bagott Glubb, moved across the Jordan River, occupied the Old City of Jerusalem, and attempted, with the assistance of Kawukji's irregulars, to besiege the Jews who had swiftly occupied British positions in and around the New City as the British withdrew. The Egyptians entered Palestine along the coastal road to Gaza and eventually linked up with the Jordanians in the siege of Jerusalem. A small Iraqi contingent also moved into northern Palestine. A Syrian force moved just across the international frontier but did not attempt to press further. The Lebanese remained prudently on their own side of the international frontier.

According to Fred Khouri in *The Arab-Israeli Dilemma,** the forces confronting one another in this war increased substantially as it progressed. In May, 1948, he estimated the collective Arab strength at 20,000 to 25,000 men and Israeli strength at 35,000 to 80,000. After the first truce, he found the Arabs to number 35,000 to 45,000 and Israelis 60,000 to 100,000. The comparable figures after the second truce were: Arabs, 50,000 to 55,000; Israelis, 75,000 to 120,000.

At no time during the war were the Arabs able to mount a successful assault against major Jewish positions or centers of population. On the whole, they remained relatively immobile, occupying the high ground overlooking the Jewish lines of communication. They hoped that they would be able to use superior numerical strength to paralyze the Jews and starve them out, but the Jews, thanks to their efficient manpower mobilization, actually fielded more men than the combined Arab armies.

The Israelis, who had formally proclaimed their state at the moment of British departure from Jerusalem, pursued quite different tactics. Their tactics were offensive. After a critical first four weeks of holding operations, during which they received the first of considerable quantities of arms and ammunition from Czechoslovakia and other parts of the world, they struck out in what has been called the "Ten Days Offensive."

I was stationed in Jerusalem at the time as correspondent for *The New York Times.* From Zone B, the last stronghold of the British army and administration in the heart of Jerusalem, the press was able to make forays out to both sides.

I got a firsthand view of the Israelis' offensive capabilities during the Palmach assault, which broke through the old city wall into the Jewish quarter and rescued most of the remaining Jewish inhabitants. The attack was prepared by a barrage of gunfire led by a giant mortar which the Israelis had built themselves to lob explosives over the old city wall.

*New York: Syracuse University Press, 1969.

Running down the road behind a group of young Palmach soldiers and through the gate they had blown open, I was amazed by the youthfulness and physical vigor of these Jewish soldiers.

Their offensive broke the siege of Jerusalem and inflicted the first stinging defeats on the Jordanians and Egyptians. In retrospect, it seems that these ten days were decisive, but the Israelis followed up after successive periods of truce imposed by the United Nations, with three more offensives. These drove the Egyptians back into the Negev Desert, knocked Kawukji's irregulars out of Galilee, and finally pushed the Egyptians back into the Sinai Desert. The Israelis captured Elat at the head of the Gulf of Aqaba, thereby establishing Israel's access to the Red Sea. Against the Jordanians who controlled the mountains of Samaria, they were notably less successful, but they did succeed in preventing the Arab Legion from carrying out its most obvious strategic objective—to cut the Israeli-held territory in half at its midpoint by driving a wedge from the region of Tulkarm to the sea, a distance of only seventeen miles. (However, General John Bagot Glubb, the former Jordanian commander, has written in his book *A Soldier With the Arabs** that he never tried to cut Israel in half as he had barely enough forces to defend Judea and Samaria.)

Why did the Israelis win and the Arabs lose? Above all, the answer must be given in terms of morale. The Israelis were inspired not only by the sense that they were fighting for survival, with their backs to the sea, but also by an awareness that they were Jewish fighting men vindicating the honor of their people. The idea that Jews could not fight, born of centuries-old ghetto tradition, was totally destroyed.

For the Arabs the reasons for fighting were not so clear as they would become twenty years later. The Egyptian army's morale was low. Its officers, the product of a corrupt social system that was about to be overthrown, had no heart for combat and little concern for the welfare of the rank and file. The soldiers of this army were ill-fed, ill-armed, and understood only vaguely why they were fighting.

*London: Hodder & Stoughton, 1957.

The Jordanians were high-spirited and superbly disciplined by comparison with the Egyptians. Some military analysts believe that they could have taken Jerusalem, split the Israeli territory in half, and inflicted a significant defeat on the Israelis had King Abdullah been willing to commit his forces to an all-out offensive. But neither he nor his British advisers were willing to take such a chance. It would have been like a gambler committing all of his resources to a single throw of the dice. The Arab Legion, which then numbered 4,500 men, was the main resource of the Kingdom, its heart and its backbone. Its real strength was therefore never committed.

To these moral considerations must be added the factors that the Israelis fought on interior lines of communication whereas the Arabs, moving in from outside the circle, did not succeed in establishing a unified command. They were divided militarily and politically.

THE SECOND ROUND

The next regular confrontation between Arabs and Israelis, in 1956, was again preceded by a long buildup of guerrilla warfare. Although there were no major operations, the borders were never quiet. A "little war" of the borders continued—the kind of war that still goes on every day of the year.

Arab guerrilla activity continued, but on a different scale and in a different manner. Attacks into Israel now took the form of unorganized, individual actions aimed at stealing, smuggling, and sometimes killing Israeli citizens. Israel would respond to these attacks with periodic army raids designed to pressure Arab governments to clamp down on border crossings. Occasionally, groups of angry Israeli settlers acted on their own.

With 775 miles of borders crowded with hostile refugees, many of whom knew their way through the rocky hills and desert along the borders, it was not surprising that the Israelis experienced trouble from infiltrators. Here are some examples of the kinds of actions that took place, taken from an article I wrote in *The New York Times* magazine of June 4, 1953, while I was stationed as a correspondent in Israel.

A group of seven guards outside the copper mines in Wadi Timna, north of Elat, in the Negev, are sitting in the darkness, gossiping. Everything has been quiet for weeks, and they have laid their rifles on the ground at their sides. Suddenly there is a volley of gunfire, and several men slump to the ground. The others seize their rifles and fire back into the darkness. Minutes later, five of the guards are dead and the Arab assailants are gone, probably over the border from which they came. . . .

The only daughter of a Jerusalem physician, graduate of a Swiss university, is proud to do her bit for Israel by serving as a shepherdess at Sde Boker, the settlement farthest into the heart of the Negev. She stands by the roadside 300 yards from her settlement, watching her flock, as the sun disappears below the horizon. Then there is a shot, and a crowd of Bedouin, who had been hiding in a dry creek bed, swarm out, round up the sheep and drive them off into the desert. The shepherdess is dead. Next day an Israel Army patrol catches up with the Bedouin; in a running fight one Israel soldier and two Bedouin are killed. The flock is recovered. . . .

A police patrol ambushes a band of infiltrators near Tulkarm, and one Arab is shot dead. In his clothing a document is found, in Arabic: To whom it may concern: The holder of this document, Mahmud Suleiman, of Nablus, is on active service.

(Signed) Second Lieutenant (signature illegible), on behalf of the Intelligence Office of the Western Area.

Multiply the thefts by thousands, the killings by hundreds, and the acts of sabotage and espionage (of growing frequency lately) by scores, and you begin to get an idea of what infiltration is. Incensed by this unceasing harassment, Israeli settlers have struck back. They organized reprisal expeditions in this fashion: From captured marauders the settlers would learn who the organizers of infiltration were. A party of kibbutzniks armed with Sten guns, hand-grenades and charges of dynamite would set out by night, swoop into an Arab village, and blow up the houses of the reputed infiltrator-bosses.

As reprisals followed infiltration back and forth across the border, many Arab villagers began to live in fear of attack almost as continuously as the Israelis in border settlements. They organized a National Guard which stands watch at night, peering into the darkness for hostile movements as tensely as their Israeli counterparts on the other side.

The Arab raids of this period had no official backing by the states of their origin. On the contrary, the governments involved took measures to prevent their occurrence. In 1954 one-half of the prisoners on the West Bank of the Jordan were incarcerated for infiltration. The death toll from guerrilla activity was running five to one against the Arabs on all frontiers, according to Kenneth Love in *Suez: The Twice Fought War.** The largest single act of Arab terrorism took place in March, 1954, when eleven Israelis were killed in the eastern Negev by irate Bedouins whose movement had been restricted by Israeli settlement policies. Israel responded with an attack on the Jordanian village of Nahhaleen.

These raids were a nuisance, but not a serious threat to the Israeli Government. Political leaders could make as much of them as they wanted. When David Ben-Gurion headed the State of Israel, he chose to react strongly. By reacting harshly to individual acts of terror, he hoped to pacify Israel's borders and achieve far-reaching political and territorial gains as well. For example, he initiated notable military reprisals against the refugee camp of el Bureig in Gaza and against the Jordanian village of Qibya. Twenty persons were killed in the first attack, twenty-six in the second.

With the temporary retirement in November, 1953, of Ben-Gurion and the elevation of Moshe Sharett as premier, relations between Israel and the Arab world improved considerably. Although disorganized and ineffectual, Arab forays continued. No large-scale army raids were deemed necessary by the Sharett Government.

Ben-Gurion's return to the Cabinet in February, 1955, signaled a return to the policy of large reprisal raids, the most important of which, the raid on Gaza, was staged at the end of the same month. As in the case of earlier raids, the Israeli Government disclaimed responsibility.

The Egyptian reaction rather than the scope of the Gaza raid set it apart from previous raids. Two Israeli platoons killed thirty-eight Arabs, a smaller number than in the raids on Qibya two years before.

But to the Egyptian leadership, Gaza was the turning point.

*New York: McGraw-Hill, 1969.

Nasser later told an interviewer that it was this raid—coming at a time when his policy had been conciliatory—that made up his mind to acquire arms from the Soviet Union. He also organized his own commandos for counterraids. Border raids became national policy on both sides. The level of violence escalated into the Anglo-French-Israeli drive to the Canal in 1956.

A number of factors were working in the Middle East to bring about a second round of conventional warfare in 1956. Primary among them was the belief on the part of Israeli officials that a preemptive strike into Egypt was essential to the safety of the Jewish State. Nasser had denied the use of the Gulf of Aqaba to Israeli ships, which negated plans for developing the Port of Elat and the southern region of the country and prevented oil shipments from entering the country via this route. In addition, Israel was concerned about the size of the Soviet-Egyptian arms deal. Israeli intelligence held that if the Egyptians had time to integrate these new weapons into their army, they could become a serious threat. Nasser's growing stature as leader of the Arab world also worried the Israelis; they looked for an opportunity to cut him down. Furthermore, Egyptian-backed commando raids were growing more frequent and more effective along the Gaza Strip and in Sinai. The disturbing thing to the Israelis about these raids was that, instead of using Egyptians, Nasser had armed the Palestinians in Gaza to do the raiding.

As early as October, 1955, Ben-Gurion asked his Chief of Staff, Moshe Dayan, to formulate plans for a preemptive strike. The timing of the plan had to await favorable international circumstances. In the fall of 1956 circumstances were favorable.

Before any plan could be carried out, Israel needed heavy military equipment. But her sources of supply were limited by the fact that Britain, France, and the United States at this time interpreted their Tripartite Declaration of May, 1950, as a commitment to maintain a military balance. This was in addition to a pledge by the three Western powers that they would not permit any armed aggression across existing armistice lines in Palestine and would take action against an aggressor "both within and outside the United Nations."

To break the bonds of these restrictions, Israel, after vainly knocking on all Washington doors, turned to France. Informal contacts between French and Israeli officials had been taking place since the first round of warfare in Palestine. As early as November, 1954, France agreed to sell Israel warplanes within the limitations of the Tripartite Declaration. Soon thereafter, the two countries, obviously disregarding the 1950 Declaration, were talking secretly about additional shipments to assist in an Israeli operation against Egypt.

France was prepared to help Israel because of Egypt's support for the Algerian rebels, who had been in revolt against France since 1954. French officials believed that Nasser's defeat would be a severe blow to the Algerian rebellion. The immediate cause of French as of British military intervention was, however, Nasser's nationalization of the Suez Canal in July, 1956. This had been Nasser's reaction to the withdrawal of Western backing for the Aswan High Dam project. The French and British took the view that Egyptian control over so vital a waterway through which most of their oil shipments were delivered might prove capricious, and that they could not accept it.

These two Western powers, who formerly had controlling interests in the Canal, and who considered their security directly linked to its smooth operation, planned to reverse Nasser's action. Militarily unprepared, they laid their plans for invasion while seeking an acceptable solution through diplomatic channels.

Secretary of State John Foster Dulles led the Western powers in proposing a plan that would have recognized Egyptian sovereignty over the Canal, including the right of nationalization, but which would have established international control over operation by the "user" nations. But this was unacceptable to Nasser.

The idea of coordinating a French and British landing with an Israeli offensive appealed to the French leadership of Prime Minister Guy Mollet, Foreign Minister Christian Pineau, and Defense Minister Maurice Bourges-Manoury. They calculated that an Israeli drive into Sinai could be used as pretext for Anglo-French landings to protect the Canal.

Secret transfers of French weapons to Israel began in August,

1956. On October 1, Moshe Dayan and Shimon Peres, the Director-General of the Defense Ministry, who had laid most of the ground-work for these transactions, presented to French authorities their final "shopping list," and it was accepted.

The British, whose relations with Israel had been strained since the days of the Mandate, were more circumspect in their relations with the Israelis. At no time did they give military or logistical assistance to the Israelis. Unlike the French, who had actively supported Israel from the start, the British at first supplied infor-mation only. Thus, the French leadership laid the groundwork for collusion while the British leaders, Prime Minister Anthony Eden and Foreign Secretary Selwyn Lloyd, did not actively enter into deliberations with Israel until mid-October.

Despite the delivery of French weapons and numerous verbal assurances, the Israelis still did not have the binding assurance of Western support that they wanted. Ben-Gurion flew to France on October 22 to complete the bargain. At Sevres, the Israelis received a declaration of intent on paper, signed by Mollet and Patrick Dean, the British Deputy Under-Secretary of State, as well as a French assurance of air cover of Israeli territory.

So, in the fall of 1956 circumstances were favorable for the Israeli preemptive strike combined with the Western Powers' Suez opera-tion. Britain and France were directly involved in the planning and coordination. The United States, however, was embroiled in a Presidential campaign. While President Eisenhower could not be expected to support the invasion, the French and British expected him to play a neutral role in the affair or at least not oppose his Western allies. Here they miscalculated.

From the Israeli standpoint, the need for a preemptive strike was underlined by the announcement on October 23 of the formation of a united military command consisting of Egyptian, Jordanian, and Syrian forces under an Egyptian Commander in Chief. This enhanced the likelihood of integrated Arab military action.

The Sinai campaign began on October 29 with a paratroop drop at the Mitla Pass, thirty miles east of the Suez Canal. Israeli military plans were shaped by two factors. They had to create a threat to the Canal, and thus a credible pretext for Anglo-French intervention. At the same time, they had to be able to pull back if British and French support should collapse. When the British and the French fulfilled their part of the bargain with an ultimatum on October 30 calling for both Egyptians and Israelis to withdraw to a distance of ten miles on either side of the Canal, while British and French forces occupied the Canal Zone, the Israelis dropped all restraints and threw themselves into the attack.

The Israeli campaign called for the capture of the Mitla Pass by paratroop units who would be joined by an armored column. A second armored column would sweep westward to the Canal along a more northerly route, using the village of Quseima as a jumping-off point. Another offensive would capture the town of Rafa and cut off the Gaza Strip from Sinai, then move toward the Canal and Port Said. A final drive would aim at the capture of Sharm el-Sheikh and control of the Straits of Tiran on the southernmost tip of the Sinai Peninsula.

In all of these operations the Israelis, facing under-strength detachments of demoralized Egyptian soldiers, met with complete success. In a seven-day war, Israel obtained all of her military aims: the opening of the Gulf of Aqaba, the control of Sinai, the occupation of Gaza, and the destruction of Fedayeen bases on her southeastern flank. The costs of the operation for Israel were extraordinarily low—172 killed and 817 wounded.

The period immediately following the 1956 invasion of Egypt by Israel, Britain, and France is notable for two extraordinary examples of how effective diplomatic pressure by the United States, combined with other powers, can be. These examples would be of great relevance to the comparable situation that arose after the 1967 War.

Fearing that President Eisenhower and Secretary of State Dulles might obstruct them, the British and French had deliberately avoided informing Washington of their plans. Although it seems difficult to believe that the C.I.A. did not know what was afoot—and there is evidence that some did know—the President and Secretary of State registered shock and distress at the news of the invasion and began international moves to frustrate it.

The United States combined with the Soviet Union to oblige

Britain and France to break off their amphibious operation in the Suez Canal Zone and to withdraw from Egypt. Whether it was U. S. pressure or Soviet saber rattling that brought the British and French governments to reverse gears is a matter for debate. Certainly the Soviet pressure, which amounted to a threat to fire guided missiles at Western population centers, sent a shiver of apprehension through Washington. American experts on Russian affairs were not sure whether the Russians were bluffing or not—as the Russians were not sure how far the Americans would go in the Cuban crisis of 1962.

Apart from its worry about the danger that the Anglo-French action might trigger a world war, Mr. Dulles' State Department was convinced of the invasion's uselessness. The Department's Arabists, who for once were making policy, were not at all sure that the Anglo-French-Israeli operations would topple Nasser and, if they did, that an alternative more desirable from the Western point of view could be found. Finally, they hoped, by opposing the invasion, to gain some credit for the United States.

The pressure worked. By December 22, the British and French were entirely out of the Suez Canal area. But on February 2, when the General Assembly of the United Nations passed its sixth resolution demanding immediate withdrawal of the Israelis and restoration of the armistice, together with the stationing of U. N. troops on the armistice lines, the Israelis were still sitting tight in the Gaza Strip and Sharm el-Sheikh. U. S. pressure on Israel mounted.

President Eisenhower, in a cable to Premier Ben-Gurion, warned that Israeli defiance "could seriously disturb the relations between Israel and other member nations [of the U.N.] including the U.S." The Israelis replied with public affirmations of their willingness to live without American aid and by initiating an intense lobbying campaign in Washington. The Israeli press pilloried as an "Arab lover" Dag Hammarskjöld, Secretary-General of the U.N., who was working closely with the White House.

On February 11, Dulles handed Israeli Ambassador Abba Eban an *aide memoire* which represented what the U. S. was willing to do for the Israelis in return for Israeli withdrawal. This was as far as the United States was willing to go, and it was along these lines that settlement was finally reached. In return for "prompt and unconditional Israeli withdrawal," the United States was willing to announce that it considered the Gulf of Aqaba "international waters through which no nation had the right to prevent free passage." Furthermore, the United States was prepared "to exercise the right of free and innocent passage and to join with others to secure general recognition of this right." In other words, the United States was willing to put an American ship through the straits and to commit its prestige and authority to maintaining freedom of passage. In the end this was the main thing that the Israelis gained from their 1956 adventure in Sinai. In addition, they were assured that the United Nations would station forces in Gaza which would prevent Fedayeen raids across that border for the next decade.

But the Israelis did not give in until the Eisenhower Administration had increased its pressure almost to the point of a U.N. vote for cutting off all forms of support, both public and private, to Israel.

At first Ben-Gurion responded with a reassertion that there was "no basis for restoring the status quo ante in Gaza" and with a proposal that the United States join Israel in working out a plan to solve the refugee problem in Gaza.

With Ben-Gurion's memorandum in hand, Secretary of State John Foster Dulles and Henry Cabot Lodge, then American Ambassador to the United Nations, flew immediately to see President Eisenhower, who was at Secretary George Humphrey's plantation in Georgia. The occasion was historic. From accounts given by Eisenhower and Sherman Adams in their memoirs, we learn that Mr. Lodge announced that the sanctions issue was sure to reach the General Assembly during the coming week, and that if it came to a vote the United States would either have to join the majority against Israel or stand out as Israel's special champion. He said that the United States had done all it could to make Israel's withdrawal easy. Anything more would play into the hands of the Soviet Union in the Middle East, driving the Arabs to see Russia as their only hope and dooming the Eisenhower Doctrine before it had started. The Doctrine, in the form of a Presidential message on January 5, 1957, and endorsed by Congress, sought to strengthen the American position in the Middle East by authorizing the use of American armed forces to defend any Middle Eastern nation requesting aid against "overt armed aggression" by a power "controlled by international Communism." It also authorized special military and economic aid in the area.

The point here is that in Dulles' mind East-West relations, in which he expected the Eisenhower Doctrine to play a key part, were of overriding importance. That is, overriding the political importance of Zionist pressure in Washington.

Eisenhower wrote in his memoirs that it was clear to him that a mere threat to cut off United States aid would be ineffective because American aid to Israel and Egypt had already been suspended. It would have to include suspension of private assistance as well.

At that moment, the President and his advisers had before them income tax figures showing that private gifts to Israel amounted to 40 million dollars a year and sales of Israeli bonds to 50 or 60 million dollars—all tax deductible.

At a meeting with legislators at the White House a few days after the meeting at Humphrey's Georgia plantation it became apparent however that the President could not expect Congressional support for his pressure on Israel. He would have to carry the burden alone.

His next move was a cable of warning to Ben-Gurion which he paraphrased in a broadcast as follows: "I believe that in the interests of peace, the United Nations has no choice but to exert pressure upon Israel to comply with the withdrawal resolutions."

Ben-Gurion, in an address to the Knesset, the Israeli legislature, protested the "injurious proposals by the United States government," but a few days later, while a sanction resolution was being prepared for voting at the United Nations, he ordered the withdrawal. The Israelis were out of Gaza, and the United Nations Expeditionary Force (UNEF) moved in on March 6, 1957.

THE THIRD ROUND

After the United States compelled Israel to withdraw from the territories conquered in the Sinai campaign, Israel enjoyed ten years of peace along her borders. Peace, however, is a relative term in the Middle East. The calm along Israel's borders was occasionally shattered by sporadic acts of violence. But there were no organized, clandestinely backed Fedayeen attacks, as had been the case before the 1956 War.

Nasser was determined to deny the Israelis any pretext for attacking his inferior army. The Egyptian leader declared in Gaza on June 26, 1962: "I do not agree with becoming involved in semi-military operations. If I were engaged in such operations, how could we guarantee that Ben-Gurion would not also be engaged in semi-military operations? . . . I would be gambling with the fate of my country and I would be exposing it to another disaster similar to that which occurred in 1948."

With Egypt preventing commando activity, the focus of the Arab-Israeli conflict shifted to the Syrian border. The immediate issue was the 100-square-mile demilitarized zone which stretches along most of the Syrian-Israeli border around the Sea of Galilee. Border conflict took place in the familiar pattern of an accumulation of incidents, such as Syria-based shelling of kibbutzim and patrol boats followed by an Israeli retaliatory raid.

A far more serious development was the renewed attacks by Fedayeen from Syrian bases. Just as in 1956, organized raids played a key role in initiating a conventional war. Still, the origins of the 1967 War were infinitely more complex than those of the previous two rounds of conventional warfare, which can be fairly simply explained. There can be no categorical answers to the assessment of blame and motive. The best approach to the most recent war is to review as objectively as possible the events and various interpretations of blame and motive which preceded the June War.

Guerrilla attacks, covertly sponsored or tolerated by Arab governments, have always been deemed unacceptable by the Israeli government, which has adopted a policy of retaliation against the sponsoring or tolerating Arab country. It was the Syrian Arab Republic which decided in 1965 to risk the Israelis' retaliation by sheltering a nascent band of guerrillas called Fatah. The origins of this organization can be traced back to the aftermath of the 1956 War in the Gaza Strip, where Yasir Arafat had lived just after the 1948 War. There, a group of Palestinian Arabs, who were disenchanted with official Arab support and military performance, began to build up a force of their own, using guerrilla tactics. The guerrillas were beset by difficulties with supply, financial backing, building trained cadres, and official opposition from Egypt, Jordan, and Lebanon.

The attitude of the Syrian Government was different. The Syrians had been the first, in 1965, to support the doctrine of a "people's war" to regain Palestine. A coup changing the ruling faction of the Baath Party in February, 1966, led to even greater support for the Palestinian guerrillas. The new leadership—Colonels Salah Jadid and Hafez al-Assad and their civilian frontman, Nureddin al Atassi —took a more direct role in supplying, training, and equipping the Fedayeen. The Syrians' official attitude was irrevocably at odds with that of their Arab neighbors. The Syrian Prime Minister told a press conference in October, 1966: "We are not sentinels over Israel's security and are not the leash that restrains the revolution of the displaced and persecuted Palestinian people."

Before the June War, commando attacks did not constitute a military threat to Israel. According to Israeli Defense Forces figures, until the 1967 War there were only fourteen casualties and 122 cases of sabotage. The importance of guerrilla activity lay in its political rather than its military reverberations. Guerrilla actions, regardless of their degree of success, forced the Arab States to assume more belligerent postures toward Israel. No Arab state can retain popular support if it does not pay at least lip service to Palestinian rights, and Syria's espousal of an activist "people's war" seemed to many Arabs, especially the young, more attractive than Nasser's policy of temporate action to "liberate" Palestine.

Once again, the predictable pattern of violence followed. From February to August, 1966, the Israelis reported ninety-six incidents. Israeli concern was not so much over the damage (only five Israelis were killed in these actions) as it was over the frequency of their occurrence and the backing they received from Arab states. A major Israeli reprisal was aimed at a Syrian water diversion project, and was followed, as usual, by a brief respite before the guerrilla operations resumed.

In the fall of 1966, guerrilla raids resumed at their earlier rate—

about twenty-five incidents per month. Israel's retaliation this time was aimed not at Syria but at the Jordanian town of Samu. The Samu raid was particularly violent, with tanks and airplanes being used in broad daylight by the Israelis.

The ensuing period of quiet lasted until December, when particularly severe raiding and shelling flared up across the border from Syria. On April 7, the Israeli Air Force chose to respond to Syrian shelling of the Kibbutz Gadot, and the Syrians chose to meet the incoming Israeli planes with their MIGs. In the ensuing battle, six MIGs were shot down and the Israelis pursued the Syrian aircraft all the way to the outskirts of Damascus. The Syrian leadership interpreted the violence of the Israeli reprisal as an attempt to topple their regime.

President Nasser's prestige had taken a severe beating in the wake of the Israeli raids against Jordan and Syria. As leader of the progressive forces in the Arab world, the Egyptian leader was generally expected to be in the forefront of the struggle against Israel. Still, Nasser did nothing in response to the Samu raid. Less explainable was his failure to respond to the Israeli attack against Syria, with whom he had signed a mutual defense pact five months earlier. Nasser was pilloried for his inactivity. A headline in the Jordanian paper *al-Quds* (Jerusalem) asked, "What steps has Cairo taken?" Nasser was accused of hiding behind the United Nations troops stationed on his common border with Israel. Rather than fighting Israelis, the Egyptian army was fighting fellow Arabs in the Yemen. For many of his critics in the Arab world, the Yemeni War symbolized Nasser's fall from grace. Undoubtedly the need to restore his sagging prestige was a crucial factor in Nasser's decision in mid-May to answer the Syrian call for help.

The Syrian leadership was certain that it was going to be the prime target for a massive Israeli attack aimed at toppling it and the nascent guerrilla movement it sheltered. The air attack on April 7 and harsh public warnings from Israeli Premier Levi Eshkol and Chief of Staff Rabin gave support to this belief.

In the second week of May, Nasser was faced with Syrian and Russian intelligence reports of Israeli troop concentrations preparing for an imminent strike into Syria. On May 14, all Egyptian forces were placed on maximum alert, and two divisions moved into Sinai. The Russian motives in passing this information to Nasser remain one of the key unanswered questions about the June War. Many students of this period have concluded that the information was false, and, furthermore, that the Russians and Egyptians probably knew it to be false.

Three explanations of the Russians' action seem plausible. First, they may have truly believed that an Israeli attack was coming, although not necessarily at that moment. By relaying the information to the Egyptians, the Soviets would be warning their allies in advance and setting in motion measures of defense.

Second, the Russians may have passed along the information as a signal to the Egyptians that they could expect Russian backing in the expected period of high tension. This explanation implies that the Russians, believing that they would benefit most from a crisis in the area, willingly played the role of instigator.

Third, a possible explanation revolves around the Russians' stake in their Syrian client. The Syrians faced a serious internal crisis in April and May and the Russians may have drummed up the possibility of an Israeli attack in order to take the pressure off the Syrian leadership while bringing in the direct support of Nasser.

Nasser responded cautiously but positively to the Syrian call for help. As stated earlier, the President's need for a political victory and the reinforcement of his position as vanguard of the Arab left was the primary motivating factor. No doubt, the desire to deter an Israeli attack on Syria, and support he expected from the Soviet Union, also played a part in his decision to act.

Placing the Egyptian army on maximum alert was but one step in a chain of military maneuvers which culminated in the third round of conventional warfare. In the most visible manner possible, Egyptian combat units began their trip through Cairo to the Suez front.

Nasser was then faced with the problem of the United Nations Emergency Forces. On May 16, the Egyptian Chief of Staff, in a letter to their commander, requested partial withdrawal of UNEF. The letter itself was imprecise in meaning and highly irregular as diplomatic procedure. In reply, the UNEF commander told the Egyptians to deliver their request in all-or-nothing terms to the Secretary-General. This the Egyptians did, on May 18, calling for the removal of all UNEF personnel. The Secretary-General was faced with a *fait accompli*, as local Egyptian commanders were in fact taking control of observation posts all along the border. Without resorting to procedural delays he submitted to the Egyptian demand.

By May 21, Egyptian troops had completed their occupation of all UNEF positions, including the most strategic one at Sharm el-Sheikh commanding access to the Gulf of Aqaba, and the port of Elat. On May 22, President Nasser announced that Egypt had closed the Gulf to all Israeli shipping, and to all cargoes of strategic material bound for Israel, an act which the Israelis had publicly declared to be *casus belli*.

In a matter of days, the Egyptians' role had escalated from that of foil to that of confronter of Israel. If the manner in which Egyptian soldiers moved to the front was theatrical, the eventual size of the troop movement was more serious. By May 17, 30,000 Egyptians were emplaced in Sinai. On May 19, Israeli intelligence estimated the force at 40,000 and reported that Egyptian troops in Yemen were being transferred to Sinai. Two days later, Chief of Staff Rabin estimated the level of Egyptian troops in Sinai at around 80,000.

Why did Nasser make these moves? The first, simplest, and perhaps the most correct explanation is that the process of escalation had a momentum and a logic of its own. Nasser needed to make his response to the Syrian request a credible one and, at the same time, to answer his Arab critics who caustically noted the protective shield of UNEF. For these reasons the Egyptian President asked for partial removal of the international force. It was perhaps unfortunate, unnecessary, and fateful that U Thant asked Nasser to put his demand in all-or-nothing terms, and that Nasser, feeling he could not back down, called for complete withdrawal. With UNEF gone, Nasser no longer had any excuse not to close the Gulf to Israeli shipping. The Arab leader must have known his action amounted to throwing down the gauntlet to Israel. By suggesting at the last minute that the issue be submitted to the international court at The Hague, Nasser once again raised the possibility of a diplomatic solution. But probably he already realized that Israel would opt for a military one. He must have assumed that the Egyptian forces in Sinai, which he continued to reinforce, were capable of absorbing the first Israeli blow and could hold out until the Soviet Union came to Egypt's support or Great Power intervention stopped the war altogether. Egypt and its leader might then claim a diplomatic if not military triumph.

A second explanation of Nasser's actions is based on his sincere desire to eliminate the consequences of the 1956, if not the 1948 War, and the chronic Arab propensity to self-delusion. It can be argued that Nasser saw conditions being forged for a successful campaign against Israel—unification of Arab ranks behind Egyptian leadership, and favorable international circumstances. This time, England and France would not be in collusion with Israel. The United States was embroiled in a war in Southeast Asia, and Russia could be relied on for solid diplomatic support. As Cairo's passionate propaganda escalated, the Egyptians and their leader began to believe the rhetoric of Arab militance.

A third explanation insists on the propriety of Nasser's actions and their nonbelligerent nature. According to this interpretation, Nasser's strategy was primarily one of deterrence. His declaration of restraint—that he would refrain from firing the first shot—his realization of the limited military capacity of the Egyptian army, and his call for the adjudication of the Aqaba dispute are the salient facts, according to this explanation. It is said that Nasser was only reopening a legitimate question of international law which had been closed by force in 1956.

Turning now to the Israeli side of the war, we find two general interpretations of Israeli action leading up to the Six Day War. The first stresses Israeli aggressive designs in the area. A combination of Israeli activists intent on obtaining the gains relinquished in 1956, it is said, sought to provoke a regional crisis which would give the Israeli army the opportunity to strike. By calculated leaks, the activists are said to have led the Arab countries to believe that a large-scale retaliation was in preparation, thereby provoking Arab military movements that would justify mobilization of the Israeli Defense Forces. One distinguished writer, Maxime Rodinson, in *Israel and the Arabs*,* says the Soviet misinformation on Israeli troop buildups came from activist Israeli sources in the military. There is a curious parallel here between this interpretation of Israeli behavior and the interpretation of Nasser's behavior, which postulates that he was intent on destroying Israel, or at least regaining Egyptian control of the Gulf. Both assume aggressive intent, leaving the only substantive question one of timing.

A second interpretation of Israeli behavior is that it should be understood in terms of reaction to Egyptian moves, with each Israeli action adding to the momentum of the next.

Israel began mobilization in response to Egyptian troop deployments, but in the light of the theatrical nature of Cairo's initial action, this mobilization was only partial. Expanding between May 16 and May 27 as the military preparedness of the surrounding Arab countries increased, Israeli mobilization had a momentum of its own. It provided military leaders with a strong argument that delay in a preemptive strike would jeopardize the safety of the Israeli State. On the one hand the enemy's forces were gathering. On the other, with such a high proportion of able-bodied, productive men playing some military role, mobilization meant a critical slowdown of the Israeli economy.

After Nasser closed the Strait of Tiran, debate raged in Israeli public and private sectors over how, and when, to resolve the crisis. Until the Strait was closed, Premier Eshkol resisted pressures for an immediate military response. He urged mutual troop withdrawals. On May 23, after closure, Eshkol called on the Great Powers and the United Nations to remove the blockade. Still not prepared to deliver a military response, Eshkol sought Great Power backing and sent Foreign Minister Abba Eban to London, Paris, and Washington to win support.

Upon Eban's return from his three-nation trip, the Israeli Cabinet met on May 27 to decide on whether to give the U.S. some time to open the Gulf through diplomatic pressure, or whether to go to

*New York: Pantheon Books, 1969.

war. The Cabinet vote ended in a tie, with Eshkol himself now voting to go to war. But at this meeting an essential coalition partner, the National Religious Front, let it be known that it did not trust Eshkol's military judgment. This group insisted that Moshe Dayan be named Minister of Defense, and refused to vote for war until he was appointed.

Premier Eshkol decided to temporize, but faced mounting pressure from the military and the public. In halting fashion, as though unsure of himself, he delivered a speech calling for renewed diplomatic effort to bring the crisis to an end.

On May 29 the internal political wrangle was finally resolved, and Eshkol agreed to appoint Dayan Minister of Defense in a "wall to wall" cabinet including all political factions except the Communists. The cabinet reorganization satisfied the Israeli General Staff and dissident political groupings, including the National Religious Front. The only decision left open at this point was the timing of the preemptive strike. The new cabinet was announced on June 1.

Meanwhile, the Arab states continued to integrate their diplomatic and military positions. On May 30 King Hussein flew to Cairo to sign a treaty of common defense, and Nasser's hegemony seemed complete. Hussein was also reconciled with Ahmed Shukairy, the head of the Palestine Liberation Organization, whom he disliked both personally and as head of a group that might make claims upon his territory. Iraq formally agreed to the common defense treaty on June 4.

By this time, Egyptian officers had already been transferred to the Eastern Front and two Egyptian commando battalions had been flown into Jordan and were deployed on the West Bank by June 4. The next day, the third round of conventional warfare started.

On the basic assessment of responsibilty for the June War various authors give varying interpretations. Some believe that Israel alone was responsible because an activist clique genuinely wished to launch a preemptive strike to regain that which was lost in 1956. Others believe that responsibility rests with Nasser, that he became instigator by closing the Strait of Tiran to Israeli shipping, which Israel had given notice would be a *casus belli*. Nasser is seen as committed to eliminating the consequences of the 1956 War, if not the 1948 War, and selecting the propitious time to achieve his goals.

But the weight of expert opinon is that neither side wanted war, and that neither picked the time for it. The third round has variously been called "a chain reaction war" by J. Bowyer Bell of the Harvard Center for International Affairs; the result of a "snowballing process of miscalculation" by Winston Burdett of C.B.S.; and "a textbook case of miscalculation" by Walter Laqueur, director of the Institute of Contemporary Studies in London.

All these authorities hold that events moved in such a way that the leaders of the two sides no longer had control over events. Tactically all the players in this act of the Arab-Israeli tragedy were somewhat to blame for the outbreak of war: The Israelis for their unduly harsh public statements about the threat from Syria, which led to partial Egyptian mobilization; the Syrians for their lack of restraint in border incidents with Israel, which went beyond the sponsorship of guerrilla operations to the shelling of civilian targets inside Israeli territory; and the Egyptians for their unwillingness to stop the process of escalation when it was still possible, after the first partial mobilization in the Sinai. But when this war is examined from the viewpoint of larger strategic objectives, things are rather different.

What are the intentions of nations? Always they must remain somewhat inscrutable. But there appears to have been an underlying *Israeli policy* to wage periodical preventive wars against the Arabs, and an even more fundamental *Arab determination*, always rhetorical but subconciously persistent, to destroy Israel. My belief in this *Israeli policy* and *Arab determination* does not rest on documentary evidence but on my judgment of Israeli and Arab interpretations of history.

One must distinguish Nasser's public and private position, his propagandistic and real positions. In public he often seemed bellicose. This was a part of the public image he deemed necessary in the Arab world. But in private he spoke more moderately and rationally. In a meeting with him in 1959 at his Cairo home, I found that Nasser projected a kind of boyish charm and sincerity. I understood immediately the many persons who had met him and spoken of his winning personality.

In retrospect, I believe that the personality the Egyptian leader showed in private reflected his intentions more truly than the bombastic speeches he felt he had to make. But he was also not without deviousness, often becoming the prisoner of his public statements.

Nasser's objectives in 1967, as I see them, were tactical. He can be taxed with overplaying his hand. He hoped by his brinkmanship to gain diplomatic advantages, and if it should come to war, I believe that he thought Egypt could withstand the first Israeli onslaught after which, while the war went on inconclusively, the Great Powers and the United Nations would intervene to stop the bloodshed. Egypt, the victim of aggression, would then gain handsomely through diplomatic channels. But Nasser miscalculated there, too. The one thing he did not reckon with was total, unlimited Israeli victory at the first blow—a victory so swift and decisive that the international community looked on bemused and incapable of intervening. If this interpretation is sound, the main responsibility for this round of war is Israel's—but, given the ultimate Arab objectives, one can hardly blame her.

The war began with a crippling series of Israeli air strikes against Egyptian targets. Israel unleashed virtually all of her aircraft at 7:45 A.M. on June 5, leaving just twelve fighters behind for air cover. Pilots flew at least five missions that day, taking off in waves after service intervals of only eight minutes. At midday, Israeli planes struck at Jordanian and Syrian targets. On the first day of the war, over 400 Arab planes were knocked out in approximately 500 sorties. In all, 452 Arab aircraft were destroyed in the war, and of these, thirty-one were lost in air combat.

With complete mastery of the air, Israeli victory on the ground was a matter of time. The Israeli attack first centered on the Sinai front. Using many of the same commanders and routes as in 1956, Israel won complete control of the peninsula in three days. Armored divisions pushed to the Canal at Qantara, Ismailia, and Suez on June 8. One day previously, Sharm el-Sheikh was captured by paratroopers, assuring Israel control of passage through the Gulf.

With the Sinai campaign under control, Israel then turned to the Jordanian front, where primary emphasis was on the capture of the entire West Bank. In two days of fighting, Israeli units were successful, and on June 7, Israeli Defense Forces entered Nablus, Jericho, Ramallah, and most importantly, Jerusalem. On June 8, both sides accepted the U.N.-sponsored cease-fire.

A cease-fire on the Syrian front did not prevent the Israelis from launching their final offensive on June 9. Syrian resistance collapsed after Radio Damascus inexplicably and incorrectly announced the fall of Kuneitra. On June 11, Syria and Israel again agreed to another cease-fire.

The third round of conventional warfare had ended. Once again, the Israelis showed that Arab rhetoric was no match for a highly motivated army, an extraordinary officer corps, ruthless military execution, and control of the air.

Neither the Egyptians nor the Jordanians have issued official statistics on their human losses in this war. A widely accepted figure for the Egyptians, however, is 25,000 killed and wounded. The Jordanians unofficially estimate 500 to 700 killed and 2,000 wounded.

The Israeli statistics, not surprisingly, are more precise. They have reported 759 men killed in the June, 1967, War. By comparison, Israeli casualties in the 1956 campaign were 191, and for the 1948 War, 4,487.

Because of its fateful importance I will save the account of the fourth Arab-Israeli war for Chapter 14.

11

The Rise and Decline of the Palestinian Commandos — Part I

The emergence of the Palestinian commandos was the most intriguing development in the Arab world between the Arab-Israeli war of 1967 and the fourth Arab-Israeli war in 1973.

The commandos—often known as the "Fedayeen," meaning "those who are prepared to sacrifice their lives"—introduced a new dynamic into the life of the Arab world. Their activity—even when reduced by the buffeting they suffered at the hands of King Hussein in 1970 and 1971—and their ideologies, inconsistencies notwithstanding, serve as catalysts in Arab life and especially on the far left of Arab politics.

Oversimplifying the complex but often vague thinking on the Arab side, one may say that since the arrival of Jewish immigrants in Palestine, Arab guerrilla activity has had twin objectives: at least to stem the influx of Jewish immigrants and prevent the Jews from creating a Jewish State, at most to destroy and expel the Jewish community.

The new, post-1967 commandos refined these objectives. Distinguishing between Zionism and Judaism, they said, as formulated by Fatah, the largest group, that they meant only to destroy the "Zionist, racialist, theocratic state of Israel." Most of them maintained that they were not opposed to the Jewish people in Palestine. Although the various movements of commandos differed as to precisely whom among the Jews in Palestine they would tolerate, whether all now present or only those who came before 1948, the new commandos, again according to Fatah, defined their goal as the establishment of a "unitary, democratic, and nonsectarian Palestinian State."

In the mood of despair which possessed the Arabs after the 1967 War, the commandos served the Arab peoples as a psychological crutch. After the terrible defeats of the regular armies, the humiliation of the Arab governments, and indeed, of the entire "establishment" in the Arab world, here was one group of Arabs who were not defeated, who were able to go on fighting, and who were able to twist the tail of the Lion of Judah. If, as Gamal Abdel Nasser once wrote, there was "within the Arab circle, a role wandering aimlessly in search of a hero," that role had now found its hero in the form of the commandos. Nasser may have meant that Egypt should play the role, and it may be that he himself played the role during his lifetime. But with Nasser gone, the only possible stand-ins were the commandos.

Inevitably, the commandos became the darlings of all the Arab "media." Later, things would change somewhat, but in the immediate aftermath of the June War, no Arab government could co-opt or constrain this movement.

In contrast to earlier commandos or guerrillas in this area, many of whose leaders were non-Palestinians, the most vibrant faction of the new commando movement was Palestinian. The principal movement, Fatah, insisted on its Palestinian character, and non-Palestinians in its ranks were treated as guests. The Popular Front for the Liberation of Palestine (PFLP) and Saiqa acknowledged Pan-Arab principles but were mainly Palestinian. The smaller groups were almost entirely Palestinian except for the self-consciously Pan-Arab movement called ALF, the Arab Liberation Front, sponsored by the Iraqi branch of the Baath Party. The Syrian authorities also introduced a good many Syrians into the ranks of Saiqa, and the Popular Democratic Front for the Liberation of Palestine (PDFLP) was led by a Christian, East Bank

Jordanian. As time went on, the new commandos' Palestinianism created tensions between themselves and the surrounding states, especially Jordan and Lebanon, within whose borders they tended to organize the Palestinian refugees into a "state within the state."

This movement today numbers between 2,500,000 and 3,000,000 people who, according to unofficial estimates, in March, 1973, were scattered throughout the Arab world as follows:

		UNRWA Registered	
East Bank of the Jordan River	700,000	562,038	
West Bank of the Jordan River	675,000	282,179	
Israel	350,000	—	
Gaza	375,000	325,078	
Lebanon	275,000	180,648	
Syria	175,000	172,391	
Egypt	25,000	4,000	(including the Gulf States)
Iraq	10,000	—	
Persian Gulf	170,000	—	
	2,755,000	1,532,287	(March 31, 1973, including 5,953 residing elsewhere)

These figures include Palestinians who have become naturalized citizens in their countries of residence—more than 40,000 in the case of Lebanon. Another 100,000 Palestinians are scattered throughout western Europe, mainly West Germany, in the United States, Latin America, and Australia.

The effect on the Palestinians of the disastrous war of 1948 and their ensuing dispersal was traumatic. For two decades they remained in something like a coma. I do not mean that there were no stirrings among them. There was in fact an attempt after the 1948 War to continue the guerrilla campaign begun by Fawzi al-Kawukji. One of the leaders was Wasfi Tal, later Premier of Jordan, who was assassinated late in 1971. The movement petered out for lack of support, and in the face of the disapproval of the host governments. There were no more concerted movements until Fatah and its earliest rival, the Palestinian Liberation Front (predecessor of the postwar PFLP) sprang into action just before the June War.

For two decades the name of Palestine was almost lost. It was even omitted from most maps. The Palestinians became a deeply dejected people dependent on international charity for the support of their majority.

The refugee camps dot the landscape of the Arab countries surrounding Israel. They are not model housing settlements—nor are they rampant slums. Suffice it to say that they are not comfortable places to live, especially in winter. Standards of nourishment, sanitation, housing, and education are austere but adequate.

The United Nations Relief and Works Agency (UNRWA), two-thirds of whose costs are paid by the United States, is charged with care of Palestinian refugees. Each month a person eligible for refugee aid receives 22 pounds of flour (sometimes partly replaced by pulses), 1.1 pound of rice, 1.3 pound of sugar, and 13 ounces of oil. This amounts to approximately 1,500 calories per day during the summer and 1,600 calories per day in the winter—barely enough for subsistence. But small children and pregnant mothers can receive more, and some members of almost all the large, cohesive Palestinian families find work and can supplement the family diet.

As of March, 1973, 830,000 individuals were receiving rations, a substantial reduction from June, 1970, when more than 1,160,000 Palestinian refugees were receiving UNRWA rations of some kind. The reduction was effected by striking from the lists the names of recipients who died. The refugees avoid reporting deaths, and it had taken years to correct the lists.

UNRWA also provides basic medical and educational services, including vocational and teacher-training programs. The eight vocational training centers teach thirty-eight different skills, from mechanics to beauty shop operations and secretarial services. While education in all its forms is the Palestinians' preferred escape route from camp life, the vocational schools are the great hope of those who do not qualify academically. By learning a trade, a young man can liberate himself from the tragic limitations of the majority of the older generation of camp dwellers, peasants whose only knowledge is how to till the soil.

A visible improvement in camp life has been the disappearance of the tent camp. In 1969 and 1970 the last tents came down and were replaced by tin huts built by UNRWA itself or with special donations by NEED, an American charitable group, by the West German and Italian governments, by British charities, and by Catholic and Protestant groups.

Progress on this front, as in the sanitary and educational areas, has been hampered by lack of funds for UNRWA operations. Each year since 1970 UNRWA has run a deficit of as much as 6 million dollars which had to be met by special fund drives. In 1972, thanks to a 4 million dollar gift in the form of flour, sugar and rice from the European Economic Community, the deficit was only 700,000 dollars.

The inhabitants of these camps sometimes express shame at the squalor of their habitations, and resentment of the affluent foreigners who, for twenty-five years, have come to take pictures, express sympathy, and move on. To visit the camps is often embarrassing and occasionally intimidating.

Why do these people then remain in the camps? For the older generation of peasants there is no alternative because their only skill, farming, is in surplus supply in the Arab countries. There are also political pressures on them to remain as a living assertion of the Palestinians' determination to accept no solution to their problem except return to the homeland. Accepting resettlement would also raise difficult problems for most Arab host countries. Egypt is already overpopulated. Lebanon's system is based on a Christian-Moslem balance that would be upset by a Moslem Palestinian influx. Jordan's resources are slender. Only Syria and Iraq could sustain substantial numbers. The refugee population grows steadily. Every year people do leave the camps, but their number cannot overcome the high birthrate of the Palestinians. UNRWA health services aggravate the problem by lowering the death rate.

In mid-1973 there were sixty-three established refugee camps, ten of which were established after the 1967 War in an attempt to care for the new wave of refugees that the war created. Here is the breakdown by country of the camps:

Country	Number of Camps	Inhabitants
East Bank Jordan	10	222,298
West Bank	20	73,041
Gaza	8	198,919
Lebanon	15	90,949
Syria	10	48,296
Total number of refugees living in camps:		658,855

The figures for refugee camps are somewhat smaller than the total of UNRWA-registered refugees and much smaller than the number of Palestinians, yet the refugee camps persist and grow, and are breeding grounds for hatred and political radicalism.

The foundations of the Palestinian national revival were laid by the element among the Palestinians who did not vegetate in the camps during the two decades after 1948. As of mid-1973, there were about 1,500,000 refugees who drew no rations either because for some reason they were disqualified, or because they chose to look after themselves. These were the ones who had "made it" on their own.

You meet them all over the Arab world and beyond. These are the Palestinian success stories. Most sensational is the story of Yusef Baydas, who built a financial empire in Lebanon called Intrabank. Intrabank unfortunately crashed in 1966, but Beirut's fashionable Rue Hamra remains lined with solid business houses and a few modest "skyscrapers" built by Palestinians. The best doctors and engineers, and also plumbers and electricians in Beirut, Amman, and throughout the Persian Gulf are Palestinians. In the Gulf they run the new bureaucracies of the oil sheikhdoms. They are the radio station managers, the entrepreneurs, the teachers and technicians, the advisors to the sheikhs. They form a kind of elite which stirs not a little envy among the people with whom they live. They are sometimes maligned as the "Jews among the Arabs," people who get up too early in the morning, work too hard, and succeed too well. Many also become involved in political activities of all kinds, so that the Palestinians as a group are often suspected of coups, attempted coups, plots, and subversion.

The Palestinians are as active culturally as they are economically. They are publishers, writers, artists, composers, newspaper editors. They were caught up in a general drive toward self-improvement. It is said that there are nearly 80,000 Palestinian university graduates, and that in 1972 no less than 35,000 Palestinians were attending institutions of higher learning.

This is the group, the bootstrap Palestinians, who energize the Palestinian national movement and the commandos. Some of them seem possessed of a new purposefulness and dignity, making it respectable, even honorable again to be a Palestinian. Fatah's radio station, Saut al Assifa, "Voice of the Storm," conveys their attitude in a song of which the refrain is: "I am an Arab, my address is Palestine."

For some years after 1967 commando exploits gave all the Palestinians—those in the camps as well as the more successful ones outside—a new sense of dignity that contrasts with the wailing and the breast-beating braggadocio of an earlier period. If there is anything new here, it can probably be summarized as a "revolt against Levantinism" much as the new character of the "Sabra," the second or third generation of Israelis, lies in revolt against the ways, values, and culture of the Diaspora.

What is Levantinism? Perhaps "not quite genuine," the merchant falsely extolling his wares, a veneer of European manners covering Oriental emotionalism, noise, instability—the antithesis of military values such as would be required in a persistent commando campaign.

A true sense of the way the commando movement evolved can best be conveyed in terms of the lives of its two most prominent leaders, Yasir Arafat and George Habash.

Yasir Arafat grew up in Jerusalem amidst serious disturbances in his neighborhood near the Wailing Wall. His father's house had been one of a group of twelve, including a mosque and a religious school, just south of the Wailing Wall which have lately been demolished by the Israelis to expose an additional forty meters of the wall. His mother was related to the Husseinis, and probably through this connection the young Arafat became personal secretary to Abdel Kader al-Husseini, the one member of this aristocratic family who fought personally against the Israelis.

A few years before the 1948 War the young Arafat, then in his late teens, and his father joined a Palestinian militia group called al-Jihad al-Muqaddas (the Holy Struggle) led by Abdel Kader al-Husseini. Their particular task was running arms across the border from Egyptian Sinai. After Abel Kader was killed in 1948 in the battle for Qastel, a strongpoint on the road from the coast to Jerusalem, the Arafats departed from Jerusalem with thousands of other refugees for Gaza, where a part of the family owned property. In Gaza the young Arafat became associated with the Moslem Brotherhood, which had organized a volunteer guerrilla force.

Gaza was the center of support for the Brotherhood Volunteer Battalions at this time. Although his associates now say that he did not become a member, it is certain that the Brotherhood influenced Arafat and many other Palestinians who later joined in the organization of Fatah.

Active in the area between Gaza and Hebron, the Brotherhood helped support and supply the Egyptian units at Falluja, where one of the officers was Gamal Abdel Nasser, then, according to some sources, an active member of the Brotherhood.

Looking back on his formative years, in an interview in Amman in October, 1968, Arafat observed that "Since I opened my eyes to this world, I was able to hear the sound of bullets." It is likely that as a boy the future commando leader heard about the exploits against the British—and the Arabs—of the Jewish paramilitary groups, Haganah, Irgun, Stern. It would have been natural for him to yearn to do likewise, or better, with the Arabs against the Jews.

"Of course," he said, "I joined the fighting of 1948 just as thousands of my brethren . . . because we believed it was a fight to defend our existence and the existence of the Arab people." The interview took place in one of the small, bare rooms of the headquarters Fatah was using at that time in a stone villa on Jebel Luwebdeh, a few hundred yards from the American Embassy. He sat at a small wooden desk, the afternoon sun shining upon him.

As he grew accustomed to his visitor he seemed to relax, and removed the heavy dark glasses which had become his trademark. With his large, brown eyes, he gazed searchingly at the visitor. He spoke quietly, even gently. For a man who has spent much of his life "underground," his manner with strangers is not easy at first. He conveyed a quality of sweetness. As I pressed him for the personal side of his story, he smiled broadly showing his full, sensitive lips and regular teeth. He wore a heavy, brown sweater in the chilly atmosphere of the stone house, a tattered red-covered notebook in his left breast pocket visible above the edge of the sweater. His trousers were of the wooly British battledress type, his boots black and heavy. He spoke in Arabic, through an interpreter most of the time, although his English is good.

Soon after the Arab governments had signed armistice agreements with Israel, Arafat moved from Gaza to Cairo to study engineering at King Fuad University.

At the university Arafat was elected chairman of the Palestinian Students' Federation from 1952 to 1956, and thereafter became chairman of the Palestinian Alumni Federation, linking Palestinian university graduates all over the Arab world and beyond. This is one of the explanations for the number of intellectuals in Fatah's leadership. During his student years Arafat remained friendly with the Moslem Brotherhood. It is interesting to reflect that both Nasser's Free Officers' Movement, which made the Egyptian revolution, and Fatah, which seeks to make the Palestinian revolution, began in friendly association with the Moslem Brotherhood but soon discarded its theological ideology for a more secularized and vaguely socialist conception. Whereas Nasser's regime, engaged in a bitter struggle for control of the revolution, eventually suppressed the Moslem Brotherhood, Fatah remains friendly with the remnants of that organization.

His associates deny that he had any connection with the short-lived Egyptian-sponsored commandos who raided Israeli territory from the Gaza Strip during the period preceding the War of 1956. But some Fatah and other commandos got their first training in these units, which popularized the name "Fedayeen," which became a collective description of all commandos.

In 1956, Arafat, who had received some training at the Egyptian Military Academy during his student years, and had led commandos against the British in the Canal Zone, fought with the rank of lieutenant in the Egyptian Army at Port Said and at Abu Kebir, and served as a demolitions expert.

In the meantime, in Gaza, the Palestinians, who had not previously been allowed by the Egyptians to organize independently, formed their own underground during the short Israeli occupation. These cells formed in Gaza in 1956 persisted and became the nucleus for Fatah and its various rivals in spite of the fact that the Egyptians, after the experience of the 1956 War, were anxious to avoid provoking the Israelis and for the next ten years eschewed all commando activity and arrested anyone suspected of such intentions.

The nucleus for the future Fatah organization was formed at this time by Arafat with Khalil al Wazir (later Abu Jihad) and Salah Khalaf (later Abu Ayad). With Salah Khalaf and Zuhair al Alami, Arafat traveled in 1956 to Prague as representatives of the General Union of Palestinian Students at an International Union of Students conference.

After graduation, Arafat was employed as an engineer for a time at el Mahalla al Kubra, in Egypt, until in 1957 he got another job in Kuwait running a contracting company, later working for the Department of Public Works. Here he entered into a new world of Palestinians drawn by the oil boom—an elite of skilled workers, technicians, teachers. The Kuwaitis at that time did not care how the Palestinians organized themselves as long as they did their work and kept out of Kuwaiti politics. For once the Palestinians were free.

One day in the summer of 1957 a dozen men met outside the town of Kuwait, on the bare beach near the water, a few hours before sundown. Most were from Gaza but some had come for the meeting from Iraq, Jordan, Lebanon, and Syria. Their names included the three associates of Cairo days, plus Faruq al Qaddumi (later Abu Lutuf), Muhamed Yussif al Najar (later Abu Yusif), Khalid al Hassan (later Abu Said), and Kamal Adwan. These seven men and Arafat remained the core of Fatah leadership—a factor of cohesion and stability that explains the persistence of this organization. (Until recently, when Israeli raiders in Beirut killed Abu Yusif and Kamal Adwan. It is not hard to imagine what this meant to Arafat and his colleagues, nor pleasant to speculate what vengeance they will exact.)

Huddled together for security on the Kuwaiti beach, they founded an organization to liberate Palestine. It was to be called Fath, a name composed of the initials, spelled backwards, of the words *Harakat Tahreer Falasteen*, the Movement of the Liberation of Palestine, and prounced "Fatah," with the emphasis on the first syllable.

The word "Fath" had special significance for the founders, for it meant "victory," and was an allusion to the Koranic account of the promise given by God to the Prophet Mohammed when he was in Medina. God promised him victory over his enemies if he would return to Mecca. He returned and was victorious.

Equating the Palestinians' return to Palestine with Mohammed's return to Mecca, el Fatah radio now opens its program from Cairo each night as follows:

"In the Name of Allah, the Beneficent, the Merciful, Lo! We have given thee (Mohammed) a signal victory . . ."

Arafat, often known by his pseudonym "Abu Ammar," insisted that Fatah must not follow any particular ideology except the Liberation of Palestine and that it was the duty of Palestinians to put aside their political party loyalties and unite for this single objective.

Fatah ideology has scarcely changed since then. In his interview with me, in a sudden burst of perfectly fluent English, Arafat said: "Our ideological theory is very simple. Our country has been occupied. The majority of our people have been kicked out by Zionism and Imperialism from their homes.

"We wait and wait and wait for the justice of the United Nations, for the justice of the world, while our people are suffering in the tents and caves. But nothing of this was realized. None of our hopes. But our dispersion was aggravated. We have believed that the only way to return to our homes and our land is the armed struggle. We believe in this theory without any complications and with complete clarity and this is our aim and our hope."

While Arafat was still in Kuwait it was Nasserite doctrine that the Arab states should prepare for an inevitable decisive confrontation with Israel at some unspecified date in the future but should avoid military involvement in the meantime. By contrast, Fatah began with the assumption that the Arab countries and their armies had failed and that the Palestinians must take their fate into their own hands.

Fatah also rejected a related scheme for a "war of surprise," possibly a "blitzkrieg" of one week, that would eliminate Israel in a single rush. If the war of liberation were to wait indefinitely for a buildup, or if the Israelis were to be finished off in a week, then the Palestinian people would have no function in the struggle and there would be no cure for the psychological and spiritual sickness that had kept them dormant for two decades. Furthermore, if the guerrillas were to wait for the eventual "war of surprise," that is, until the Arab armies were strong enough to oppose the Israelis, the Arab states, out of psychological or moral faults, might never prepare themselves. They must be dragged into it.

How Fatah went about realizing its own concept of the liberation of Palestine may be illustrated by Fatah's training of commandos and of Palestinian youth. I was one of a small group of correspondents invited to visit a Fatah training camp in Jordan early in 1969. The correspondents were cautioned to avoid in their stories any indication of its location and to take care in the pictures they took to avoid long shots that would identify the landscape or close-ups that would identify the individual commandos. Although they wanted publicity, secrecy of this kind remained important in their minds.

In a heavily wooded glade redolent with the perfume of wet pine trees, the Fatah commander, a thoroughly military, mustachioed type of near middle age, welcomed us to his tent. He willingly described the three-months' training course his men must follow before joining one of the "Asifa" fighting units. And he happily put some of his men through their paces. His relative willingness to submit to scrutiny was the measure, I thought, of the self-confidence Fatah had by this time attained.

He said his men had to pass three tests, medical, physical fitness, and psychological, before beginning their course. At the end they would face another test, including a week of maneuvers almost without sleep. If they failed they might be allowed to repeat some part of the course, or be assigned to nonmilitary tasks.

"The first week," he said, "is devoted to instilling military attitudes, acceptance of orders, accustoming the men to hard living conditions. There are political lectures on international politics, our role in liberating Palestine, instruction in first aid, and field hygiene, and exercise, a half hour of intensive workout gradually stepped up to a full hour.

"That first week the fighter is watched. If he is able he is promoted to the second week, with tougher physical training and instruction in the use of all kinds of weapons . . . especially our automatic rifle, the Kalashnikov."

He proudly described this Russian-made weapon as "the best all-round weapon in the world, slightly lighter and longer in range than the Israeli 'Uzi'."

In subsequent weeks, the commander continued, physical training and weapons instruction become progressively more advanced. All kinds of weapons are included, with a special course on how to deal with paratroopers, helicopters, and tank attacks. Much attention is given to hand-to-hand combat, he pointed out, "for there may be conditions when a man finds himself without any weapon, or out of ammunition, or with only a knife. A man must also know what to do if he is lost in the mountains, how to live off the land."

Another course of instruction, he added, deals with planting mines, and demolition with explosives. All men are also taught a few key phrases in Hebrew and all drills are rehearsed at night.

The commander called out a platoon that had had forty days' training to set up exercises and to run an obstacle course under live fire. It was the sort of thing any commando training would include. The men performed with zest and style.

During another visit to an Ashbal paramilitary youth training center, I glimpsed a fragment of what a new Palestinian state might become.

The Ashbal camp, across the road from the vast Baqaa refugee camp inhabited by 36,000 sullen refugees, was a somewhat surprising island of cheerfully "swinging" teen-agers. Very serious, they did their "swinging" with submachine guns around the flag of Palestine (the same as Jordan's, three green, white, and black horizontal stripes, but minus the white star within the red triangle).

Intended for boys eight to fourteen years old, Ashbal was started in early 1967. It had more than a score of camps by the end of 1970. This particular one drew 5 to 10 percent of the boys of the adjoining refugee camp. It required only that participants also go to school.

"We are not just a paramilitary organization," explained the head of Fatah youth services. "Rather this is a morale building and educational movement to prepare the well-rounded future citizen of Palestine—equipped and trained to defend his nation but also to be a good, productive citizen. We encourage the artist, the engineer, the architect, as well as the fighter among our young men."

The hut near the entrance to a field was all the center then had in the way of buildings. But a cultural center for meetings, movies, and stage shows was being built.

The boys raced across the field from the scene of a series of explosions, practicing evacuation of wounded under fire. They marched on the double, or jogging, in platoon-sized groups, each chanting or singing:

"To the left, Asifa,
To the right, Asifa,
At the front, Asifa,
At the rear, Asifa."

Another group went by, its leader calling out questions and the platoon answering at the top of lusty lungs:

"It has been told . . .
What?
That we are the Fedayeen . . .
What Fedayeen?
The Fedayeen of Asifa . . .
What Asifa?
The Asifa of the revolution . . .
What revolution?
The revolution of the return . . .

What return?

The return to Gaza, Jaffa, Haifa . . ."

The Ashbal continued running the obstacle course. The best of them were to graduate to training in the use of rifles, submachine guns, machine guns, and bayonet drill.

Ashbal was only one of the elements of the Palestinian infrastructure which Fatah and other groups, notably PFLP, had at this time, in 1969 and until September, 1970, built on Jordanian soil. On the periphery of the services already provided by UNRWA Fatah had also established its own clinics, hospitals, convalescent homes, and special schools for the children of its own "martyrs"—those who had been killed in action.

Of special significance were the "Popular Resistance Militia," whose men report for training by Fatah professionals in their spare time and return to their homes at night. Difficult to distinguish from regular Fedayeen, because they wore the same variegated kind of outdoor clothing, with a fondness for leather jackets, big sweaters, and khaki, the militia, numbering many times more men than the regular commandos, played a vital role in the various confrontations between the Jordanian Government and the commando movement.

In addition to Arafat and Fatah, one must take note of a second commando leader, George Habash, and his organization, the Popular Front for the Liberation of Palestine (PFLP). Slightly older than the general run of commando leaders—he was forty-seven in 1973—he gives the impression less of a guerrilla leader than of a distinguished, rather scholarly physician—which he is. An Arab Christian of Greek Orthodox background, he was a student of medicine at the American University of Beirut in 1948. Stirred by the approaching crisis as the time for British withdrawal from Palestine approached, he returned to Lydda, the town where he had been born, and where his father was a grain merchant. Suddenly engulfed in the war, he fled with thousands of others along the highways under a pitiless sun to Ramallah in the Arab-held part of Palestine. He saw old men and women drop by the wayside and die of exhaustion and mothers struggling to keep their babies alive. The flight of the Palestinians was the turning point of his life.

He resolved to combine his medical career with political activity to avenge his people.

This was the origin of the Arab Nationalist Movement (ANM) which much later merged with Fatah's prewar underground rival, the Palestinian Liberation Front, to form the PFLP. At first Dr. Habash's thinking was almost entirely nationalist. Marxist ideas crept in only gradually, and the doctor's dogmatic Marxist critics maintain that he remains today more of a pragmatist or opportunist than they would like. They complain, for instance, that he does not hesitate to take money from wealthy merchants who have no love for Marxism but who feel that a contribution could earn them protection at some future date.

After graduating from AUB, Dr. Habash established his practice in Amman but found it expedient to move on to Damascus after he had been implicated in the antiregime riots of 1957. In both towns his clinics became known as places where the poor could expect free attention.

After the rise of the Baath (Arab Socialist Renaissance Party), Dr. Habash found Damascus inhospitable. His ANM had become, along with the Baath and the Nasserite movement, one of the competitors for the attention and loyalty of Arab youth. Prior to the 1967 War, Dr. Habash argued against the use of commandos to fight the Israelis. He was more interested in political organization than in guerrilla warfare. But after the 1967 War, his views changed and he participated in the founding of the PFLP out of a union of three smaller groups, over which he in time assumed total command. Then the widespread organization of the ANM, especially among Palestinians, served him well.

In May, 1968, when Dr. Habash was in Damascus to inquire about a supply convoy that had been confiscated, he was arrested and imprisoned on a charge of plotting to overthrow the government. After he had been held six months, his men succeeded in staging a daring rescue. They seized him as he was being transferred from one prison to another during the confusion of an attempted coup, and escaped to Jordan. During Dr. Habash's absence, a dynamic ideologist, Nayef Hawatmeh, a young East Bank Christian Jordanian, had effectively usurped the leadership of the

PFLP. Hawatmeh's faction is interesting in that it represents the most extreme Marxist-Leninist element among the commandos. Their differences with Habash soon deteriorated into street brawls and were resolved by the formation of a new group whose name differed from the old one only by adding the word "Democratic." Habash's men made fun of the Hawatmeh crowd for their bookishness and supposed ineffectuality as guerrilla fighters. But the importance of the new Popular Democratic Front for the Liberation of Palestine (PDFLP or, more frequently, PDF) was unquestionable. They served as a focus for young European leftist intellectuals who were beginning to take an interest in the Palestinian national movement and even offer their services as volunteers. The Europeans identified more easily with PDF's purely Marxist or Maoist concepts than with Fatah's Palestinian nationalism.

Another group that split away from the main PFLP adopted the name of Popular Front for the Liberation of Palestine, General Command, headed by Ahmed Jabril. At the opposite end of the political spectrum from Hawatmeh's group, they were composed mainly of former professional army officers. The main PFLP organization headed by Dr. Habash maintained its dominance by dint of his leadership and originality. The PFLP sponsored a long series of imaginative exploits, beginning with the hijacking in July, 1968, of an El Al airliner flying from Rome to Tel Aviv. While other groups also participated from time to time, almost all the hijackings were carried out by PFLP, including the fantastic exploit of September 6, 1970, when PFLP commandos attempted to hijack no less than three aircraft, two of which (a TWA 707, a BOAC VC–10) were landed on a half-forgotten airstrip in Jordan, while the third (a Pan American 747 jumbo jet) was flown to the Cairo Airport, where it was blown up after the passengers had been released.

A fourth aircraft (an El Al Boeing 707) escaped because Israeli guards managed to thwart the hijacking. Finally, a fifth plane belonging to BOAC was hijacked on September 9 and landed on the airstrip near Zurqa in Jordan. The PFLP blew up the three jet airliners on the Jordanian airstrip after exchanging fifty hostages for the freedom of seven commandos held in West Germany, Britain, and Switzerland, including Leila Khaled, who had participated in two hijackings and was captured in Britain when the second attempt failed.

The PFLP also at one time held more than fifty foreigners hostage in the Intercontinental and Philadelphia hotels in Amman threatening to blow them all up if the Jordanian Army shelled refugee camps. In May, 1969, the PFLP blew up a section of TAPLINE, the pipe that carries Saudi Arabian oil produced by the Arabian American Oil Company (ARAMCO) from Dahran to the Mediterranean, putting this American-owned pipeline out of commission for more than one hundred days. Later, the Syrian Government took advantage of what appears to have been an incident in which a French contractor broke the pipeline with a bulldozer to keep the pipe closed more than three months and to exact substantial increases in transit fees.

In yet another exploit, PFLP in September, 1969, sent a group of teen-agers to European capitals, where they threw grenades at El Al offices in Brussels and the Israeli Embassies in Bonn and The Hague, causing damage but no fatalities.

Discussing the philosophy behind these operations, Dr. George Habash, the PFLP founder, and his most brilliant ideologist, Ghassan Kanafani, editor until his assassination in 1972 of *al-Hadaf*, of Beirut, made these points to me:

The movement has no illusions about being able to hurt Israel seriously, much less defeat the Israelis, with such exploits as the attacks on El Al or other aircraft. But this kind of action focuses world attention on the Palestine national movement and what the commandos like to call the "revolution." The point is that if the world has refused to take note of the Palestinians as a nation, the PFLP would force it to do so—if only with a sense of outrage.

The PFLP sent its teen-agers on perilous missions to Europe and its young girls—always modishly attired and impeccably polite—to participate in the hijackings because "we want the world to know that the whole Palestinian community, women and children as well as men, is imbued with revolutionary fervor. And we want it to know that they are modern people and that they are civilized." The PFLP was anxious to convey the idea that these people were not the usual stereotypes of the Arab: the primitive Bedouin with his camel plodding through the desert, the tourist guide cadging tips from tourists outside religious shrines, the refugee forever exchanging one miserable hovel for another in his camps. The. frequency with which these leaders of the PFLP came back to the concept that the world must accept the Arabs "not as savages with knives between their teeth," but as "modern people," their resentment of Westerners' "folkloric" associations with the word "Arab," reflected, in my opinion, a profound Arab inferiority complex vis-à-vis the Israelis and Europeans.

Another central theme in PFLP ideology is anti-Americanism. "Israel is America. America is Israel," one of the PFLP slogans reads. Dr. Habash, in an interview with me in July, 1970, insisted that although he had nothing against the Americans as people, ultimately all American interests would have to be driven out of the Middle East. Dr. Habash put it this way: "We are facing Israel here but Israel is actually a base for America. . . . It's simply a matter of economic interests. You are backing Israel because through Israel you can strike any radical national movement which will shout that our petrol is for us. We expect much more from America. Our expectation goes up to the extent of Sixth Fleet interference, and bringing American troops into the country." Thus, America must be economically and politically excluded from the Middle East for the PFLP vision to become reality.

It is worth noting, as a commentary on the mental processes of this important commando faction, that Dr. Habash twists the facts as they are understood by more objective observers to suit a Marxist-materialist interpretation of history. He insists that the United States supports Israel as a means of protecting its economic interests in the Middle East, even though it is the paradoxical truth that the United States does this in spite of its interests and for reasons of internal politics and sentiment.

The two largest and most important commando organizations, Fatah and the PFLP, have during most of their history interacted in such a way that Fatah, the larger group, numbering perhaps 10,000 followers at its height, was constantly forced to the left by its smaller and more radical rival, the PFLP, whose membership was never more than one third as large as Fatah's.

For example, during the confrontation of February, 1970, in Amman, the PFLP launched an assault against the government radio station. PFLP could muster only a few hundred men, but the boldness of its move obliged Fatah to back it up and to commit a thousand men or more. Later this relationship between the two movements changed. Fatah's leadership under the heading of "Black September" became the more radical, or more accurately, the more violent in the course of 1972 and 1973.

In their adversity, after expulsion from Jordan, as the Lebanese Government encountered increasing pressure to restrict Fedayeen activities, the two organizations worked more closely together. Here is an organizational breakdown of the commando movement as it existed in the fall of 1970. All the movements together had about 20,000 members, while popular militia groups comprised another 20,000. As listed by William B. Quandt in his book, *The Politics of Palestinian Nationalism,** the groups were as follows:

COMMANDO GROUPS	MAJOR SOURCE OF AID
I. *Large Groups (5,000–10,000 armed men)*	
1. Palestine National Liberation Movement—Fatah (Military forces—al-Asifa)	Diverse (Libya, Syria, Kuwait, Saudi Arabia, Algeria, private Palestinian)
2. Palestine Liberation Army (PLA) Popular Liberation Forces (PLF)	Arab League through Palestine Liberation Organization (PLO)
3. Vanguards of the Popular Liberation War (Saiqa)	Syrian Baath Party
II. *Middle Groups (1,000–3,000 armed men including militia)*	
4. Popular Front for Liberation of Palestine (PFLP)	Iraq
5. Popular Democratic Front for the Liberation of Palestine (PDFLP)	Syria

*Berkeley: University of California Press, 1973.

III. *Small Groups (100–500 armed men)*

6. Popular Front for the Liberation of Palestine— General Command (PFLP—GC)	Syria; later Libya and Iraq
7. Arab Liberation Front (ALF)	Iraq
8. Organization of Arab Palestine (OAP)	UAR
9. Action Organization for the Liberation of Palestine (AOLP)	UAR, Kuwait
10. Palestinian Popular Struggle Front (PPSF)	Miscellaneous
11. Popular Organization for the Liberation of Palestine (POLP)	UAR, miscellaneous
12. Al-Ansar	Arab Communist Parties

The twenty-seven members of this supreme executive body were as follows:

PLO Executive Committee

Yasir Arafat (Fatah)
Yasir Amr (pro-Saiqa)
Kamal Nasir (Independent)
Khalid al-Hassan (Fatah)
Faruq al-Qaddumi (Fatah)
Hamid Abu Sittah (pro-Fatah)
Muhammad Yusif an-Najjar
    (Fatah)
Yusif al-Barji (Saiqa)
Ahmad ash-Shihabi (Saiqa)
Billal al-Hassan (PDFLP)
Husayn al-Khatib (pro-Saiqa)
Zuhayr al-Alami (head of the
    Palestine National Fund)

Independents

Ibrahim Bakr
Abd al-Khaliq Yaghmur
Khalid al-Fahum

*Chairman of the Palestine
    National Congress*

Yahya Hammuda

Commander of the PLA

Abd ar-Razzaq Yahya

*Representatives of the commando
    groups*

Salah Khalaf (Fatah)
George Habash (PFLP)
Dafi Jamani (Saiqa)
Munif ar-Razzaz (ALF)
Nayef Hawatmeh (PDFLP)
Ahmad Jibril (PFLP-GC)
Isam as-Sartawi (AOLP)
Ahmad Za'rur (OAP)
Bahjat Abu Garbiyya (PPSF)
Abd al-Fattah Yasir (POLP)

12

The Rise and Decline of the Palestinian Commandos—Part II

The landmarks at the beginning of the Palestinian commando movement after the 1967 War are the Battle of Karameh of March 21, 1968, in Jordan, and the establishment of a commando camp on the slopes of Mount Hermon with the covert approval of the Lebanese Government in the late summer of 1968.

Before Karameh, commando operations, whether by Fatah or other groups, were indeed, as the Israelis sneered, "mere pinpricks." The commandos confined themselves to laying mines, sniping, and occasional ambushes and firing across the border.

But the Battle of Karameh was a great deal more significant than the Israelis will admit—and a great deal less than the Arabs claim. The facts of the battle, as they can be gleaned from the conflicting reports from the two sides, appear to be as follows. In the early morning hours, a column of tanks and infantry estimated by the Arabs at 5,000 to 15,000 men but which was probably a reinforced brigade of 4,000, supported by paratroopers and air strikes, crossed the Damia and Allenby bridges and attacked Karameh village, situated a few hundred yards from the river, where the mountains of Moab dip below sea level near the Dead Sea. The village consisted of a refugee camp partially deserted because of Israeli shelling, and at the edge of the camp a long street of miserable shops built of cinder blocks and corrugated iron. The Israelis had reason to believe that this was the base for many commando operations and were determined to wipe it out.

Whether by design or spontaneously, the commandos at Karameh did not, when attacked, follow the classic guerrilla tactic of fading away when confronted by superior force. Well buttressed by the Jordanian army, they made a stand. There was street fighting, hand-to-hand combat, and the Palestinian commandos and Jordanians hung on. Fighting raged for fifteen hours in and around the village, but the Israelis finally gained control, killing or capturing all Fedayeen and blowing up storehouses and other buildings. But resistance from the hillsides above the village never stopped. The Israelis claimed to have killed 150 commandos and 100 Jordanian troops. They also claimed the capture of 138 prisoners. Israeli casualties were listed as 21 dead with 70 wounded.

For the Israelis to admit that they lost 21 men was unusual, and attests to the fierceness of the battle. The commandos claimed that the Israelis had in fact lost 200 men, plus 45 tanks and 4 aircraft, while the guerrillas had lost 59 men. Whatever the precise facts, the Arab version won credibility because for the first time in twenty years of raiding the Israelis were forced to leave behind some of their damaged equipment and dead. The abandoned jeeps and tanks were paraded through Amman and filmed for Arab television. Ever since, whenever the Palestinians or other Arabs do well in withstanding an Israeli attack, the inevitable comparison is "like Karameh." The battle has come to symbolize the Arabs' and especially the Palestinians' ability to stand up to the best the Israelis can send against them. Or, as a Fatah officer once put it to me: "It proved that the Israelis are not supermen."

Karameh launched the commandos onto a wave of popularity in the Arab world. In Beirut, boys deserted their classes and hitchhiked to Amman to volunteer. In Kuwait and Riad and Tripoli the sheikhs wrote checks. And in Jordan, Yasir Arafat coolly organized the forces of Fatah, which was the main beneficiary of so much enthusiasm.

Fatah's forces grew from a few thousand at the beginning of 1968 to about 10,000 late in 1970. The other groups grew more slowly. The PFLP enjoyed a surge of popularity among Palestinians in Lebanon because it handed out arms and organized in the camps while Fatah was fighting against the Lebanese army in October, 1969. The membership of Saiqa appears to be largely determined by the Syrian Government, which can influence members of the Palestine Liberation Army or the Syrian regular army to "volunteer."

Up to September, 1970, confrontation with the Jordanian Government operations by Fatah and by the other groups increased steadily in intensity and scale but fell off sharply after they were badly beaten by the Jordanian army. On July 11, 1970, the Central Military Office of the Palestinian commando movement issued statistics to show a rapidly increasing level of operations against Israel in 1969 and the first half of 1970.

The study, prepared by the Palestine Armed Struggle Command, said there were about 6,000 operations between 1965, when the movement took shape, and the end of 1969, with 3,900 in 1969 alone.

During the first half of 1970, 450 to 550 operations were carried out monthly, the report said. It indicated that the average number daily rose from one in 1965, to three in 1968, to sixteen in 1969, and then to twenty-five during December, 1969. El Fatah, the principal commando group, was said to have carried out 61.3 percent of all the operations.

Asserting that Israeli casualties had risen steadily in comparison with those of the commandos, the study said 960 commandos had been killed between the 1967 Arab-Israeli War and the end of 1969. It claimed that 1,347 Israelis had been killed in 1969, compared with 383 commandos.

One may assume that the commando figures are exaggerated with respect to number of operations and Israeli casualties, but they do indicate the trends.

By comparison, the Israelis reported between June 11, 1967, and August 7, 1970, 642 persons killed on the borders of Israel and 2,333 wounded. Of these, 337 were killed in the Suez area.

During the period between the War of Independence and the

Suez campaign of 1956, the Israelis recorded 1,176 dead in frontier incidents of one kind or another. Between the 1956 campaign and the 1967 War, 893 more Israelis were killed. The Israeli figures are probably accurate.

The growth of numbers and resources of the commandos in Jordan enabled them to become something like a state within a state. They had their independent government, sources of revenue, schools, hospitals, Red Cross, and even administration of justice. They sometimes set up their own roadblocks and ignored those of the government. Undisciplined commandos and sometimes men posing as commandos, searched houses, made arrests, extorted money, and committed crimes. Inevitably, there was a showdown. On November 2, 1968, when the Jordanians marked the anniversary of the Balfour Declaration with demonstrations in front of the mosque in central Amman, one group of demonstrators broke away and came perilously close to launching an attack on the American Embassy. They were restrained at the last minute by the personal intervention of Suleiman Nabulsi, the former Premier who had once been accused by King Hussein of organizing a revolt against the monarchy, and had for some years been expelled from the kingdom. Mr. Nabulsi, now the most prominent officially tolerated leftist, was apparently anxious to avoid another showdown with King Hussein's regime. He saved the American Embassy but was unable to prevent the fighting that grew out of Balfour Day from flashing around the seven hills of Amman to such an extent that the Jordanian army found it necessary to move into the city and impose a military stranglehold.

This incident led to the first of a series of confrontations followed by agreements between the commandos and the government of Jordan. The most important aspect of the agreements was that they constituted official recognition of the commando movement by the Jordanian Government, which had up to that point given it only a de facto toleration. Even after the agreement and late in 1970, the Jordanian Government's radio never mentioned the commandos as such but merely alluded to them vaguely as "the resistance." The commandos for their part agreed to respect Jordan's sovereignty, abide by its laws, and police their own members to prevent infractions. They remained free to conduct operations across the border against Israel but promised not to fire across the border.

Although it was never formally acknowledged by either side, agreements were also reached after this or subsequent confrontations barring the commandos from raiding Israel in the region of Aqaba and Elat at the head of the Gulf of Aqaba. The rationale behind this agreement was that Aqaba was too vital to the existence of Jordan to risk provoking major Israeli reprisals in that area.

The agreements reached after Balfour Day, 1968, soon broke down and were followed by a series of new confrontations and agreements in 1969 and 1970. But the sense of the agreements remained always the same. As the number, resources, and activities of the guerrillas expanded, and as Israeli defenses hardened, commando tactics also changed. They had begun before Karameh with hit-and-run ambushes, sniping, the laying of mines and careful avoidance of casualties. Gradually, introduction of Soviet- and Chinese-made automatic weapons and long-range rockets had added new dimensions to guerrilla possibilities. Techniques of penetrating enemy territory for sabotage improved. Larger confrontations were risked. Fatah and other groups attempted small sieges of Israeli army posts and isolated villages. For example, in early 1969 Fatah took and held the village of Hamma in the Golan Heights for four hours.

But in the course of 1969 the commandos also began to realize their limitations. Israeli defenses became steadily more effective. An electric fence stretching from north to south, parallel to the Jordan River, made it almost impossible for the guerrillas to penetrate more than a few hundred yards' depth without Israeli detection.

In fact, the guerrillas were not able to move on to the next tactical phase prescribed by the Fatah theorists. This was to have been the mounting of bases inside occupied territory. From secret hideouts these were supposed, in theory, to evolve into open bases sufficiently armed to survive in the way of a Barzani in the Kurdish Mountains, of the Yemeni royalists, of the Sudanese Negroes in their southern jungles, and the most revered and classic example of the National Liberation Front (FLN) in Algeria in their vast and rugged homeland. As the months slipped by, many guerrilla lead-ers accepted as fact that the geography of Palestine makes exact emulation of any of these precepts impossible. The space of Pales-tine is too limited, its mountains too accessible, too readily encom-passed by Israeli security.

Whereas in 1969 Fatah launched operations with grandiloquent names such as "Scorched Earth" and "Bayonets of Fatah," in which up to 500 men were said to have been employed in direct confrontation, towards the end of the year and in 1970 the com-mandos appear to have gone back to their old tactics. It would seem that although the volume of activities increased, the comman-dos' striking ability gradually declined between 1968 and 1970. The percentage of actual river crossings declined with the construction of the Dayan Line along the river, and an increasing percentage of operations were shellings from the eastern bank.

The difficulties encountered in the Jordan Valley undoubtedly made the prospect of a new front in Lebanon most attractive. So, late in the summer of 1968 Yasir Arafat succeeded in persuading Premier Abdullah Yaffi of Lebanon to allow a small force of sixty men representing Fatah to establish themselves on the slopes of Mount Hermon in the southeastern corner of Lebanon. The move was secret at the time but was of course known to key political leaders. It was obviously considered by Mr. Yaffi to be good poli-tics at a time when the commandos were gaining so much popularity. He hardly imagined, one supposes, that the comman-dos would one day become strong enough, with their leftist allies, to threaten the governments of Lebanon as well as Jordan. The demographic structure of Lebanon was quite different from that of Jordan, where one million Palestinians equal or slightly outnumber the Jordanians, differing from them only as first cousins may differ. But in Lebanon the 275,000 Palestinians are a small minority in the state's population of 2,520,000, and are regarded very much as outsiders.

Whether the Palestinian commandos should be allowed to oper-ate freely from Lebanon against Israel became a central issue in Lebanese politics as the first sixty men on the slopes of Mount Hermon increased to several thousand and spread out in a geographical area known as the Arkoub in the southeastern corner of the country.

A Beirut demonstration, in which the commandos and their allies demanded freedom of operations, led to serious rioting in April of 1969, and the Lebanese government fell in a welter of charges of incompetence and police brutality. It took the Lebanese most of the rest of that year to put together a new government as they wrestled with the commando issue. Before it was resolved, a small war broke out between Fatah and the Lebanese army. On October 20 the Lebanese army, having failed to persuade the commandos to withdraw from certain villages in the south-central plain of Lebanon, forced them out of the village of Majdal Bani Selim. Further clashes followed in the next thirteen days, mainly along the commandos' lines of communication between the Arkoub and the Syrian border. Commandos, heavily reinforced by Saiqa from Syria, occupied a dozen or more Lebanese border posts and police stations along the eastern fringe of the country and in the north. In the town of Tripoli, left-wing Lebanese sympathizers staged an uprising, dominating approaches to the city with sniper fire from a Crusader castle that overlooks the town on the outskirts of Tripoli. PFLP guerrillas seized refugee camps and cut the highway.

After thirteen days of desultory clashes and maneuvering, the fighting ended inconclusively, but with the Lebanese army on the whole in dominant positions. The Lebanese army commander in chief, Major General Emile Bustani, flew to Cairo to sign an agreement with Yasir Arafat under President Nasser's auspices. The agreement differed little from those previously reached by the commandos with Jordan, except that it restricted the commandos more severely. They were to operate only from the Arkoub—not from the south-central plain. They were not to fire across the border, but only after penetrating Israeli territory. They were to keep out of Lebanese towns and not to show themselves in uniform or carrying arms. They were given their own private route from the Arkoub to Syria, using secondary roads, as a line of supply, which became known as the Arafat trail.

The agreement formally acknowledged the right of the commandos to operate from some parts of Lebanese territory, and this was for them a major success. On the other hand, this right was placed under definite limitations. While Lebanon in effect abandoned its sovereignty to the commandos in the Arkoub, the integrity of the country survived this test of strength in a larger sense. The Lebanese army, whose officer corps is predominantly Christian, while the men in the ranks are predominantly Moslem, held together and proved itself to be an effective military instrument. Even though Christians generally favored the army while Moslems supported the commandos, this confrontation did not develop into a confessional struggle as in 1958, and this was for the Lebanese a major success, albeit negative.

From their Lebanese bases, Fatah and the other groups succeeded during the first half of 1970 in carrying out a number of deep-penetration raids, some extending as far south as the Haifa area and some inflicting quite painful casualties on Israeli settlements.

As the commandos developed their campaign against Israel from Jordan and later Lebanon, the Israelis not only developed their defenses in the Jordan Valley and along the northern borders, but also hit back with massive reprisals intended to oblige the two Arab governments to bring their guerrillas under control and to prevent them from penetrating Israeli territory.

The commandos began to penetrate the refugee camps and make them a basis of support and recruitment after Karameh, but could not move decisively until the confrontation between the Lebanese army and Fatah in October, 1969. Up to this time, the camps in Lebanon were under the thumb of army security. The "Deuxieme Bureau"—Lebanese army intelligence—operated in every camp. Refugees were even required to obtain a permit to travel from Sidon to Beirut.

I described the situation late in October in a dispatch datelined from Burj el Barajneh, an UNRWA camp on the outskirts of Beirut, as follows:

> At this camp, the Lebanese and Palestinian commando flags fly side by side. But the guard at the gate with a Kalashnikov auto-

matic rifle is a Palestinian commando and inside the camp, authority is entirely in the hands of the commandos.

Within the limitations of space, military training is in progress
in and around the camp, which is on the outskirts of Beirut.

Accompanied by an information officer and two young men
who have been conducting military training, visitors climb over a
wall of sandbags around a strongpoint flanking the entrance and
a playing field used for military training.

The camp has an official population of 20,000 but actually
contains about 30,000 people in a labyrinth of twisting lanes,
tracks, and huts. It has been expanded bit by bit over twenty-one
years, reaching a jumble of cinder blocks, bricks, and corrugated
iron.

In one place a man has built an annex, in another, extended a
wall. Another has used cinder blocks to raise the roof of his house
to build a loft. All this individual enterprise makes the camp even
more crowded.

Wherever there is a foot of unused ground, someone has planted
a bush or vines that spill over the walls even in winter. Wherever
there is a ledge, the Palestinians have set cans of flowers that
alleviate the grimness.

The lanes between the houses have been paved with concrete,
with gutters down the middle for drainage. Children are everywhere. A goat placidly munches in a corner. A donkey with a load
forces its way through the narrow streets, squeezing passers-by
to the walls.

It has been like this for more than two decades, or rather has
been growing steadily worse. But now there is something new. The
atmosphere is electric. The tempo of life has stepped up. Girls
carrying cinder blocks on their heads hurry to new construction
sites. Buildings long prohibited by the authorities are going up
double-time. One is a a headquarters for the Popular Front.

No one pays any attention to men carrying automatic rifles.
Many men and boys wear khaki or fatigues. A boy, Ibrahim,
eleven years old, appears. He wears around his neck a bullet that
he says was awarded to him on completing a course of instruction
for Ashbal, or lion cubs, at a camp in Jordan.

Ibrahim appears to be a mascot among the armed men of this
camp, who on Sunday completed two weeks of military training.
The training consists mainly of physical exercises, running, rope

climbing, jumping from heights, as well as some hand combat, weapons drill, and target shooting.

Ibrahim's sister, who is sixteen, says that she has just finished a Popular Front "public health course," mostly first aid. She glows with pride as she announces that she will now begin training as a guerrilla.

In November, 1969, UNRWA reported that fourteen of the fifteen refugee camps in Lebanon had been taken over by the commandos. The army security and gendarmerie have not returned since. Internal security is maintained largely by representatives of the commandos. During the two weeks of confrontation and the month that immediately followed, there was an atmosphere of revolutionary fervor in the camps. During this period, military training began. The agreement eventually reached between the Lebanese Government and the commandos prohibited training in the camps, but allowed it at mutually agreed sites. The Lebanese army and gendarmerie never regained control over the interior of the camps; they had to keep their posts outside. From this period on, the commandos dominated the camp dwellers, organizationally and emotionally.

The Israelis' first major reprisal against Lebanon was brilliantly executed, and had wider repercussions than the Israelis could have anticipated. It consisted of a massive airborne raid against Beirut International Airport on December 29, 1968, in reprisal for a PFLP attack on El Al aircraft at Athens Airport. The Israelis landed with helicopters and systematically blew up thirteen Lebanese-based Middle East Airlines, Trans Mediterranean, and Air Libyan planes on the ground. International reaction was almost universally unfavorable to the Israelis. It was said that the Israeli action was out of proportion to the provocation. Furthermore, this violence against an unresisting civilian enemy, including an airline in which the United States and other Western powers had a large interest, struck many observers as unnecessarily brutal. Certainly the Beirut raid went far at that time toward weakening Israel's propaganda advantage in the "media" of the Western world. The Israelis could certainly not count any longer on automatic approval of their actions.

Tactically, the Israeli reprisal raids were illusory. Bombing and rocketing supposed commando camp areas or villages allegedly used by the commandos had little effect. The guerrillas had little in the way of fixed assets and usually suffered minimal casualties.

A sweep by Israeli ground forces into the Arkoub in May, 1970, did little to stifle the ardor of guerrilla operations. More effective was a bold decision by the Israeli High Command two weeks later to occupy observation posts actually inside the Lebanese border and to maintain continuous patrols on Lebanese soil. The Israelis also built service roads from the Golan Heights across the border, right into the Arkoub so that Israeli patrols could at any moment strike at commando bands attempting operations into Israel.

In some respects, however, the Israeli policy of violent reprisals succeeded. In principle, both the Lebanese and Jordanian host governments have always maintained that it was not their role to act as Israel's policeman. They insisted that the Palestinians had a right to fight for their own country. But the Lebanese army's fitful attempts to contain the commandos were quite obviously related to fear of Israeli reprisals. In Jordan, Major General Nasser ben Jamil, King Hussein's uncle, who for a long period was commander in chief, issued numerous orders meant to inhibit commando penetrations. In particular, he attempted to appease the Israelis after they had, in August, 1969, destroyed a section of the East Ghor Canal, a project built with American capital and technical skills, thereby threatening the country's richest agricultural land with drought. Under United States pressure, the Israelis let the Jordanians repair the Canal, but a few months later destroyed it again. This time much of the Jordanian's irrigated crops dried up before the Israelis, again under U.S. pressure, allowed repairs.

In Jordan, 1970 was the year of the great September confrontation between King Hussein and the commandos. In February and again in June violence had broken out between the army and the commandos on various pretexts which were in themselves not important. Important was the fact that on both sides, among the commandos, especially the PFLP, and in the army, there were elements eager for a showdown. Some of the commandos no doubt imagined that the time was approaching when the monarchy might be overthrown, while in the army some officers were convinced that, if given a chance to act forcefully, they could put an end, once and for all, to the commando threat on the domestic front.

Fearful of a bloodbath, King Hussein refrained in February and June from allowing the tanks of the Third Armored Division to occupy the capital as they had done on previous occasions. They were kept at a distance in a circle around the city so that the encounters between them and the commandos took place for the most part in the less-populated suburbs. They did not intervene even when the PFLP in June took over the two largest hotels of the capital, the Intercontinental and the Philadelphia, and held captive eighty foreigners, including fifteen Americans. The PFLP held them as a guarantee that the army would not bombard the refugee camps in which the commandos had their headquarters and a large part of their military supplies and manpower, not to mention their families. The price the King paid for his restraint was progressive erosion of his authority. In order to buy peace, he was obliged to make one concession after another.

A code of laws, which did little but recapitulate existing law, was issued after a winter during which lawlessness by commandos, or men calling themselves commandos, had upset many people in Jordan. There had been holdups, fake collections of funds, unauthorized roadblocks, clashes between the army and men carrying arms without authority. But the commando leadership rejected the new code and the February confrontation ensued. In the end the government was obliged to fall back once again on the old and ineffective formula of commando self-discipline.

In June, renewed disorders were brought to an end by the King's promise to dismiss two men: the commander in chief, his uncle Major General Nasser ben Jamil, and the commander of the Third Armored Division, Zaid ben Shaker. Nasser ben Jamil had long been a *bête noir* of the commandos. They called him an old rogue who had amassed a great fortune by smuggling, and they regarded him as their most uncompromising enemy in the royal family. At his direction, an elite internal security force known as Saiqa (meaning lightning—unconnected with the Syrian commando organization) was organized in the winter of 1969–1970 with the special purpose of keeping the commandos under control. Nasser ben Jamil created a "special branch" of intelligence operatives to watch or subvert the commandos. Whereas King Hussein always insisted that he was not opposed to the commandos inasmuch as they fought the Israelis, and coined the phrase "we are all Fedayeen," his uncle ben Jamil made no bones, at least in private, about his conviction that the commandos must be broken before they broke the monarchy.

For King Hussein to dismiss his uncle from this high post was obviously galling. Ben Jamil not only was his uncle but had been extraordinarily loyal over the years, a tower of strength in times of trouble—morally and financially. But he had to sacrifice his uncle and to officially dissolve the "special branch" he had created and arrest its chief. As on the occasion in 1956 when he had to dismiss another commander in chief, Glubb Pasha, political necessity—the survival of the monarchy—came first. In 1956 King Hussein was under pressure from the Nasserites and had to prove by firing Glubb Pasha that he was a good Arab nationalist; in 1970 he was under pressure from the Palestinian guerrillas. He had, by firing ben Jamil, to prove that he was not against the commandos. But King Hussein was biding his time.

In all the confrontations up to September, 1970, the great superiority of the army's force had never been brought to bear against the commandos. Why the King at last, in September, abandoned this restraint is not entirely clear. But it seems more than likely that he was driven to it by the most spectacular of all the PFLP's exploits. This was the hijacking of four international airliners. The PFLP held hostage aboard these planes, parked on a remote desert airstrip, seventy passengers. After some had been released on September 12, fifty-four remained, including thirty-seven United States citizens, eight Swiss, and eight Germans. Thirty of the Americans held dual United States and Israeli citizenship. When fighting broke out between the PFLP and the army, the hostages were spirited away to secret hiding places in refugee camps.

The commandos appear to have succeeded in attaining their

immediate goal in the hijackings. They obtained the release of Leila Khaled in London and six others in West Germany and Switzerland. Miss Khaled had been taken prisoner after an unsuccessful attempt to hijack an El Al aircraft; the others had been sentenced to prison terms for attacks on El Al aircraft in Europe. But this time they went too far. Most of the commando leadership felt that the PFLP exploit was counterproductive. In the Central Committee of the Palestinian Movement, PFLP was suspended temporarily. King Hussein was forced to act as he had never acted before, and his actions brought about a turning point in the history of the commandos and of Jordan.

On September 15 he dismissed his Cabinet and formed a new government consisting entirely of military men headed by Brigadier Mohammed Daoud; Field Marshal Habis Majali became commander in chief and military governor in Jordan, with absolute powers, and military governors were appointed to all provinces. The King also reinstated General Zaid ben Shaker—who had been dismissed in June at the insistence of the Palestinians—as deputy chief of staff.

After the Jordanian army had eliminated isolated guerrilla posts in the south, it began, just after dawn on September 17, to move into Amman with armored support. This was the key move it had so long refrained from making.

The commandos resisted and struck out from their centers of strength in the northwest, around Irbid, and clung to their strongholds in the refugee camps around the Seven Hills of Amman. It looked, for a few days, as though the commandos were taking over the country, except for parts of Amman and the sparsely populated southern provinces. In fact, the commandos took over Irbid, Jerash, Ramtha, and numerous other smaller towns in the northwest. Then beginning on September 18, the army, now exerting its full strength, went systematically about the task of regaining all the positions the government had lost in and around Amman and the towns to the north. It threw the weight of its armor into a major offensive against guerrilla supply routes from Syria and Iraq. It moved also against Irbid, which had become the center of commando-controlled territory. Then the Syrian army suddenly intervened. Large armored units, estimated to have included 250 tanks with Palestine Liberation Army markings, crossed the border into Jordan on September 20. They were met and turned back the next day by the 40th Armored Brigade, estimated to have only fifty Centurions and old Patton tanks, but effectively supported by the Jordanian air force.

According to King Hussein, in an interview in New York in December, 1970, it was intervention by the Jordanian air force, using its British-built Hawker Hunter fighter bombers with its American-built F-104s flying cover, that turned the Syrians back. It was the first combat operation for the F-104s. The fact that the Syrian air force did not intervene, apparently on orders of General Hafiz al-Assad, was of course equally significant. There is reason to believe that General Assad, then Minister of Defense and Commander of the Air Force, a moderate and a political pragmatist, disapproved of this intervention, which he regarded as a foolish aggrandizing maneuver by his political enemy, Salah Jadid, the Assistant Secretary General of the Baath Party, a power-hungry ideological extremist.

Wider international forces may also have been at work to cut short Syria's military adventure in Jordan. The Israelis contributed by threatening to intervene militarily against the Syrians if they did not withdraw. And the United States, by means of public statements and ostentatious naval maneuvers, in effect brandished the striking power of its Sixth Fleet in the Mediterranean.

How close the United States came to intervening in Jordan to frustrate Syria's adventure and stop the commandos was revealed in a dispatch by Benjamin Welles to *The New York Times* on October 8. In a reconstruction of the crisis, Mr. Welles recalled that King Hussein, having formed a military government, on September 17 struck out against the commandos and that President Nixon, talking to a newspaper editor in Chicago that same day, said that the United States might intervene if Syria or Iraq threatened King Hussein's government. During the next two days, reports filtered in to Washington that the Syrian army had crossed into Jordan with at least one hundred tanks, and on Sunday, Joseph J. Sisco, Assistant Secretary of State for Near Eastern and

South Asian Affairs, called in the Soviet Chargé in Washington, Yuli M. Vorontsov, to warn him that Israel would probably attack if the Syrians continued their invasion. He called on the Soviet Union to use its influence to persuade Syria to withdraw.

Also on Sunday, Mr. Welles reported,

> a message from King Hussein asking the United States and Britain to consider what quick military support they could send him. His appeal, which some officials here termed "panicky," was made over an open, nonconfidential telephone line from the Palace to the United States Chancery in Amman, then ringed by armed Palestinian guerrillas.
>
> On Monday September 21 the issue clearly was whether the United States should intervene to shore up King Hussein's government and, simultaneously to try to rescue the hostages in guerrilla hands.
>
> The decision was taken to coordinate U.S. actions closely with those of the Israelis, who had already begun a partial mobilization in movement of tanks towards the northern part of the Jordan River Valley.
>
> The White House ordered publicity on the movement of the second Sixth Fleet carrier—the *Saratoga*—to join the *Independence* off the Lebanese-Israeli coast; on the dispatch of the helicopter carrier *Guam* with 1,500 marines to join the Sixth Fleet; on the alerting of two airborne battalions of the Eighth Infantry Division in West Germany; on the alerting of the 82nd Airborne Division in Fort Bragg, North Carolina.

Mr. Welles reported that on Monday morning, September 21, President Nixon assumed direction of diplomatic activity. On the evening of the same day, Mr. Welles continued, "there was the first glimmer of Soviet cooperation." Mr. Vorontsov called on Mr. Sisco to repeat Soviet warnings against "all" outside interference, to disclose that the Soviet Union was in touch with Syria, and to urge the United States to restrain Israel from intervening.

By this time the Israeli-United States coordinated threat of intervention, combined with a determined attack by Jordanian armored and air forces, had proved successful. The Syrians were withdrawing and the guerrilla threat to the kingdom had been beaten back. The guerrillas still controlled one third of Amman and most of the north, but they had been seriously weakened.

There had been much sound and fury on behalf of the commandos in the Arab world. President Nasser had transported units of the PLA by air from Egypt to Syria. Libya and Kuwait had cut off their subsidies to Jordan. President Gaafar al Numeiry of Sudan had denounced King Hussein for "genocide." But the Iraqi Government did not fulfill earlier promises to support the Fedayeen with the 12,000-man Iraqi contingent. The real attitude of the Arab regimes toward the Fedayeen remained, as always, ambiguous.

The September confrontation ended in the classic pattern, with King Hussein and Yasir Arafat on September 27 concluding yet another agreement in Cairo under President Nasser's auspices. Nasser, in his last political act—he died the following day—sought to maintain the political and military integrity of the commandos and the post-1967 political alliance between Egypt and Jordan as well. A high-level committee composed of Tunisian Prime Minister Bahi Ladgham, Sudanese President Gaafar al Numeiry, General Mohammed Sadeq, Egyptian Chief of Staff, and the Kuwaiti Foreign Minister Abdul Kareem al-Sheikhly, flew to Amman to supervise implementation of the agreement, beginning with mutual withdrawal of commandos and army personnel from Amman. Although they had the backing of all Arab States, King Hussein boldly continued his pressure on the commandos. The Jordanian government proceeded on the correct assumption that the Arab governments would talk but not do anything to support the commandos.

Only gradually did it become clear that the outcome of this confrontation was different from the others. This time the commandos had been badly beaten. They were shaken by the bombardment of the refugee camps and heavy casualties among their men. Whether the King and his government had also scored a true victory remained to be seen. Some observers argued that the bitterness caused by the violence of the army's crackdown could eventually be the regime's undoing.

Indignation among Palestinians and others against the army's strong-arm tactics was more than offset by the realization that the King and his army were capable of striking and asserting their will to survive, and this demonstration commanded respect. Many a Palestinian who before the confrontation might have lent his support to Fedayeen or militia would now think twice before doing so. As might be expected, commando attacks against Israel came nearly to a standstill immediately after the crackdown and increased only gradually thereafter. The commandos were indeed in a state of shock.

But King Hussein and his Premier, Wasfi Tal, were not finished. In a series of short campaigns during 1971 they accomplished all that they had failed to accomplish in September, 1970. First they cleared the cities and the north of regular guerrillas, then disarmed the militia. They wiped out the remaining guerrilla bases in the countryside, and in July, in a final sweep through the mountains around Irbid, the Jordanian army drove the remaining commando units out of Jordan.

In its next stage the story of the Fedayeen again shifts to Beirut, which became headquarters for a new phenomenon known as "Black September."

Widely believed at first to be a new commando organization, Black September turned out to be an organization dedicated to murderous aspirations against civilian targets all over the world. Its name alluded, of course, to King Hussein's September, 1970, campaign which broke the back of the commando organization in Jordan.

As these operations unfolded, and scraps of information formed a total picture, it became apparent that Black September actions were not a product of centralized planning or bureaucratic direction. Rather, they were highly personalized enterprises in both planning and execution which leading figures in Fatah reported to Yasir Arafat and Fatah headquarters only when they needed money. Whether Arafat himself has taken direct part in any of the operations is uncertain.

The first in the series was the assassination of Premier Wasfi Tal of Jordan during a visit to Cairo on November 28, 1971. The Premier had been the guiding hand in King Hussein's campaign, from July to September, which drove the Fedayeen out of Jordan. He was, furthermore, much more than a friendly political ally of King Hussein. He was a neighbor in the suburban community of Suweillah, and a friend, one of the few people whom the King could trust implicitly.

Another such man was Zaid Rifai, long the chief of the King's personal staff, whom Hussein had sent as Ambassador to England. On December 15, as he was being driven home, to Palace Gardens in Central London, gunmen waiting at a point where his car had to slow down to pass through a gate, opened fire with machine guns. Rifai escaped with an injury to his hand.

These two events ruptured the tenuous ties still remaining between Fatah and the Jordanian Monarchy. Hitherto, the King had treated Fatah as the one commando organization with which it was possible to come to terms. From then on, however, it was war to the end. Saudi Arabian, Egyptian, and Syrian attempts to arrange a reconciliation that would permit some commando units to return to Jordan were in vain.

In February, 1972, Black September carried out a strange series of operations in West Germany, where there are about 20,000 Arab workers and 16,000 Arab students, including about 3,000 Palestinians. These are undoubtedly a source of recruits for Fatah in its European operations.

Five Jordanians said to be friendly to the Israelis were assassinated in Cologne. Oil tanks were bombed in the Netherlands and in Hamburg, West Germany.

The summer of 1972 began with one of the most gruesomely bizarre terror operations of all. On May 30, three young Japanese of extreme leftist, radical backgrounds, who had been recruited by Fatah, landed at Tel Aviv Airport. They entered the terminal, pulled out automatic rifles concealed in their clothing, and proceeded to shoot everyone in sight. The twenty-four persons killed and eighty wounded were mostly Christian Puerto Ricans on a pilgrimage to Jerusalem.

Black September had attempted another hijacking on May 8. Two men and a woman diverted a Sabena airliner enroute to Libya and tried to trade the lives of the passengers for the freedom of commandos in Israeli captivity. Israeli paratroopers overcame the commandos after slipping aboard in the guise of Red Cross workers, and saved the passengers.

On September 5, Fatah blew up more oil tanks at Trieste, Italy. Precisely what the rationale behind this blowing up of oil tanks may be is not clear. Presumably the commandos are trying to hurt American oil companies who, they believe, own the oil involved.

On September 10, at Munich, Black September commandos committed what to most people appeared as an unimaginable crime. They broke into the quarters of the Israeli Olympic team, killing two of its members, and took the other nine men hostage. Their attempts to win the freedom of Palestinians imprisoned in various parts of the world and to make their getaway aboard a Lufthansa aircraft went awry when German police tried to catch them off guard and shoot them down. In the ensuing gunfight, the Palestinians blew up their hostages with hand grenades. Five Palestinians and one West German also lost their lives. This atrocious deed is bound to live in the minds of Israelis, and for the lives of their innocent young athletes the Israelis are sure to exact a terrible price.

Meanwhile, since February Black September operatives have been mailing time bombs to Israeli diplomats all over the world. The letters came from Amsterdam, from Malaysia, and India. At least half a dozen went to Israeli diplomats at the United Nations. Numerous Israelis have been injured. One, the Cultural Attaché in London, was killed. Postal workers all over the world also have been injured. Most of the bombs consisted of tubes or sheets of plastic explosives; some contained deadly cyanide gas.

On January 27, 1973, in Madrid, an agent of Israeli Intelligence, Barouch Cohen, was shot dead. In the following months, Black September attempted to kidnap the Jordanian Cabinet in the Prime Minister's office where it meets. One of the Fatah leaders, Abu Daud, and fifteen men accompanying him, were caught in Amman while they were still reconnoitering their target. Abu Daud, undoubtedly after torture, subsequently broadcast a detailed account of his own exploit, along with everything he knew about all other Black September operations.

Another profoundly shocking Black September operation took place in Khartoum, beginning March 2. The commandos managed to invade the residence of the Saudi Arabian ambassador, who was holding a farewell party for the American Chargé d'Affaires, George C. Moore, combined with a welcome for his successor, U.S. Ambassador Cleo A. Noel, Jr. The commandos took prisoner these two men and the Belgian Chargé d'Affaires, Guy Eid, along with the Jordanian and Saudi ambassadors and the Saudi ambassador's wife.

The commandos' demands, which are perhaps revealing, included the release of Sirhan Sirhan, the man who assassinated Robert Kennedy; seventeen terrorists led by Fatah leader, Abu Daud; and several Jordanian military men led by Major Rafeh el-Hindawi, all under arrest in Jordan for anti-Hussein plots; about fifty other terrorists and political prisoners in Jordan; two West German anarchists, Andreas Baader and Ulrike Meinhoff, who have perpetrated bombings in Germany, and a number of Arab women terrorists in Israeli prisons.

As all these demands were rejected, the commandos, apparently on instructions from their leaders in Beirut, killed their two American hostages and the Belgian, Guy Eid. This is by no means a complete list of Black September operations. Furthermore, there were a number of Black September operations that failed. One of these was the attempt on December 31, 1972, to take captive the staff of the Israeli Embassy in Bangkok, Thailand. In this case, the intervention of the Egyptian ambassador was successful in winning the release of the captives.

On April 10, 1973, a group of young commandos, who may not have been connected with Black September, but whose methods were similar, attempted to blow up the residence of the Israeli ambassador in Cyprus and then to shoot up an Israeli El Al jet aircraft at the airport. The Israeli guard aboard the aircraft returned the commandos' fire. One commando was killed and the Cypriot police captured the other three.

Needless to say, the Israelis have not been slow to strike back. First of all, there seems to be in progress a well-publicized counter-terror in which individual Palestinians are mysteriously shot down.

Second, in mid-September and in November, 1972, the Israeli air force carried out punishing raids on Fatah camps in Jordan, including, on the later date, a four-day sweep through the Arkoub Province of southeastern Lebanon, where the commandos have been well entrenched for several years. This time the Israeli operation had the desired effect in that the Lebanese army moved into the Arkoub on the heels of the withdrawing Israelis, assuring that the commandos did not return. Third, one must mention a tragic accident in the last week of February, 1973, that was not intended in any way as a reprisal but which inevitably took its place in the psychological climate of the period. A Libyan Boeing civilian aircraft, piloted by a Frenchman, lost its bearings on its way from Tripoli to Cairo and flew over occupied Sinai. Intercepted by Israeli Mirages, the pilot and crew at first thought they were being escorted by friendly Egyptian aircraft. The pilot did not understand the Israelis' signals that he should land. The Israelis, meanwhile, fearful that this might be a suicide plane intended to crash on an Israeli military strongpoint, or even on Tel Aviv with a load of explosives, tried to force the plane down by firing at the area between its wings and body. Understanding at last that he was dealing with hostile Israeli fighters, the French pilot tried to make a forced landing. The plane burst into flames. One hundred and six persons lost their lives.

Although the Israelis were contrite once the plane's "little black box" had been recovered and the pilot's confusion became clear to all, Libyan and other Arab radio stations inevitably spoke of "murder."

A most remarkable air and sea raid was conducted on the night of February 20–21 against the commando base scattered between two refugee camps in northern Lebanon. The Israelis landed naval commandos and paratroopers by rubber boat and helicopter. They went into the refugee camps at Nahr el Bared and al Badawi, about ninety-five miles north of the Israeli border. It was the Israelis' deepest penetration into Lebanon. The Israelis, according to Arab radio stations, killed eighteen commandos and thirteen civilians; the Israelis admitted eight of their men were wounded.

Probably, as the Israelis claimed, there were some middle-to-high echelon PFLP and Fatah leaders among the casualties. In addition, according to Washington intelligence sources, the Israelis were looking for George Habash, who had been keeping under cover for some months. He is said to have restricted his activities to a few hours a day because of a heart condition.

Then, on April 10, the Israelis staged the most daring of their commando-style raids. This time, instead of using helicopters, they sent men into Beirut disguised as tourists. These men rented cars and duly appeared on the seashore to meet the men in rubber boats coming ashore. They landed at a little beach popularly known as the "beach of death" because of its treacherous currents and scrambled up the fifty-foot earthen bank onto the promenade along the most fashionable part of Beirut's waterfront, within 100 yards of a Lebanese army barracks, jumped into their cars, and headed straight for the homes of leading members of Fatah and of the PLO, and several other points of importance to the commandos.

When it was all over, the Israelis had withdrawn, without serious casualties, and three key men in the Fatah-PLO leadership and forty others connected with them were dead. The three were Kamal Nasir, spokesman for PLO, and, according to the Israelis, key man in over-all leadership, Mohamed Yusif Najar, better known as Abʼi Yusef, the Chief of Intelligence of Fatah, according to the Israelis, and Kamal Adwan, probably the number three man in Fatah who, the Israelis say, was in charge of operations inside Israel and the occupied territories.

That the Lebanese army, gendarmerie, and, in particular, police, the vaunted Squad 16, Beirut's special riot police, made no move whatsoever to intercept the Israelis, coming or going, must be interpreted in terms of Lebanon's place in the Arab world. Obviously the Lebanese did not even try to stop the Israelis and, according to well-placed Lebanese, the only casualties were suffered by police trying to prevent Fatah from interfering with the whole operation. It is probable that the Israelis hoped to catch Yasir Arafat, who was in fact visiting Abu Yusef a short time before they struck. Even so, the operation must rank as one of the most devastating ever perpetrated by the Israelis. It cost the Lebanese Premier, Saab Salaam, his premiership, for he could not explain to the satisfaction of the Arab world why Lebanese forces had not even tried to intercept the raiding Israelis.

Once again, the Israeli reprisal seems to have had the desired effect in triggering Lebanese repression of the Fedayeen. The sequence of events was somewhat as follows: Three Black September men attempted to fly to Europe with baggage stuffed with explosives and weapons. They were stopped at the airport and arrested. Fatah demanded their release and seized several soldiers as hostages. On this occasion the Lebanese army was not to be trifled with. It struck back, surrounding the refugee camps at which the army men were held prisoner. In one moment, it seemed, fighting broke out all over the country. The army found itself bombarding and even bombing and strafing refugee camps. The Syrians began infiltrating members of the Palestine Liberation Army, including armored units, across the Syrian border. It looked like October, 1969, all over again, or perhaps like September, 1970, in Jordan. But for every initiative in this situation there was a limitation. The Israeli Government let it be known in no uncertain terms that if the Syrians invaded Lebanon Israel would intervene to protect the Lebanese; the message was much the same as one put out in September, 1970, when the Syrians rather more seriously started some 250 tanks, with PLA markings, across the Jordanian border. The Syrians, once again, turned back.

The Lebanese army could go only so far. Its manpower is only 10,000 to 15,000, compared with the 50,000 to 60,000 of the Jordanian army. Furthermore, the Lebanese are not capable of defying the Arab community of states, and almost all the states at this time were vociferous in the support of Fatah.

As for Fatah, it was restrained by the knowledge that Lebanon was the last base from which it could carry on more or less free operations, and Fatah no longer possessed the kind of manpower it had in Jordan. Now its population base consisted of approximately 300,000 Palestinians in Lebanon, of whom 180,000 are readily accessible to the commandos in fifteen UNRWA camps. Finally, Fatah knows that if it goes too far in Lebanon, it will not only lose the support of the Moslems who are normally predisposed in favor of the commandos, but it may also stir into action considerable paramilitary forces of the Christian community, tough mountain boys who have managed to stay out of the fighting in the previous minor civil wars of Lebanon.

In June, 1973, then, where do the Fedayeen stand? In numbers, compared to the year 1970, they are reduced at least by half. In resources, they have probably lost more than that, having angered King Faisal for seizing the Saudi Arabian Embassy in Khartoum, and having angered President Qaddafi by the seeming inactivity of commando units so far as incursions into Israel are concerned.

In their frustration, Fatah, with about 5,000 members, has, as we have seen, resorted to bloody operations against civilian targets abroad. PFLP has chosen to go underground. The PDFLP with only 500 or 600 men, led by Nayef Hawatmeh, has broken away from the PLO leadership, and Arafat has said that he considers them out of control. Saiqa, with 3,000 to 4,000 men, is whatever the Syrian government wants to make of it. It can assign men to the commandos from the PLA or from other sources, and it controls the resources available to the commandos, as well as all their operations from Syrian territory. Generally, since the most recent series of Israeli aerial reprisals against Syrian targets in November, the Syrians have chosen to keep Saiqa quiet, except, of course, for the tentative foray into Lebanon in April.

As for the PFLP, General Command, led by Ahmed Jabril, it numbers 400 or 500 men and is the only one of the commando groups that apparently still attempts to conduct military operations into Israel and occupied territory. Led by a group of former professional officers, its military expertise is probably superior to that of any of the other groups.

All of the other commando groups have either disappeared or merged. The Palestine Liberation Army (PLA—a regular army formation) remains intact, with most of its main units numbering perhaps 3,000 men in Syria and several thousand more in Iraq and in Egypt.

In judging the terror operations perpetrated by the Palestinian commandos, it is well to remember that in the years before the State of Israel was created, Jewish terror organizations, Irgun and Stern, did rather similar things. Also, it would be well to bear in mind a statement made by Shafik Hout, the head of the PLO office in Beirut to the *Times* of London on October 14, 1972: "We have to shock the West out of its guilty conscience about the Jews and into recognizing the plight of the Palestinian people. That is why Lydda and Munich were such tactical successes. They showed we were prepared to die for our cause."

Finally, it remains true that the Palestinians scattered throughout the Middle East have gained a new sense of national belonging and a pride in their identity as a result of the commando operation. The commandos are now widely accepted in the Arab world as the spokesmen for the Palestinian people. They have established a political presence, with official representatives and information offices in several Arab and European countries, as well as in New York and Washington. The commandos have staked a claim to a Palestinian voice in any final settlement of the Middle East conflict.

The Fedayeen were completely upstaged by the big guns of the regular armies in the fourth Arab-Israeli war. This was not their style of fighting and there was not much they could contribute. A few commando groups managed to fire some rockets across from Lebanon into Israel until the Lebanese, fearful of Israeli reprisals, drove them out of the frontier area. The Fedayeen will come into their own more politically than militarily when and if discussion of the future of the Arab West Bank of the Jordan comes before the settlement conference. The purists of the most radical groups will go on opposing the formation of any kind of a Palestinian State that is not a total restoration of the old Palestine. But a great many others, I am sure, will opt for the half loaf, or even one-quarter of the loaf of Palestine.

For the long look forward, I shall save my comments for Chapter 16, "Solutions." But I should point out that the title of the present chapter was carefully chosen and does not read "The Rise and Fall of the Fedayeen" but "The Rise and Decline of the Fedayeen." The Fedayeen are in a decline but are by no means finished. A great deal more will be heard from Fatah and Black September; and the political importance of all the groups, and especially of PFLP, will probably grow.

13

The Great Powers
in the Middle East

Before I draw conclusions about the Arab-Israeli conflict, it is necessary to look at the role in the Middle East of the Great Powers —the United States, the Soviet Union, Britain, France, and Communist China.

When I first went to the Middle East in the early 1940s, Britain was the force that prevailed from the Turkish border to the Southern Sudan, from the Mediterranean to Persia—and especially so after the British had driven the Vichy French out of Syria and overthrown the pro-German Shah in Persia. World War II had produced this last great episode of empire in the Middle East.

United States interest in the Middle East is very recent. It began at the end of the nineteenth century with philanthropic, religious, and educational missions. Their fruits were such admirable institutions as Robert College in Istanbul, the American University of Beirut, the American University in Cairo, and many others. When the King-Crane Commission in the 1920s conducted a survey to discover the wishes of the people of Palestine they discovered that the predominant sentiment was that the United States, which had no interests in the Middle East, and was trusted, would make an ideal trustee for Palestine.

However, by the late 1940s the United States became intensively preoccupied in the Middle East with two things: oil and Israel. The American interest in oil has been described earlier in Chapter 8.

After World War II the British faded fast. The landmarks of their failing strength were withdrawal from Palestine in 1948, withdrawal from the Suez Canal Zone in 1954, the expulsion of Glubb Pasha from Jordan in 1957, the overthrow of the pro-British monarchy in Iraq in 1958, the withdrawal from Aden in 1967, and, finally, the withdrawal from the Persian Gulf at the end of 1971.

France was eliminated as a Middle Eastern power somewhat earlier, at the end of World War II, when Syria and Lebanon, over which France had exercised a League of Nations mandate, became independent. But French cultural influence persists, especially in Lebanon. The French, who had been aligned against the Arabs as long as France was fighting to hold on to Algeria, enjoyed a period of political influence in the Arab world after General de Gaulle turned French policy around and refused in the years following the 1967 War to supply military aircraft to Israel.

As the British presence declined, those of the United States and the Soviet Union rose. And as the United States' commitment to Israel has grown, so have Arab rage and threats of reprisal against American interests.

Why, then, does the United States follow so paradoxical a policy? The answer is to be found, surely, in the nature of Israel and of the United States. In Israel, Americans see what appears to be a little democracy fighting against great odds, a land of refuge for millions of Jews who fled from persecution, a country peopled by idealists. They admire Israeli efficiency, at least by comparison with the Arabs. They see Israel as a David defying Goliath.

It is true that for the past several years David has seemed to become Goliath, and many of the left-wingers and liberals of Europe and the United States who formerly gave their allegiance automatically to the Zionist cause have shifted their sympathies increasingly to the weaker states among the Arabs surrounding Israel. But the old image of Israel remains deeply embedded in American consciousness. It must be remembered that the United States is the center of gravity of the whole community of Jews in the world. Before World War II the center of the Jewish world was eastern Europe. But Hitler changed everything. While Israel today exercises a certain leadership, no fewer than six million Jews—the largest Jewish community in the world—are at home in the United States. Economically and culturally, this is the new Jewish center. It is American Jews who annually contribute millions to the support of Israel. While United States government support has not been negligible—about 1.3 billion dollars—private purchases of Israel bonds have amounted to 1.5 billion dollars since 1951, and contributions to the United Jewish Appeal rather more than that. Even larger but confidential sums have been spent for military aid, including a remarkable open-ended credit of 500 million dollars for arms purchases voted by Congress in 1970.

Added to this is the fact that millions of Christian Americans believe in the fulfillment of Biblical promise, and will always give the Israelis the benefit of the doubt in any contest with the Arabs. Then you begin to realize the built-in strength of Israel in the United States.

There is one way in which the United States could resolve the dilemma created for American policy by conflicting American interests in oil and Israel. That way is peace, or, more precisely, settlement. And the United States has in fact, with great sincerity, yet astounding impotence, devoted itself to the cause of Arab-Israeli settlement since the creation of the State of Israel first became an issue before the United Nations. The United States sponsored the U.N. project in 1947 to partition Palestine and to internationalize Jerusalem. The United States provided the mediator, the late Dr. Ralph Bunche, who succeeded in ending the 1948 War with armistices, and the United States gave its backing to the United Nations Concilation Commission in a vain attempt to transform the armistices to peace agreements. The United States lent financial backing to the United Nations Relief and Rehabilitation Administration (UNRRA) to the extent of 70 percent of total expenses in all the years since the 1948 War. John Foster Dulles, in the mid-1950s, asserted that the United States would be willing to underwrite the cost of the resettlement of Arab refugees, whether they returned to Israel or settled elsewhere. Since the war of 1967, the United States has continued its unavailing search for settlement and an approach to peace, and has made elaborate efforts to get the belligerents to talk to each other. I have written about this in detail in Chapter 14, "Solutions."

When the United States was not busy trying to square the circle of Arab-Israeli hostility, it was maneuvering to keep the Russians out of the Middle East. Mr. Dulles tried unsuccessfully to persuade King Farouk to join a Middle East command, and then conceived the "northern tier" of nations. This became the Baghdad Pact, and later CENTRO. It was Mr. Dulles who, in President Eisenhower's name, pressed a souvenir pistol into the hand of President Nasser in the hopes that he would, after all, join the Western Alliance. When all else had failed, the United States tried to persuade the Arabs to crusade against "international communism" by means of the Eisenhower Doctrine, which promised economic assistance. But so far as the Arabs were concerned, only frustration and resentment resulted, and for this simple reason: the Arabs would not—politically and emotionally could not—collaborate with the principal backer of the State of Israel. The more the United States became involved with Israel, the more the Arabs turned to the Soviet Union.

While the United States' interest in the Middle East was growing, so was that of the Soviet Union. A difference between the two was that, while for Americans this was a new sphere of interest, for the Russians it was very old. For centuries past the rulers of Russia have, for political as well as religious reasons, been generous patrons of the pilgrimage to Jerusalem. The various Orthodox churches of the Middle East were favored by the Tsars, and again by the Soviet Union, which has sought to maintain its influence by making donations to Orthodox charities and educational funds, and offering important clerics opportunities to visit the Soviet Union. When the State of Israel was established, the Soviet Union managed to take over the Russian Orthodox churches in the Israeli part of Jerusalem and Palestine and make them bases from which to exert influence.

The almost proverbial Russian aspiration to warm water ports —that is, ports that would not be closed by ice in winter—was reflected at the beginning of World War II in a draft agreement between the Soviet Union and the Axis powers, worked out by the Nazi foreign minister, Joachim von Ribbentrop, and the Russian foreign minister, Vyacheslav Molotov. A secret protocol to the draft stated that "the Soviet Union delcares that its territorial aspirations center south of the national territory of the Soviet Union and in the direction of the Indian Ocean."

In another document, Molotov informed the German ambassador in Moscow that "the area south of Batoum and Bakou in the general direction of the Persian Gulf is recognized as the center of the aspirations of the Soviet Union." What were the Russians after? Warm water? Strategic position? Access to India and the Indian Ocean? Oil? Perhaps all of these combined into a compulsive urge to expand, not only for reasons of aggrandizement but also in order to protect the "soft underbelly" of Russia, the southern provinces inhabited by Moslems who might be influenced by the Moslems of the countries on Russia's southern flank.

Since World War II, the element of oil has been immensely enlarged. It would be unrealistic to imagine that the Russians have not studied very carefully what the great storehouse of energy in and around the Gulf could mean to them. I believe that the Russians see the Gulf as a center of potential power.

But the first significant Soviet move in the penetration of the Middle East after World War II was the 1965 arms deal with Egypt. This was a key development, causing the withdrawal of United States aid for the Aswan Dam, which the Russians then took over, and the nationalization of the Suez Canal, which led to the 1965 War. The arms deal, hugely popular among all Arabs, swung Nasser and the Russians into political orbit in the Middle East. After that, several attempts were made by Communist parties to win control of Middle Eastern governments, but all failed. Thus, in 1957 the Communists seemed close to dominance in Syria, but were headed off by the union of Syria and Egypt in the United Arab Republic. In 1958 the overthrow of the monarchy in Iraq brought Abdul Karim Kassem to power, and it seemed in the ensuing years as though the Communists were on the verge of taking control. But after Kassem's overthrow in 1963, the Baathist Party decimated the

Communists. Yet another attempt by Communists to seize power took place in the Sudan in 1971. But once again they failed. The common denominator in all of these cases is that the Soviet Government quickly accommodated itself to failures and hesitated only briefly before entering into relations with anti-Communist regimes. Obviously, for the Soviet Government, the Communist parties were expendable.

More important than the Communist parties as tools of penetration in the Middle East are military and economic aid, and the growing presence of the Soviet fleet. While the United States Navy's fire power and numbers will probably remain greater than that of the Russians in the Mediterranean well into the 1970s, the Russians with their smaller, faster vessels and ship-to-ship missiles are already a serious challenge. The United States could not afford to engage in another operation such as landing in Lebanon in 1958 without worrying very seriously about Russian reactions.

The Russians have made themselves the principal arms suppliers to all the Arab countries except Jordan and Lebanon and, of course, Saudi Arabia and the Gulf sheikhdoms. As of June, 1973, Saudi Arabia and the Gulf sheikhdoms (except Kuwait) were the only countries of the Middle East that had no relations with the Soviet Union. Even Lebanon decided late in 1971 to buy some Russian weapons. Economic and military assistance of the Soviet Union plays a vital role in the lives of Egypt, Syria, and Iraq in particular. The Soviet Union beyond a doubt derives great influence therefrom. But the course of Soviet penetration in the Middle East has not been entirely smooth. The Soviet role is neither as well rooted or as controlling as that which was formerly played by the British in the Middle East. The main reason is, undoubtedly, that times have changed. The Arabs are more self-consciously independent today than they ever were before, and the Russians could not possibly build up in a few years the kind of position the British developed over centuries. There is unmistakable evidence that the Russian are heavy-handed in their dealings with proud and sensitive "underdeveloped" peoples. This is amply illustrated by the story of the expulsion of the great Soviet military aid mission in Egypt in July, 1972. Eight months after he came into power, President Anwar Sadat found himself challenged by a somewhat un-coordinated attempt led by Aly Sabry, the leading Soviet leftist in his regime, and other leftists, to stage a coup d'état. Sadat headed them off, and in the process consolidated his own power position.

The Soviet Union was clearly taken aback by the disappearance from Egyptian government of those whom the Soviet Union re-garded as its friends. Concerned that Egypt might shift politically so far to the right as to break ranks with the other socialistic regimes of the Middle East, the Russians quickly sent a mission to Cairo armed with a Treaty of Friendship for President Sadat to sign. Sadat did sign, but it is probable that the Russians did not benefit themselves by insisting on this display of overt friendship. Sadat was annoyed as he found himself again under criticism from the right.

Soon thereafter, a Communist coup d'état in Khartoum over-threw President Numeiry. Sadat, who saw in the coup an attempt by the Russians to restore their position in the area, reacted strongly against the revolutionaries, and was relieved when Numeiry succeeded in a bold counter coup which ousted the Com-munists. In the months that followed tension built up steadily between the Soviet military technicians and advisors, numbering about 14,000 persons, and the Egyptian army. Sensing their govern-ment's shift to the right, perhaps, Egyptians at all levels began to show increasing resentment against what they called Russian arro-gance. At the highest level, Egyptian officers—and President Sadat himself—began demanding that the Soviet Union supply Egypt with a better grade of sophisticated weapons to equal those sent by the United States to Israel. The Russians countered that first the Egyptians must learn to train properly, keep more regular hours, study more faithfully their instructions.

Apart from trying to persuade the Russians to supply Egypt with the latest offensive weapons, President Sadat was trying to per-suade the Russian Government to make a real issue of the Middle East at the summit meeting between President Nixon and First Secretary Leonid Brezhnev, which was then in preparation. That is, he wanted the Russians to insist that the United States put pressure on Israel. He wanted concessions in the matter of withdrawal from occupied territory to be used as a condition of Soviet agreement on other issues.

The Russians may have led President Sadat to believe that they would do so. But they did not. When Sadat learned that during their meetings with President Nixon in Moscow, the Russians had not pressed his case, he was angered. This was May, 1972. Still, Sadat did not give up. He calculated, apparently, that the Russians, having let him down in the realm of diplomacy, would make up for it in the supply of offensive arms. He sent Prime Minister Ahmed Sidky to Moscow in a last effort to get the arms he wanted. But the Russians remained unresponsive. Sidky cut his trip short and Sadat called in the Russian Ambassador, telling him and his aid mission and advisors to "Get packing." He told the Russians to evacuate all their advisors and announced that facilities designated for Soviet use would be returned. In the end almost all Russians did leave. Observers who had imagined the Russians to be entrenched beyond recall were amazed.

The expulsion of the Russian experts and technicians in 1972 was, of course, a great humiliation. In the months that followed, a few of the Russian technicians returned and helped the Egyptians to take over operation of the Sam 2s, Sam 3s, and SA-6s which previously had been manned by Russians. But the Soviet position remained fundamentally altered. It had been shown that the Russians could be deprived overnight of the main base for their activities in the Middle East. Although the Russians tried to compensate by increasing their activities in Syria and Iraq, the lesson was not lost on the other Arabs. The Soviet Union's voice in Middle Eastern affairs would never again be quite so loud and overbearing as it had been.

It seemed for a moment during the fourth Arab-Israeli war as though the Russians might massively reestablish their position in Egypt as a consequence of the war. The huge Russian resupply operation, followed by confrontation with the United States, during which the Russians threatened to fly in airborne units numbering 50,000, seemed to foreshadow an entirely new role for the Russians. But it did not happen. President Nixon's worldwide alert deterred the Russian airborne influx, and President Sadat did not admit large numbers of Russian technicians to return even in the darkest days of the war.

As Secretary of State, Henry Kissinger moved into the diplomatic picture with proposals for a ceasefire and then an Arab-Israeli settlement. The Russians were upstaged. While the United States was able freely to deal with the Egyptians as well as the Israelis, the Russians could deal only with their clients, the Egyptians. And it began to look as though the Egyptians preferred dealing with the Americans. The Egyptians moved with alacrity following Dr. Kissinger's visit to restore diplomatic relations with Washington, which had been interrupted since 1967.

14

The Fourth Arab-Israeli War

At 2 o'clock in the afternoon of October 6, while Israelis were celebrating Yom Kippur, the holiest day of the Jewish year, the armies of Egypt and Syria attacked Israel simultaneously and with complete surprise.

Demonstrating that they had been truly well-trained by the Russians, the Egyptian assault units moved across the Suez Canal on rafts and in rubber boats with perfect timing and precision. With intended significance the Egyptians had named this "Operation Saladin," after the great Arab general who began destruction of the Crusaders. While artillery and ground-to-air missiles provided a dense umbrella in the manner prescribed in the Soviet textbooks, the Egyptians added a touch of originality of their own. They turned huge water hoses against the towering sand banks along the Suez Canal behind which was sheltered Israel's Bar Lev fortifications. The powerful jets of water scoured away the sand much faster than any mechanical excavator. They opened a breach to which Egyptian engineers connected first one, then two, then more bridges of pontoons.

The Israeli Air Force responded to this audacious assault in its usual fashion. American-built Phantoms and Sky Hawks bore down from the sky in wave upon wave with cannon, missiles, and bombs. To the horror of the Israelis, however, only a few of their aircraft got through to the targets. Plane after plane went down in flames, literally impaled on the wall of explosives the Egyptians raised to defend their pontoon bridges and their bridgehead.

The Israeli Air Force already knew something of the effectiveness of Sam 2s and Sam 3s, which it had encountered when the Israeli Phantoms hit the outskirts of Cairo a few years earlier. But now there was obviously something more. That something more, it was soon learned, was the presence of the SA-6, a weapon the Russians had not supplied in Vietnam. Employing at least three different radar wavelengths—one for high altitude, one for low altitude, and one for locking onto the target—the SA-6s proved a baffling target for the Israeli Air Force.

As the Egyptian army pushed forward to consolidate its bridgehead, Israeli tanks encountered another particularly effective Soviet-built weapon. This was the Sagger anti-tank missile, which proved capable of stopping even the big American-built M-6os. Egyptian anti-tank crews had been well-trained. They stood their ground in a way the Israelis had not expected. The whole Egyptian army displayed a new discipline and spirit.

The success of Egyptian arms at the Canal hit Cairo with an intoxicating rush of euphoria. This was no false, manufactured victory. This was the real thing. The Egyptians had proven for all the Arabs—or so it seemed—that they were the equals if not the superiors of the Israelis. This is the psychological triumph—the fact of having grabbed back and hung on to a few square miles of Sinai desert—that made the whole campaign worthwhile for President Sadat.

The Egyptian offensive, and a similarly successful attack by the Syrians on the Golan Heights, took the Israelis—and the Americans—by surprise. However, Israeli intelligence was quite aware that something was afoot on the Arab side of the border. This activity even had been confirmed by American satellite photographs in the last days before the war. There was no failure of intelligence gathering but perhaps of intelligence-interpreting, or of the decision-making process at the highest level. The Israeli leaders may have deliberately decided that in this war they would not expose themselves to the charge of aggression. They may have been convinced that they could handle the Arab attack without undue difficulty.

Whatever the truth may be, the fact that the Israelis were taken by surprise, that they did not in good time launch a preemptive attack, became a major issue in the December elections in Israel. The hero of the 1967 War, General Moshe Dayan, and his Premier, Golda Meir, were held responsible by their political opponents for the heavy loss of Israeli lives in this war.

The Egyptians moved forward a distance of only about ten miles beyond the Canal. Some military analysts have talked about the mystery of why the Egyptians did not strike out more boldly to seize the Mitla and Giddi passes in the mountain range that parallels the Canal, where they could have established strong defensive positions. I suspect that the answer is quite simply that they feared getting too far ahead of the curtain of missiles that had proved so effective in the first hours of their Canal crossing. The moment they got ahead of their missiles they found themselves outgunned and outmaneuvered by the Israelis' American tanks.

I also believe, however, that President Sadat's objective in this war was strictly limited. It was to cross the Canal, inflict maximum casualties on the Israelis, to seize and to hold a chunk of the Sinai desert, and to wait for the shock effect to galvanize the Great Powers into action—to break the stalemate and force the Great Powers to implement U.N. Resolution 242 of 1967. Realizing the potential for East-West confrontation if they were involved in this war, the superpowers would be obliged to act. If these were his objectives, President Sadat succeeded beyond his wildest dreams— but that is getting ahead of the story.

Developments on the Syrian front were basically similar. The Syrians at first regained much of the Golan Heights; then, while the Egyptians hung on in the Sinai desert, the Syrians fought a losing battle to maintain their initial gains. Little by little, and at heavy cost to themselves, the Israelis pushed them and their Iraqi and Jordanian allies back from the Golan Heights, back to a point within 20 miles of Damascus.

In one of their most sensational operations, the Israelis carried out a helicopter assault on positions high on Mount Hermon, the 9,000-foot peak that occupies the junction area between Israel, Lebanon, and Syria. Thus the Israelis regained positions from which they could oversee the entire battlefield and observe movements far inside Syria.

The Israelis might have pressed on in an attempt to capture Damascus and perhaps to destroy totally the Syrian Army. But instead they turned southward in an attempt to drive out the Egyptians. The Israeli riposte proved as daring and brilliant as the original Egyptian assault. It proved that even if the Egyptians could fight well, the Israelis could fight better. On the night of October 15, nearly ten days after the start of the war, Major General Ariel Sharon, the maverick of the Israeli Army, who had led his reserve armored division right across the Negev Desert, and who had almost recklessly hurled his tanks against the Egyptians, suddenly broke through to the great bank of sand along the eastern shore of the Canal. His engineers told him it would take many hours, perhaps days, to dig through this bank to the water. But here General Sharon had a surprise. He directed his engineers to find the red bricks he had set up in the sand months before when he was in command of the Israeli sector. They marked an area where he had the sand carefully thinned down in anticipation of just such a day as this.

General Sharon's men looked for and found the red bricks. It was like a chapter out of a fairy story. The engineers quickly cleared the sand, and the general and his tanks, with rafts and rubber boats, stood at the water's edge.

Ordinary caution and certainly all the conventional military strategy required him to wait for reinforcements. Instead, at 1 o'clock in the morning of the 16th, he crossed the Canal.

General Sharon's gamble proved successful. There was almost nothing on the west bank to oppose him and he was able to fan out quickly to the north and south. The general later complained that his timid colleagues in the Israeli high command had held up his operations for 36 hours. But for this delay, he maintained, he would have occupied Suez before the cease-fire of October 22 and would have isolated the Egyptian Second Army opposite Ismaelia as well as the Egyptian Third Army opposite Suez.

The heaviest battles of this war were fought as the Egyptians attempted in vain to pinch off General Sharon's salient. They attacked from north and south and at one time came within one thousand yards of the Israelis' main line of communication.

General Sharon's personal tank was stocked with caviar and champagne and a bottle of cognac so that he was amply equipped to celebrate his success. For an Israeli such behavior is atypical. As a nation they do not particularly indulge in alcohol. But in the case of Ariel Sharon, all could be forgiven because of his brilliant success.

The October ceasefire was formulated by the Security Council of the United Nations after Secretary of State Kissinger had flown to Moscow to consult Leonid Brezhnev, the Russian Communist Party Secretary. Its text, which became of great political importance, reads as follows:

"The Security Council,

"1. Calls upon all parties to the present fighting to cease all firing and terminate all military activity immediately, no later than 12 hours after the moment of adoption of this decision, in the positions they now occupy;

"2. Calls upon the parties concerned to start immediately after the cease-fire the implementation of Security Council Resolution 242 (1967) in all its parts;

"3. Decides that immediately and concurrently with the cease-fire, negotiations start between the parties concerned under appropriate auspices aimed at establishing a just and durable peace in the Middle East."

The significant points here were the renewal of Security Council insistence on Resolution 242 and the fact that it did not "call upon the parties" but "decides" that immediately the parties should sit down "concurrently with the cease-fire" and start negotiations "under appropriate auspices." The auspices were not defined but State Department officials have told me it meant the Soviet Union and the United States.

Thus simply, in a few words, can great issues be resolved by determined men seizing events at floodtide.

It took two more Security Council resolutions, on the 23rd and 25th, to end the fighting.

It was Sharon's men who immediately after the original cease-fire rushed on to Suez, occupied all but the residential part of town, and cut the road connecting Cairo to the positions of the Third Army with its 20,000 men on the east bank of the Canal. They claimed they had a right to act as they did because they said, the Egyptians had never stopped shooting.

In the words of one Israeli officer, the issue after the Third Army had been cut off was this: "If we force them to surrender, we win. If they hold out and we have to go back, they win."

The United States Government had no interest in forcing any such sharp conclusions. For the Egyptians to be forced to abandon their hard-won position on the east bank of the Canal would have been to deprive them of the new-found self respect that might enable them to negotiate directly and as equals with the Israelis. On the other hand, the United States also did not want to deprive the Israelis of their success in forcing a crossing of the Canal. The United States Government therefore exerted its first heavy pressure on the Israelis in the days that followed the cease-fire to force them to allow 125 trucks with food, water, and medicine to pass through the Israeli lines to the Third Army under supervision of the International Red Cross.

The cease-fire was signed by Lieutenant General Mohamed Abdel Ghany el-Gamazy and Major General Sharon Yariv on November 11 in a tent at kilometer 101 on the Suez-Cairo road, 63 miles from Cairo. For the first time since the 1949 armistice agreements, Israeli and Egyptian officers met to sign an agreement and discuss its implementation. General Ensid Siilasvuo, representing the United Nations, presided at the head of a U-shaped table. The six points of the agreement were the following:

"Egypt and Israel will observe the cease-fire.

"Both sides will discuss the return to the positions that their forces held on October 22, when the United Nations called for a cease-fire. [Egypt says that Israeli forces extended their bridgehead on the western bank of the Suez Canal after the truce was called.]

"The city of Suez, which is surrounded by Israeli forces, will be supplied, and wounded civilians evacuated.

"The Egyptian forces on the eastern bank of the Canal will be supplied.

"The Israeli checkpoints on the Cairo-Suez road will be replaced by United Nations checkpoints.

"All prisoners of war will be exchanged."

The scene was memorable. The tall, lean Egyptian and the dark, solid-looking Israeli met on a dusty, sundrenched plain in front of a tent which flew three United Nations flags. Since this was currently Israeli-controlled territory, the Israelis had set up bottles of an Israel orange drink on the tables. The unsmiling Egyptians did not touch it.

The Egyptian was accompanied to the signing by another officer and two men in civilian clothes; the Israeli by five officers. Outside were another 200 Israelis in dark olive uniforms and 30 Egyptian military police in red and white helmets. But blue-helmeted Finns in the service of the United Nations, big, blond, and very determined, maintained a ring around the tent and controlled entries and departures. A few scuffles between the Finns and people on both sides—but especially with the Israelis—established that the Finns were polite but firmer than anyone had expected.

The Israelis, mostly bareheaded, many with longish hair, sideburns, and whiskers, contrasted with the cleanshaven, well-shorn Egyptians. Losses on both sides in this war were heavy in both men and materiel. The Israelis announced after the cease-fire that they had lost 1,854 dead and about the same number in wounded. The Egyptians and Syrians combined, according to Pentagon specialists, probably lost about five times those numbers. But for Israel, with a population of fewer than three million Jews, this was tragic loss indeed. It has been calculated that if the United States were to lose the same proportion of its young men its loss would be around 140,000.

It was the Israelis' loss of basic materiel—about one third of 300 front line aircraft, and about one third of 1,500 heavy tanks, plus about 300 armored vehicles, according to the Pentagon estimates —that would have defeated them had it not been for American resupply. But America could not resupply those young men whom Israel had so lovingly nurtured. Great was the grieving for them in Israel.

While Arab losses of aircraft and tanks were higher—260 Egyptian and 200 Syrian aircraft, and 1,000 tanks of each of the Arab armies—the Arabs also had greater quantities in reserve. The Arabs, with a population of 40 million in Egypt and Syria, knew they had many young men to fill the places of the dead, but all too few with the training needed to fight such a technological war as this.

15

From "Oil Weapon" to NATO

This account of the fourth Arab-Israeli war would not be complete without four closely related stories. These are, first, the story of the Arabs' oil weapon and how effective it has been; second, the astonishing resupply operations engaged in by the United States and the Soviet Union, which made this something like a war by proxy between the two superpowers; third, the naval confrontation in which American and Soviet fleets paraded around the Eastern Mediterranean; and fourth, the destructive impact of the entire performance on the NATO alliance.

THE "OIL WEAPON"

Ever since the great Arab defeat at the hands of Israel in 1967, Arab radicals have been demanding that the Arabs use their "oil weapon" against Israel. When Egypt on October 6, 1973, suddenly attacked the Israelis and succeeded in crossing in strength to the west bank of the Suez Canal, it looked at first as though the Arabs would not need to use this fundamental economic weapon. But ten days later the tide turned against the Arabs. On Wednesday, October 18, in Kuwait, five Arab oil producing states, under immense pressure from the entire Arab world and from Egypt in particular, made the historic decision. Nothing quite like it had ever been done before in the realm of economic warfare.

During several days of debate preceding their decision, the representatives of Saudi Arabia, Kuwait, Qatar, Abu Dhabi, and Iraq devised a most clever scheme. They would all immediately cut their total oil production by five percent and would each month thereafter cut another five percent until Israel withdrew from the occupied·territories and the rights of the Palestinian people were restored. At the same time, all deliveries of oil to the United States, Canada, and the Netherlands, three nations deemed to constitute a citdel of Zionist support, were immediately embargoed.

At another meeting a week later the oil producers decided to make the immediate cut more severe—25 percent of September 1973 production. Late in November they decided, in recognition of a forthright statement by the nine Common Market countries in favor of Resolution 242, to exempt Europe from the effects of further cuts.

The Iraqis, most of whose customers are in the Communist Bloc of Eastern Europe, decided to ignore the production cut, but put into effect the embargoes.

Each country in fact administered the general decisions made in Kuwait in its own fashion. King Faisal divided the countries of the world into three categories. Some, he acknowledged, had been friendly to the Arabs. Among these he recognized Britain, France, Spain, Pakistan, Malaysia, and, of course, the other Arab countries, in particular Egypt, Jordan, Tunisia, and Lebanon: These countries, he ruled, were to continue receiving petroleum products at the same level as during the first nine months of 1973. When they had been served, said King Faisal, then whatever was left might be distributed to the rest of the world.

Dr. Henry Kissinger, the new American Secretary of State, who began his tour around the world immediately after the conclusion of the cease-fire on October 25, suggested to King Faisal that the Arabs might ease up on their production cuts and embargoes now that the fighting had ended and there was a good prospect for negotiations. But King Faisal left him in no doubt, according to the best diplomatic information in Washington, that he meant to stick it out. This was the King's day on the stage of history and he meant to make the most of it.

Few people realized how dependent the world had become on Arab oil. Not only Europe and Japan but the United States too, it turns out, desperately need the oil of Saudi Arabia in particular. Why Saudi Arabia? American needs are growing rapidly, and the only source of oil in the world sufficiently broad and deep and, above all, expansible to meet those needs is Saudi Arabia.

Here are the facts, which amount to a technical description of "the oil weapon":

The Middle East in the autumn of 1973 was producing 24 million barrels of oil a day. (A barrel of petroleum, by the way, is equal to 42 U.S. gallons.) Of this quantity, Iran was producing about five million barrels, leaving 19.1 million barrels of production by the Arab countries.

The United States, which consumes 17.3 million barrels a day, depends on the Arabs for ten percent of it, or 1.8 million barrels a day. This includes not only petroleum products shipped directly from the Arab world to the United States, but large quantities that reach us indirectly after they have been refined in Canada, the Caribbean, or the Netherlands.

Europe's situation is considerably worse. Not only does Europe depend on oil for 64 percent of its total energy supply, compared with only 46 percent in the case of the United States, but the Europeans receive 65 percent of all their oil from Arab countries. That is, ten million barrels a day.

Japan's situation is also grave. It is dependent on oil for 76 percent of its energy supply, and 50 percent of this comes from Arab sources.

The following table illustrates the United States', Western European, and Japanese dependence on Arab oil:

PETROLEUM CONSUMPTION AND ENERGY DEPENDENCY
OF MAJOR CONSUMING AREAS

	1973 Petroleum Consumption (MM bbl/day)	Percentage of total energy dependent on Petroleum	Percentage of Petroleum dependent on Arab[1] Petroleum	Percentage of total energy dependent on Arab[1] Petroleum
United States	17.3	46%	10%[2]	5%[2]
Western Europe	15.0	64%	65%	42%
Japan	5.2	76%	50%	38%

1. Excluding Iran
2. Including direct crude shipments and indirect product movements

Sources: *BP Statistical Review of the World Oil Industry 1972* and Arthur D. Little, Inc., estimates.

The impact of the embargo on the United States was much aggravated by the fact that it hit this country at a time when, as a result of mismanagement by the government certainly, and by industry probably, it was already suffering from severe shortage of petroleum products. Few Americans know in what serious trouble we were already even before the Arab oil boycott. Here are some of the sad facts: In the year of the boycott United States domestic oil production, which covers only 33 percent of American needs, had just begun a slow decline. Drilling for oil had been diminishing in this country ever since its peak in 1956. Perhaps the government did not provide the companies with the right tax incentives, perhaps the companies were less enterprising than they might have been, but the overriding fact was that the American oil industry had used up its most readily accessible supplies so that future drilling would have to take place in more remote, less hospitable areas such as Alaska and the deep waters of the continental shelf. Meanwhile, incredibly, refining capacity in the United States actually declined by 11,000 barrels in 1972. The big companies had not been building refineries in the United States because it was more profitable to do the refining elsewhere.

Meanwhile, in order to meet the burgeoning needs of the United

States, which were expanding at a rate of about four percent per annum, the United States expanded its imports of oil by 52 percent between 1969 and 1972. For the Middle Eastern area the increase amounted to 83 percent.

Since June, 1971, President Nixon had issued four statements on energy and in so doing acknowledged the new importance of this subject in American life. But somehow, in spite of a plethora of energy studies by Executive agencies, Congress, and private institutions, no decisive steps had been taken to cope with the problem by the time the Arabs struck.

The action taken by President Nixon on November 7, 1973, must be seen in the context of the fourth Arab-Israeli war—America's first act of defense against the Arabs' oil weapon. It was not a very effective act, nor did subsequent administration moves measure up to the gravity of the problem. The President raised the possibility of direct gasoline rationing, or imposition of a heavy tax, something between four percent and twenty percent of present values. But he left this to the future. Immediately he undertook a voluntary program which, in the unlikely event that it was fully effective, would save 2,350,000 barrels of oil per day, thus slightly more than compensating for the amount of oil the Arab embargo was expected to divert from this country.

The President asked Americans to lower the thermostats in their homes by six degrees to sixty-eight and to drive no faster than fifty miles an hour. These two measures were regarded as the most far-reaching, each capable of saving about 600,000 barrels of oil a day. In addition, he asked Americans to join together in pools to meet their daily commuting needs or to use buses. He asked factories and offices and stores to save ten percent of their fuel consumption by turning down thermostats or working shorter hours.

In addition, the President asked Congress to give him power to introduce year-round daylight saving time, to reduce airline flights, to ease environmental standards as regards the use of high sulphur and oil fuels, to draw up gasoline rationing plans, and to increase the use of federal oil resources, including Elks Hill Naval Reserves.

Europe, more gravely threatened than the United States because of its greater dependence on Arab oil, also moved toward conservation of resources. The British prepared for rationing of "petrol"; the Dutch banned Sunday driving. In Belgium the government took over oil supplies and production. Luxemburg closed its gas stations on weekends.

And all the Europeans, as they took these steps, were looking over their shoulders with some ill humor at Uncle Sam. The tendency was not to blame the Arabs, or even Israel, but to say that it was United States' Middle Eastern policy that was causing Europe to freeze this winter.

King Faisal had indeed foreseen these events and had tried in vain to head them off by sending messages and emissaries, his sons and his ministers, to President Nixon and the United States Government for several years past. His plea had been in effect this: Saudi Arabia now has ample income and capital for all its needs and development. It does not need, for its own purposes, to expand production of oil any more. Indeed, the inevitable rise in the price of oil makes it advantageous for us to leave the oil in the ground as long as possible. You, the United States, are urging us, however, to expand production of oil rapidly to meet your needs. We are now under great and growing pressure not to accede to your demands, and even to cut back our production, unless you are willing to adopt a more evenhanded policy in the Middle East. The pressure comes from all the other Arab countries, and from the Palestinian Fedayeen, whose feelings are strong and who are active in Saudi Arabia as well as in other countries.

King Faisal said that the United States as in other countries was asking Saudi Arabia to expand its daily production from its present level of 8.2 million barrels a day to 20 million barrels a day in 1980, largely in order to meet American needs.

The Saudis felt that these messages were not taken seriously, and they were probably right. The United States was too busy in Vietnam to listen or appreciate the danger. But no one could say that the United States had not been warned. In its economic effect the "oil weapon" is proving devastating.

American economists can be divided into those who anticipate the future with alarm and those who express great alarm. In the former groups are the White House Council of Economic Advisers and Harvard economist Otto Eckstein, who are on record as saying that if the conservation measures announced by the President are taken, along with effective rationing of gasoline or a 20 or 30 percent tax on gasoline, the loss to the national economy can be limited to something like one percent of the gross national product, the sum of the value of goods and services produced by a nation. That would still leave an estimated growth of 1.5 percent in the GNP in 1974.

But the National Petroleum Council, the individual oil companies, and the Wharton econometric team of the University of Pennsylvania are among those who are full of forebodings. Calculating the economic cost to the United States of the Arab oil cutback during the first year at 48 billion dollars, the NPC anticipates a 3.4 percent loss in the gross national product and the unemployment reaching 6.2 percent if the fuel shortage continues through the year at a level of two million barrels. Should the shortage rise to three million barrels, the anticipated unemployment would reach as high as 7.7 percent of the country's employable manpower.

The Wharton professors—Lawrence R. Klein, George R. Green, and F. Gerard Adams—predict a recession and inflation as a result of a shortage of three million barrels of oil. They speak of "a substantial upheaval in normal industrial and business operations."

Whether the Arabs' "oil weapon" is proving as effective politically as it is economically is at least open to question. While there is much talk and concern about the economic impact of the oil shortage, there is much less talk about the issues that brought on the use of the "oil weapon." One prominent American who has raised the issue publicly is Robert O. Anderson, Chairman of the Board of Atlantic-Richfield. Observing that the United States could not look for help in its present difficulties from any of its friends, he says that the United States is isolated. Under the circumstances, he suggests, the Arab request for a more evenhanded American policy was perhaps to be regarded as reasonable. "If we fail to reach a reasonable resolution of these problems with the Arab nations," he says "nothing will save us from a major and lasting change in the American lifestyle."

Some friends of the Arabs, meanwhile, worry whether King Faisal and the others would know when they had gone far enough. Use of the "oil weapon," they speculate, might go too far. On the one hand the Western world might, however painfully, learn to live without Arab oil, so that the old adage about Middle Eastern Oil, that the Arabs "have to sell it," would be put to the test. On the other hand there are fears that somehow the Western powers might eventually resort to force to bring about a resumption of the flow of the oil they need. Some recall a warning made by Senator William Fulbright, the Chairman of the Senate Foreign Relations Committee, in the summer of 1973, that the Arabs should be on their guard against the possibility that the United States, if sufficiently frustrated, would use its "surrogates," Israel and Iran, militarily to occupy the Arab oil fields.

ARMS

By the time the Arab-Israeli war of 1973 was four days old, the Pentagon was acutely aware that the Soviet Union had begun a massive resupply operation on behalf of its clients, Egypt and Syria, by air and by sea. Although there was evidence aplenty before that date, the American Defense Department dates the main Soviet effort from October 10. Through the American Embassy in Moscow and Ambassador Anatoliv F. Dobrynin in Washington, the United States tried to persuade the Russians to come to terms on some kind of limitation of their resupply effort so that the two superpowers, in the name of detente, might keep the Arab-Israeli war within reasonable bounds. But the Russians, so the State Department says, were not interested. The United States, therefore, on October 14, launched its own resupply operation.

From the beginning, the United States set aside a fleet of about twenty big air transports, including several of the gigantic C-5s capable of lifting up to 265,000 pounds and C-141s with lift capacity of 62,500 pounds. The Russians, using somewhat smaller Antonov 12s and Antonov 22s employed a larger number of aircraft. In spite of the greater distance the Americans had to fly, they showed, in the ensuing weeks, they could move more arms further and more quickly than could the Russians. Both sides also used ships, of course, and the Russians were able by this means to keep quantatively well ahead of the United States.

When the cease-fire came on October 22, the two superpowers paid no heed but went right on resupplying their clients. The Pentagon said, when the resupply race was thirty days old, that the score was as follows: The United States had moved 50,000 tons of arms and ammunition and other supplies to Israel, 22,300 tons by air, and the rest, either actually delivered or enroute, by sea. The Americans had made 560 sorties, or flights, from the United States to Israel. The Russians had sent to Egypt and Syria 100,000 tons of military supplies, including 15,000 tons by air according to Pentagon estimates. In addition to the big transports the United States flew about 48 Phantoms and flew or shipped about 60 Skyhawks to Israel.

If the persistence of resupply operations by both sides suggested something about their future intentions, it was the initiation on the Russian side that shed particular light on the nature and origins of this war. For the Russians, during the last six weeks before the war started, delivered to Egypt by sea about one hundred T-62 tanks, the best the Soviet Union has to offer. Previous to that delivery, Egypt had received only ten tanks of this model. During the same period, according to American intelligence, the Russians made heavy deliveries of aircraft and ground-to-air missiles, including the deadly SA-6, to Egypt and Syria. Considering further the departure of the families of Soviet technicians and advisers from Cairo and Damascus during the several days before the war started, one is almost obliged to conclude that the Soviet Union knew well in advance of the plans to launch an attack. To this evidence one must add the fact, reported by American satellite photography, that sometime in the last few months the Russians had delivered to Egypt about 20 Scud missile launchers with appropriate missiles which could travel 180 miles, just about far enough to reach from northern Egypt to Tel Aviv. American intelligence believes that the introduction of these missiles into Egypt may be in response to the existence of the even more formidable 300 mile Jericho missile which the Israelis have themselves developed. On a more speculative level American intelligence also has some evidence that a special, very small Soviet army unit in Egypt has in its custody nuclear warheads which could be installed in the Scuds were the Israelis ever to put nuclear warheads on their Jerichos.

The Israelis are known to have the capacity to make nuclear bombs or warheads with the plutonium produced by their nuclear research center at Dimona, in the Negev. Experts in the field believe that this 24 megawatt plant, built by French engineers between 1957 and 1964, could produce enough plutonium for one or more nuclear bombs or warheads annually of a strength equivalent to the 19 kiloton bomb the American Air Force dropped on Nagasaki in 1945.

The technology of putting together these weapons, once the materials are available, is said to be within the reach of most university-level nuclear scientists.

To be sure, the Egyptians did not use these missiles, but the fact that they were supplied suggests a departure from long-standing Soviet reluctance to provide offensive weapons to the Arabs. It raises questions for which there cannot be any satisfactory answers regarding ultimate Soviet intentions in the Middle East.

The Russians flew their Antonovs, for the most part via Hungary and Yugoslavia, to destinations in Syria and Egypt, while the United States, partly because of the inhospitality of its European allies in this matter, and partly because it was convenient, flew via Lajes airfield in the Azores to Israel.

Both sides at the height of the war included in their cargoes the heaviest tanks. Imagine flying an M-60 tank weighing 52 1/2 tons, 105,000 pounds! And that all the way across the Atlantic to the far end of the Mediterranean. Sad that such a technological feat should be in the service of war.

While the Russians were reported to be including more of their highly successful SA-6 and SA-7 missiles in their air cargoes, the United States, in the last days of the war, put great emphasis on flying to the Israelis electronic devices which might be used to incapacitate the radar controls of the Soviet missiles. The Tow anti-tank missile, the American equivalent of the Soviet Sagger, was also included in the shipments to the Israeli Army at the height of the battle. There were times, Israeli officers reported, when arms delivered by air from the United States were employed in battle within hours after their arrival in Israel. Neither side could have survived without resupply.

How could the Israelis possibly pay for such an outpouring of super-expensive toys? Technically, these deliveries were all payable within 120 days. The White House request to Congress for $2.2 billion to finance arms for Israel suggested the answer. The Israelis, who already have a debt load of several billion, will not be asked to take on more. Instead, most of the arms sent to them probably will be declared a gift by Congress.

The Pentagon estimates that total resupply to Israel will probably run to about $3 billion and that the cost of replacing these arms, many of which were taken right out of active American Army, Air Force, and Navy formations, will probably run even higher. The reason is that replacement costs have been raised by inflation. In some cases, furthermore, it will be necessary to reopen assembly lines to replace the particular items sent to Israel.

Israel's need in this war undoubtedly taught the American armed forces some important lessons. One lesson is that tanks and airplanes are no longer necessarily the kings of the battlefield, that they can, under certain circumstances, be neutralized by surface-to-surface and surface-to-air missiles. Another is that, against the possibility that the United States again may need to send such heavy loads of arms to the other side of the globe, this country requires a lot more aircraft like the C-5A.

SHIPS

It is hard to know whether the extraordinary confrontation of Soviet and American navies in the Eastern Mediterranean during and after the fourth Arab-Israeli war was intended by the two sides to exert pressure on or to reassure the various surrounding countries, or to threaten one another, or whether it was just a kind of a Pavlovian reaction to the fighting on land. In any event, the Sixth Fleet of the United States was expanded from its normal forty or fifty ships to a strength of about sixty. The Russian fleet was expanded from its usual fifty or sixty ships to something in the nineties during the first week in November. In mid-November it began to taper off and declined to the seventies toward the end of November.

For the two fleets this was a show of force. All their splendid and fearsome engines of war, including, on the Soviet side at least one of their latest cruisers noted for its speed and three missile systems, and four accompanying missile destroyers. The Russians also sent into the Mediterranean seven amphibious landing craft and two helicopter carriers, aboard which there were presumably several thousand men.

Although outnumbered, the United States undoubtedly remained superior in fire power. It counted among its ships three aircraft carriers, the *Franklin D. Roosevelt,* the *John F. Kennedy,* and the *Independence,* each with about 800 aircraft aboard and with its usual screens of cruisers and destroyers. In addition, the United States had in the Eastern Mediterranean at this time two helicopter carriers, the *Iwo Jima* and the *Guadalcanal,* between them carrying 3,600 Marines.

Not content with this demonstration of American power, the United States also at the beginning of November, ordered the aircraft carrier *Hancock,* which had been cruising with the American fleet in Far Eastern waters, to proceed into the Indian Ocean. Although relatively old and considered one of our smaller carriers, this ship would undoubtedly make a considerable impression were it to appear in the Red Sea or the Persian Gulf, and the mere fact that it might do so inevitably has its bearing on the affairs of the region.

NATO

The spectacle of the two superpowers straining every nerve in competitive resupplying of their respective clients in the Middle East and grandiosely displaying their naval might in an unparalleled confrontation within the narrow confines of the Eastern Mediterranean was a reminder to Europeans that this is still basically a bi-polar world in which the superpowers still play at brinkmanship.

A few diplomatic shocks in the few weeks of the Arab-Israeli war and its aftermath underlined the point. A *tête à tête* between Washington and Moscow always makes Europeans nervous, and the trip by Henry Kissinger, the American Secretary of State, to Moscow on October 20, at the height of the Arab-Israeli war, was no exception. Europeans in general feel that they have a vital stake in the Middle East, from which they buy most of their oil, and that they are entitled to know what is going on in the region. They would have appreciated it had one of Dr. Kissinger's deputies, Deputy Secretary Kenneth Rush, for instance, called in their ambassadors for a fill-in. But nothing happened until Dr. Kissinger himself returned to Washington.

The resupply itself, of course, caused friction. The Germans, who were especially involved because most American supplies in Europe are situated on German soil, tried to avoid trouble by closing their eyes to the American resupply operation. Although the background of Hitlerian atrocities has created a special relationship between Germany and Israel and a permanent feeling of German obligation to Israel, the Germans would have preferred to remain neutral in this conflict. Finally, German feelings boiled over in an incident that started just after the October 22 cease-fire with the appearance of an Israeli freighter flying the Israeli flag and loading tanks at Bremerhaven. A local German reporter tried to approach the ship but was turned back by American military police. He complained to the German Foreign Ministry, which soon thereafter issued a statement sharply objecting to the American resupply operation. Later the Foreign Ministry maintained that the statement was made public by mistake, that the commentary intended for internal use only was in error typed on a form intended for public distribution. One wonders.

This incident occurred just after the United States had been drawn into a sudden, almost hysterical confrontation with the Russians over an alleged Russian plan to fly 50,000 Soviet airborne troops to the Middle East. The Russians, it seems, were worried that the Israelis might entirely isolate and defeat and humiliate the Egyptian Third Army in spite of the cease-fire that had been declared.

In a note to President Nixon, Soviet Party Leader Leonid Brezhnev is believed to have said in effect that if the United States could not restrain the Israelis, they, the Russians, were going to do it themselves. He suggested the United States join the Soviet Union in sending in troops. In addition, the United States had evidence by satellite photography and other intelligence that the Russians were actually making ready to move airborne units numbering 50,000.

Intelligence analysts of the Defense Department and Central Intelligence Agency feared that if the Russians did so they might well remain in the Middle East for years, adding a new and most undesirable factor to the Middle Eastern balance of power and influence. Their presence might well lead to World War III.

At 11 o'clock on the night of the 24th of October, Dr. Kissinger met at the White House with an abbreviated National Security Council, including William E. Colby of the CIA and Admiral Thomas E. Moorer, the Chairman of the Joint Chiefs of Staff, and worked out a plan of action. He says that he and Admiral Moorer returned to the Pentagon about 11:30 and got busy working out the details of a Stage 3 worldwide alert of American armed forces. By 3:00 A.M. they had their plans ready to go and they obtained the approval of President Nixon, who strangely had not participated in this bit of crisis management but had remained in his White House bedroom. But that is another story.

A Stage 3 alert is in the middle of a scale that goes from 1 to 5 —1 being total readiness and 5 maximum unreadiness to deploy forces in combat.

The American alert was supposed to head off the movement of Soviet airborne troops to the Middle East. But the American action, of course, was far more massive than that taken by the Russians. It included an alert of SAC, the Strategic Air Command, which controls intercontinental missiles and long-range bombers, including those carrying nuclear bombs. Specially alerted was the 82nd Airborne at Fort Bragg, North Carolina. The 82nd would probably have been the unit actually sent to Israel had the Russians begun to move their troops into Egypt.

Given the circumstances, Dr. Kissinger can perhaps be forgiven for being extraordinarily irritated by the critical statement issued by the German Foreign Ministry in its effort to halt the movement of supplies toward the Israeli freighter. He argued at a news conference that the U.S.-Soviet confrontation should be regarded as transcending the feelings of NATO allies about the Israeli conflict. He added sarcastically that some of the United States' NATO allies apparently had a conception of military readiness different from that of the United States. He threatened that if the United States was not to be free to move the supplies it had prepositioned in Germany as it saw fit then the United States might have to find another location for some of those supplies. It sounded just a little bit like Secretary of State John Foster Dulles' threat in the early fifties to engage in "an agonizing reappraisal" of the alliance at the time when the French were showing reluctance to go along with the plan for creation of a European Army.

A few days later Dr. Kissinger went off to a nuclear planning group meeting at Brussels. By the time he came back he had calmed down. But the alert continued for a week.

Other members of the alliance were included in Dr. Kissinger's displeasure because they had objected to the movement of American resupply flights over their territory. The British maintain that they never actually told the United States that they could not use British ports or airfields and that they did not deny the British airfield at Akrotiri on Cyprus to the high flying SR-71 U.S. reconnaissance plane. But sometimes, even in international relations, more can be conveyed by a general attitude than by a formal statement. And there is no doubt that the British were not supporting the Americans in this Middle Eastern war. A State Department request that the British Ambassador in Washington, the Earl of Cromer, propose the cease-fire at the United Nations was declined by Britain on the grounds that the Egyptians and Syrians at the time were adamantly opposed.

Italy and Spain let the Americans know that they did not approve use of their airports for the resupply operation. Only Greece, where the American 6th Fleet had recently established a new home port, cooperated fully with the United States, and, of course, Portugal, which provided the Azores base.

The 24-year-old NATO alliance already had been under strain, and the United States had been hard at work seeking a new foundation for the relationship of the United States and Europe. The visit by President Nixon to Europe planned for the end of 1973 or the beginning of 1974 was to have been the occasion for proclaiming a new declaration of United States and European solidarity, a fitting successor to the Atlantic Charter. But the ill feeling stirred by the Middle Eastern incident shifted these plans into an uncertain future.

Some American diplomats were deeply impressed by the extent of the United States' isolation in its Middle Eastern stand. After all, there is no real reason why the Europeans should support a United States policy, the nature of which derives entirely from a paradox. This paradox is that the United States, the home of six million Jews, allows its sentimental attachment to the State of Israel to override economic interests in the vast Arab world. For the Europeans, however, the economic interest is obviously decisive.

16

Solutions

The possibility of settlement of the conflict between Jews—later Israelis—and Arabs has existed for fifty years, and still exists. It would take just a little rationality on both sides to pull it off. But the Israelis want total domination and absolute security. The Arabs demand total fulfillment of what they consider to be their rights. This situation reminds me of an old story about the Middle East.

Once upon a time a scorpion came to the Jordan River and wished to get across. But he could not swim. Then he saw a frog sitting on the shore. "Dear frog," he implored, "would you kindly carry me across the river?"

"Good heavens," exclaimed the frog, diving into the river. "I wouldn't dream of it. I know you. You might sting me."

"Oh, no," replied the scorpion, "have no fear. If I did that while we were crossing the river, then we would both perish."

"That's true," observed the frog, reassured and returning to shore. "So hop on my back, and I will give you a ride across."

The scorpion jumped on the frog's back, and they set off across the river. In midstream, the scorpion suddenly stung the frog. As the two sank beneath the waves, the frog cried out: "Scorpion, why did you do that? Now we shall both die."

To which the scorpion replied: "Well, that's the Middle East."

By recounting this hoary tale, I do not mean to equate the conflicting parties in the Middle East with treachery—though there is enough of that in the area—but rather with unreasonableness. I mean to say that one should not take the carefully reasoned arguments of experts too seriously, and should bear in mind that in the Middle East anything is possible.

There is much of the unreasonable about both sides in the Middle East. If the Arabs were "reasonable" people, they would have recognized Israel long ago. If they were "reasonable" people, the Arabs would have accepted the Eric Johnson plan for joint development of the Jordan Valley by Israel and the Arab states, and a million refugees would have been resettled by now. If King Hussein had been motivated only by "reason" he would not have gone to war against the Israelis in 1967. But the Arabs are romantics. They have romantic notions of their honor. They are a people of poets and speechmakers who substitute words for action and whose words are forever in hyperbole. Their alliances shift with bewildering rapidity—yet there are causes which they are able to serve unflinchingly from generation to generation.

And if the Israelis, or rather their Zionist predecessors, were a "reasonable" people, they would never have dared undertake such a seemingly impossible task as the creation of a Jewish state in Palestine. Or at least they would have accepted the British offer during World War I to turn a section of Uganda (some say it was really part of Kenya) into a Jewish national home. But they were and are romantics who returned after nearly 2,000 years to the land of their forefathers and are attempting to transform people steeped in commerce and intellectual pursuits into farmers. They have a tendency to first build factories in the desert, and then attempt to make them economically feasible. They have built a state on faith and credit, and in their own way—different from the Arab way, but similar—they, too, are addicted to words—usually complex and in writing. The word "Talmudic" describes a tendency among these people. The Babylonians described them as "the stiff-necked people," and stiff-necked they remain to this day.

The qualities of both peoples add up to nationalism—two nationalisms that meet head-on in the struggle for Palestine. One land, two peoples.

The Jews maintain that they have historic rights in Palestine because their forefathers conquered the land in the days of Joshua and King David, and because, according to their reading of the Bible, it had been promised to them by God. The Arabs point out that their ancestors, who in this region were non-Arabs, but who later mixed with Arabs, lived in this land long before the Jews arrived, and that Arab tribes have occupied the land continuously for thirteen centuries since the Arab conflict. They dispute the idea that God promised this land to the Jews or that He, being a universal God, could favor any one people.

With so much right on both sides, so much sentiment, so much suffering, so much injustice, I do not believe that the moral argument for one side or the other can alone lead to solutions. Basic ideas for solutions or, more honestly, approaches to solutions, have, however, emerged from the political and intellectual leadership on both sides. I think it would be useful at this point, before we examine the situation after the fourth Arab-Israeli war, to examine the thinking of the Jews and Arabs as it has developed, and to make some comparisons.

The first stirrings of Arab and Jewish nationalism manifested themselves on a cultural level after the middle of the nineteenth century. In Constantinople, Beirut, Damascus, and Cairo; in the ghettos of eastern Europe, among Jewish intellectuals in western Europe who had broken away from traditional patterns of Jewish life but who rejected assimilation by gentile life.

On the one hand we have Jamal Addin Afghani, the Arab father-philosopher who sought to revive his religion in a purer form and to awaken the Arabs as a nation; on the other, Theodor Herzl, prophet of the Jewish State, who sought to express his Jewishness not in terms of religion but of nationalism, in terms of a new state.

The Arabs wanted to synthesize their role religiously and politically with modern nationalist institutions; the Zionists, to reconstitute Jewish life in a practical expression of the nineteenth-century European concept of nationalism.

For the thinkers of both sides there developed a triangle of mutually conflicting concepts which they sought, with varying degrees of success, to reconcile: nationalism, religion, and Marxism.

While the total concern of men of action such as Weizmann, the first President, and Ben-Gurion, for many years the Premier, and later Premier Golda Meir and General Dayan, was the creation and preservation of the Jewish State, the Jewish conscience from the very beginning expressed itself in attempts by intellectuals to reach out to the Arabs—to understand, to reconcile.

By comparison, the Arabs were much less interested in the Jews. They had no problems of conscience. It was not they who had tried to exterminate the Jews. They knew their own "Oriental Jews," and they were not curious about these Jews from Europe. They were not attracted but appalled by the Jewish phenomenon thrust into their midst. Only much later did a few Arab scholars begin to study the ways of the Jewish immigrants. The strident, abrasive Israeli presence forced the Arab's attention. While some Arabs dreamed and plotted wars against the Jews, a few began to consider ways of living with them.

A cultural father of Zionism, Asher Ginzberg, better known under his pen name Ahad Ha-am, criticized the early Zionists. As he became aware of their military activities and concern for economic development, he wrote in a letter around 1922: "Now, if this be the Messiah, then I do not wish to see his coming."

Ginzberg's liberal, humanistic concerns applied to the Arabs as well as the Jews, and in this he found himself in accord with other writers, such as Yitzhak Epstein, Chaim Kalvarisky, and Moshe Smilansky, and later also with Martin Buber and Judah Magnes, who developed a deeply Semitic movement called Berit Shalom (Covenant of Peace), which became known as Ihud.

In the mid-thirties Pinhas Rutenberg sought meetings with prominent Arabs such as Musa Alami, but the 1936 Arab revolt interfered.

Chaim Arlosoroff, as head of the Jewish Agency Political Office, began preparing talks with the Arabs in the period after the revolt but was assassinated as he walked on the beach at Tel Aviv, apparently by the nationalist extremists known as Revisionists.

All of these men expressed the feeling that the Zionist State would have no meaning without an understanding, without political, economic, and educational cooperation with the Arabs.

The MAPAM Party became the champion of cooperation with the Arabs as part of the working class. But some young left-wingers felt Marxist-Zionism inadequate. A group took shape on the left called the Canaanites, led in the early fifties by the poet, Ratosh, who sought the roots of the Jewish people in their pre-Biblical past. While some supporters of this movement gravitated eventually to extremist Irgun, which claimed Arab territory from the Nile to the Euphrates, others began to identify ethnically with the Arabs. Their movement is called Semitic Action. The theory behind this movement is ethnic. It holds that the Jewish people from pre-Biblical times intermingled with all the other peoples of the Middle East, the Canaanites, the Philistines, the Phoenicians, and others, and intermingled again as the children of Israel conquered the promised land. The new left as it developed in Israel in the sixties and seventies was represented by Matzpeh, whose members have from time to time held quiet meetings with Arab fellow Marxists in Europe. Yuri Avneri, although more nationalist than Matzpeh, is a notable individual who has sought contact with the Arabs.

The only joint Israeli-Arab political party in Israel was the Communist Party. It gained a wide following among the Arabs by voicing Arab grievances and might represent a political bridge between Israel and the Arab countries, were it not for the fact that the Communist Party is illegal almost everywhere in the Arab world, and is widely denounced by other Marxists—both Arab and Israeli—for its slavish adherence to instructions from Moscow.

On the Arab side there is no parallel, except in the limited frame of Lebanon, to this rich panorama of Israeli ideology, at least not until quite recently. But this does not mean that the Arabs did not react at all to the Jewish-Israeli phenomenon.

In the days of the British Mandate in Palestine, the Arab landed aristocracy felt no constraints about meeting Jews on a social level. Personal friendships developed.

On quite another level, among Lebanese Christians, there has long been some pro-Israeli sentiment. These Christians tend to resent and fear the Arab Moslems, and have from time to time toyed with the idea they could find protection in association with the Jews. Individual Arabs also had enough contact with Israel to appreciate the Israeli way of life.

The Israelis have tried with some success since 1967 to increase the number of such individuals by encouraging visits by Arabs from all parts of the Arab world to relatives on the West Bank of the Jordan. More than 100,000 once settled on the West Bank now cross the river each year. It is quite easy for them to enter Israel, and many have done so in the last few years. I have talked to some who returned to their homes in Arab countries impressed by what they had seen and eager to come to terms with the Israelis. But I think it would be a mistake to imagine, as some of the Israelis do, that these are more than isolated individuals or that they are likely to play a role in Arab politics.

While the Zionists were struggling with the problems of subordinating Zionism to socialism or socialism to Zionism, the Arabs had only just begun to think in ideological terms. In Chapter 3 I traced the roots of Arab nationalism. Here I will recall only that in the 1920s a Syrian named Michel Aflaq went to Paris, read Kant, Hegel, and Marx, and began to lay the intellectual foundation for the Baath (Arab Renaissance) Party. There were of course some others, but few whose importance was more than local.

After 1948 George Habash began to organize the Arab Nationalist Movement. At first purely nationalist, it became closely identified a little later with the leadership of Gamal Abdel Nasser, and then, in the sixties, imbued with Marxist ideas.

Nasser, in many ways Ben-Gurion's opposite, began the practical political transformation of the Arab world. He was the Arab's man of action who tried to make a reality of Pan-Arabism by creating a United Arab Republic embracing Egypt, Syria, and Yemen and who applied Marxist socialism in his land reform measures and nationalization of banks and insurance companies, while at the same time stirring Arab emotions with bold strokes such as closing the Suez Canal and buying arms from the Soviet Union.

As already noted in the chapter on the commandos, Fatah contributed a new element to Arab political thinking by distinguishing clearly for the first time between Jews and Zionists. Fatah identified the Jews as a religious group which could be accommodated and incorporated in Middle Eastern society, thus isolating the Zionists as their enemy.

Making this distinction was an achievement for liberal, humanistic thinking. The Marxists in the commando movement, the PFLP and the PDFLP, carried the subject a stage further by considering various forms of political accommodation with the Jews, or national rights for the Jews.

I think it is relevant at this point to mention the ideas expressed to me by George Habash in a July, 1970, interview. Habash envisages a solution of the Jewish question by the transformation of the Middle East by revolution. In a unified, post-revolutionary Arab world a non-Zionist Jewish community would become one of many minority groupings living with their Arab neighbors in a state embracing all or most of the Arab Middle East. There would be no struggle between Jewish and Arab positions in Palestine because there would be neither a Palestinian nor an Israeli State.

Habash made this point to me by taking issue with my allusion to a "Democratic Palestinian State" and insisting on substituting the phrase "democratic solution for the Jewish problem in Palestine." He explained that he made this point because Israel was the enemy not only of the Palestinian people but of all the Arab people. "During the fighting, which will be a long and enduring war," he said, many radical changes would take place in all the Arab countries surrounding Israel so that "Jordan will not remain as Jordan . . . we will be having here a national liberation movement in Jordan, Lebanon, Syria, and all parts of the Arab world surrounding Israel. So when we get back Palestine, we will get it back as part of this Arab revolutionary situation . . . and in this revolutionary Arab area which will be including a good number of the Arab countries existing at present it will be easy to find a democratic solution."

Most recently Habash has been quoted at his underground hiding place discussing collaboration with "our Jewish brothers." To him, allies are to be sought in the Jewish just as in the Arab world. He believes that it is possible not only to subvert the Arab States but the Jewish State.

While the old-guard PLO (the Palestine Liberation Organization) has gone on talking about expulsion of all or some of the Jews, the leftists seem to have grasped that this is simply not going to happen in any foreseeable future. They have, more precisely, grasped the limitations of armed struggle.

After September, 1970, even PLO's Central Committee no longer opposed the efforts of Egypt and other Arab regimes to recover occupied territory "so long as these attempts do not compromise the rights of the Palestinian people" and do not interfere with the armed struggle.

This shift may have reflected a realization in the Fatah leadership of the need to normalize relations with Egypt, which remained committed to the principle of settlement, because Egypt was the major source of money and arms for the commandos.

The position of the Syrian Government, hitherto adamant in rejecting any kind of peaceful settlement, also slowly changed following September, 1970. After the new government of Hafez al Assad had in the spring of 1971 joined with Egypt and Libya to form the Federal Arab Republic, Assad acknowledged willingness to accept a political solution on the basis of the United Nations Security Council Resolution 242, provided "the rights of the Palestinians were recognized."

Although there are some tendencies toward accommodation on both sides, let me hasten to add that these have been negated in practice. On the Israeli side, the intellectuals' conscience-driven reaching out to the Arabs is overshadowed by simplistic notions among the men of action of the Establishment of "how to deal with the Arabs" that are somehow reminiscent of old-fashioned Southern racist notions of how to deal with "the niggers." This philosophy was carefully explained to me in 1950 by a high-ranking Israeli army officer. He showed me charts and statistics to prove that the way to keep the Árabs in line was to hit them. The harder you hit them, the longer they stayed in line. This was called the "theory of reprisals," and it hasn't changed in the ensuing twenty-three years.

On the Arab side, too, the notion of accommodation is marginal. Marxist theorizing involves only a handful of people. Yet it is fascinating to see Israeli and Arab intellectuals occasionally getting together, as at the June, 1973, Conference of Bologna, and it is comforting to reflect on the common denominators to be found in the thinking on the one hand of a Magnes, a Yuri Avneri, of MAPAM and Matzpeh, and on the other of Fatah, PFLP, and PDFLP.

But it would be a great mistake to expect much to come of such cerebration. Insofar as the liberal, humanist, Marxist thinkers envisage solutions that imply the abolition of the Israeli State, they are totally unrealistic. And insofar as the Arab radicals' thinking implies the overthrow of the Arab regimes, they are equally unrealistic—for the time being.

Having considered some of the ideas and attitudes on both sides, I do not believe that either Arabs or Israelis are capable by themselves of working out either an interim or an ultimate solution, because both Arab and Israeli leaders are prisoners of their extremists. These leaders are afraid of appearing to give anything away for fear of being called weak or even traitors. The Arabs in particular are victims of the habit of "overbidding"; Arab politicians perpetually vie with one another in taking the most extreme possible position with respect to Israel.

In Israel Ben-Gurion might have been capable of magnanimity, but he is old; in Egypt Nasser could have made the Arabs swallow bitter medicine, but he is dead.

The Arabs show that they are not serious about reaching a settlement with Israel by refusing to engage in direct talks. And I find it difficult to blame the Israelis for their reluctance to venture into indirect talks. It must seem outrageous to them to be treated like pariahs by the people who profess to be willing to enter into a settlement. Yet, in the period before the fourth Arab-Israeli war, the reluctance of the Israelis to pay more than lip service to the U.N. Security Council's November 1967 resolution, their rejection of the Rogers proposals, and their attempt to "create facts" by building in occupied territory, showed that they were more interested in imposing their rule by force than in coming to terms.

It is my thesis, therefore, that only the Great Powers working together can break the vicious circle, particularly the United States and the Soviet Union. Britain and France and now, since its admission to the United Nations, Communist China will play supplementary roles.

Even though the Israelis became ever more deeply entrenched in the occupied territories, and a new belligerent generation which had not tasted defeat was growing up in Arab lands, certain circumstances have favored settlement ever since the Arab-Israeli war in 1967. These circumstances, were, first, the relationship existing between the United States and the Soviet Union and, second, the political situation within the Arab world.

Let us examine the first point. Important developments are most likely to occur in the Middle East when the United States and the Soviet Union agree. This happened in 1948 when the Israeli State was born. It happened again in 1956 when the United States and the Soviet Union agreed that Israel should be forced back from the Sinai Peninsula.

It could have happened just after the 1967 War. And it might still happen after the fourth Arab-Israeli war. During these years the United States and Soviet interests in the Middle East coincided in several significant respects. Above all, both countries apparently wanted a settlement. Especially during the period preceding the explusion of the Russians from Egypt, both countries feared that an Arab-Israeli confrontation could lead to a confrontation between the Soviet Union and the United States and, as a consequence, to World War III.

Soviet policy in the Middle East is based on the principle of controlled tension. That is, the Russians back the Arabs, but only enough to keep the Arabs dependent on the Soviet Union, never enough to bring about Israel's defeat. In recent years, however, the tension has been increasing. Too many elements have escaped Soviet control. For instance, on the Arab side the Palestinian commandos were a law unto themselves. No one could predict how far their provocations might lead. On the Israeli side there were "gung ho" pilots who might break through to Cairo and engage Soviet pilots—that is, as long as Soviet pilots were stationed around Cairo.

Even now, a clash might at any time escalate into serious war. It is because the Russians appreciate this danger that they refused until recently to give the Egyptians offensive weapons such as long-range bombers and missiles. Their restraint, indeed, led to the Egyptian demand that they withdraw from Egypt. Although the United States has for domestic political reasons demonstrated rather less restraint in its supply of arms to Israel, the Americans' concern for protecting their economic interests by means of political settlement seems obvious.

Apart from this overriding question of war and peace, the United Sates and the Soviet Union have comparable attitudes toward the Palestinians, unfortunately for the Palestinians. From the American point of view—State Department lip service to the aspirations of the Palestinian people notwithstanding—the Palestinians stand in the way of satisfying the aspirations of Israel, the United States' client-state. From the Soviet point of view, the Palestinians are dangerous. They are irredentist, forever unwilling to abandon their claims to Palestine. Although many of them lay claim to Marxist ideology, they are disconcertingly uncontrollable. Worst of all, they are susceptible to extremism, to Maoism. Their demands are an invitation to the Communist Chinese. The Chinese have not been slow to respond.

In the last few years "detente" has become a further factor in U.S.-Soviet relations. Soviet desire to encourage U.S. trade and to discourage U.S.-Chinese rapprochement could lead to some Soviet concessions to the American point of view in the Middle East.

The second of the major points that favor political settlement is the situation within the Arab states. Moderate regimes, which are more likely than leftist extremist regimes to settle with Israel, consolidated their position throughout the Middle East between 1970 and 1972. President Sadat eliminated the leftists led by Ali Sabry. King Hussein eliminated the Fedayeen. President Numeiry of Sudan put down a Communist uprising. King Hassan of Morocco put down an attempted coup. In Syria General Hafez al Assad supplanted the leftist wing of the Baath Party. In Lebanon President Franjieh has shown himself a vigorous force for moderation more able than his predecessor to cope with the Fedayeen.

The United States and other governments have done some things to take advantage of this situation, but by no means enough.

The fundamental attempt to bring about a settlement after the 1967 War was the November 22, 1967, resolution of the United Nations Security Council, Resolution 242, the essence of which was that the Israelis were to withdraw from occupied territories while the Arabs were to renounce belligerence and recognize Israel within secure frontiers. The formula was flawed by a basic ambiguity: it spoke of withdrawal from occupied territory, even though it did not use the word "all." This point was crucial because the Arabs maintained that the text implied *all* occupied territory, while the Israelis insisted that it left the door open to their retention of some territory.

The Egyptians and Jordanians accepted the resolution. The Israelis, while not actually rejecting it, made it very clear that they would not accept total withdrawal.

The patient efforts on behalf of the United Nations of Gunnar Jarring, the Swedish Ambassador to Moscow, to implement this resolution proved futile, and the United States—after first persuading the two sides in June to accept a cease-fire—late in 1969 once again moved to the forefront with its own proposals, based on the November, 1967, resolution, for a settlement on the Egyptian and Jordanian fronts. They are worth describing in detail because in my opinion they remain the fairest, most complete proposals for Arab-Israeli settlement ever made.

Although the text of the American proposals made by Secretary of State William Rogers has never been published, I have learned from sources in the State Department that they consisted of ten points, as follows:

1. Egypt and Israel would agree on withdrawal of Israeli forces from Egyptian territory according to a set timetable.

2. Egypt and Israel would bring the state of war between them to an official end. Thereafter they would refrain from anything in the nature of aggression and would make sure that private organizations such as the commandos did nothing of the kind.

3. Secure and recognized borders would be agreed on by the two sides. These would be recorded in the final agreement, which would include demilitarized zones and special measures in the region of Sharm el-Sheikh to guarantee freedom of navigation in

the Strait of Tiran. The border between Egypt and Israel would revert to the international frontier that once existed between Egypt and Palestine in the days of the British Mandate.

4. Egypt and Israel would enter into indirect "Rhodes-type" talks to determine the areas to be demilitarized and the nature of the measures that would in a final settlement guarantee freedom of navigation through the Strait of Tiran and security in the Gaza Strip.

5. The two sides would acknowledge the Strait of Tiran as an international waterway, and Israel along with all other nations would enjoy freedom of navigation through the Strait.

6. Egypt, while exercising full sovereignty over the Suez Canal, would guarantee the right of all nations, including Israel, to pass through without discrimination.

7. Refugee questions would be settled along the lines of agreements to be reached between Jordan and Israel.

8. Egypt and Israel would acknowledge each other's sovereignty and political independence, as well as the right to live peacefully within secure boundaries.

9. The final agreement would take the form of a document signed by both sides and filed at the United Nations.

10. The agreement would be submitted to the Security Council for ratification, and the United States, the Soviet Union, Britain, and France would pledge to use their good offices to ensure adherence to its terms.

Mr. Rogers' proposals to the Israelis and the Jordanians, submitted soon after the one to the Israelis and Egyptians, followed similar principles. He made it clear that there would be adjustments on the Israeli-Jordanian border but refrained from specifying just what these adjustments would be.

In a January, 1970, speech Mr. Rogers spelled out his proposals for solving the problems of the refugees and of Jerusalem. He said, "There can be no lasting peace without a just settlement of the problem of those Palestinians whom the wars of 1948 and 1967 have made homeless," and that the United States was "prepared to contribute generously along with others to solve this problem. We believe its just settlement must take into account the desires and aspirations of the refugees and the legitimate concerns of the governments in the area."

He noted that there is "a new consciousness among the young Palestinians who have grown up since 1948, which needs to be channeled away from bitterness and frustration toward hope and justice."

About Jerusalem, he said, "Its status can be determined only through the agreement primarily of the governments of Israel and Jordan, taking into account the interests of other countries in the area and the international community."

He said the United States believed that "Jerusalem should be a unified city within which there would no longer be restrictions on the movement of persons and goods," in which "all faiths and nationalities would have freedom of access and over which an administration would preside ensuring roles for both Israel and Jordan in the civil, economic, and religious life of the city."

It is my understanding that Mr. Rogers' proposals for Egypt and Jordan envisaged demilitarization of key areas and their occupation by United Nations troops. This would apply to Sharm el-Sheikh, overlooking the Strait of Tiran, and the West Bank of the Jordan River. While the American proposals made no formal mention of the additional key issue of the Golan Heights, the mountainous Syrian frontier area occupied by Israel, I believe that the State Department has informally advocated that this territory should also be demilitarized and occupied by a United Nations force. As in the case of the 1967 United Nations resolutions that were accepted by Egypt and Jordan, Israelis, without actually rejecting the proposals, once again made it clear that they would not withdraw to the 1967 borders.

In February, 1970, Gunnar Jarring made a notable attempt to break the impasse that had been reached in all attempts to implement the November, 1967, UN resolutions as well as Mr. Rogers' elaboration of those proposals. He addressed fundamental questions to the two parties. Of the Egyptians he asked in effect: "If the Israelis withdraw from occupied territory, are you willing to sign a treaty with them?"

Of the Israelis, he asked: "If the Egyptians are willing to sign a formal agreement, are you willing to withdraw, and if so, to what borders?"

Sadat's reply was simple: "'Yes." The Israelis were taken aback. They had been saying for years that the essential ingredient of settlement was for the Arabs to be willing to sign a formal agreement. Now that it had happened the Israelis' reply was indefinite. They were plainly suspicious, reiterating that they would under no circumstances withdraw all the way to the 1967 border.

In midsummer of 1970 the United States scored a notable success in getting the two sides to accept a cease-fire during which negotiations would be resumed through Gunnar Jarring in New York. But the talks were broken off soon thereafter by the Israelis, who accused Egypt of using the cease-fire to move missile launchers closer to the Suez Canal. American Intelligence confirmed that this was indeed true.

In spite of the inadequate, unbalanced nature of United States policy in the entire region of the Middle East, it seemed for a while in 1970 and 1971, after the cease-fire had gone into effect and Egypt and Jordan had accepted the Rogers plan, that an Arab-Israeli settlement was within grasping distance. But all the State Department's talk and Mr. Rogers' proposals and maneuvers were in vain because, for the Nixon Administration, grasping at peace would be grasping a nettle. It would mean putting serious pressure on Israel. And for this the Administration did not have the political courage. It was unwilling to do in 1970–71 what President Eisenhower was willing to do in 1956, namely, to say to the Israelis: "Go back!"

In the early part of 1972 the issue revolved around whether the United States would resume deliveries of Phantom aircraft to Israel. Throughout 1971 the Administration had stood firm in refusing Israeli demands for more aircraft. But as the 1972 elections approached, the Nixon Administration weakened, although the Administration would not admit it. According to the deal that was worked out, the Israelis were to get some of the Phantoms they wanted, with an assurance that more would be forthcoming if they were cooperative in entering negotiations with the Egyptians under American auspices in New York.

But in the end the Israelis got their Phantoms, plus Hawks, and a lot more.

Some State Department and Defense Department experts on this subject feel that the decision made by the White House represented a breach in the dike and actually prevented negotiations by undermining whatever remained of Egyptian confidence in American evenhandedness. Some of the most knowledgeable of the experts have opposed selling Phantoms or other long-range jets to the Israelis ever since the Johnson Administration made the first deliveries. They have contended that sale of these deep-penetration attack aircraft represented the most serious escalation ever made in the Israeli-Arab arms race and that their appearance in the Middle East led directly to the Russian decision to send Russian pilots to help in the defense of Cairo.

Talks among the four Great Powers, and especially between the United States and the Soviet Union, continued spasmodically in 1970 and 1971, but petered out in 1972 in the face of vocal Israeli objections. The Israelis maintained that it was wrong for the Great Powers to try to work out solutions over the heads of the people of the Middle East. They insisted that only direct negotiations between the antagonists could be fruitful.

A different kind of approach, in search of a partial, piecemeal solution, got underway as a result of an informal suggestion made in December, 1969, by Israeli Minister of Defense, Moshe Dayan, that agreement might be reached on the reopening of the Suez Canal on the basis of mutual withdrawal from its banks. This idea was, of course, quite unacceptable to the Egyptians because it would have entailed their withdrawing from their own territory. But it did result in a proposal by President Sadat early in 1971 that the Suez Canal might be reopened if the Israelis would withdraw to a specified point as the first part of a phased withdrawal.

Golda Meir, the Israeli Premier, quickly replied that Israel was willing to talk about it, although total withdrawal remained out of the question. These expressions of views by Egyptians and Israelis stimulated a surge of hope in the State Department. The principle of the piecemeal approach became gospel in the State Department, and a variety of secret proposals followed. Mr. Rogers and his top

Middle Eastern diplomat, Joseph Sisco, former CIA Director Richard Helms, and the former American diplomatic representative in Cairo, Donald Bergus, who in the absence of diplomatic relations was technically a member of the Spanish Embassy, all came up with various formulae, and attempted to put pressure on the two sides. The fundamental idea was that the Israelis should go back at least to the Mitla Pass, in the mountains about one-third of the way across the Sinai Peninsula from Suez, and that the territory evacuated should be occupied by some kind of international force. The Egyptians would then clear and reopen the Canal.

The State Department proposed that the Egyptians should be allowed to send a token force of their own army across the Suez Canal since this was, after all, their own territory. But the Israelis declared that it was unacceptable that any Egyptian military at all should be allowed to cross the Canal. Nor would they accept a United Nations or any other international force. They wanted joint Israeli-Egyptian patrols. Furthermore, they demanded that Israel should be compensated for accepting a less desirable tactical position by receiving a new consignment of Phantom jets from the United States.

Because the prospects for an over-all solution seemed so dim, the State Department threw its weight behind the idea of a partial solution at Suez. Certainly its chances for success in this limited enterprise were better than they had ever been in the more ambitious enterprises of the past. But still they remained dim.

In the months before the fourth Arab-Israeli war, Arab capitals, and Beirut, of course, more than any other, were still shocked by the extraordinary boldness of the latest Israeli raid on Beirut. A feeling of helplessness and rage engulfed the Arabs. While the immediate effect was to incite the moderate Lebanese Government to take more effective action to bring the Fedayeen under control, in the long term it probably polarized political forces in Lebanon and other parts of the Arab world—the pro-Western moderates at one end of the spectrum, the anti-Western leftist radicals at the other end.

The United States quite unexpectedly opened a new chapter in its supply of arms to the Middle East by offering to sell limited quantities of Phantom F 4s, hitherto the symbol of the special relationship of the U.S. with Israel, to Saudi Arabia and Kuwait, as reported more fully in Chapter 8.

American willingness to sell this type of aircraft to Arabs served the United States, on the eve of a Security Council meeting called by Egypt and of a visit to Washington by Soviet First Secretary, Leonid Brezhnev, as a demonstration that the United States is not totally one-sided. The Israelis rose instantly to the bait. Although Israel, with 120 Phantoms, is hardly endangered, the Israeli Ambassador expressed "concern" at the State Department.

Together with the 2,500,000-dollar arms deal concluded with Iran early in 1972, these sales to America's friends in the area probably represented one effort by the U.S. to develop an alternative to the British presence in the Gulf, which had ended in 1971.

Tension between Israel and the Arabs, especially Egypt, was on the rise again. Egypt's President Sadat, hard pressed on the home front, was threatening a resumption of the "war of attrition" across the Suez Canal if Egypt could not obtain redress for the losses suffered in the 1967 War.

It was a time also of rising uneasiness in the United States over the energy shortage. As the United States, for the first time, was becoming aware of its growing dependence on the Middle East, and in particular on the countries of the Persian Gulf for its supply of oil, there was talk in the United States of "brownouts" and of gasoline rationing. Yet, who was to blame? Israel? The Arabs? Or had the United States mismanaged its relations with the countries of the Middle East? Or its own resources?

All facets of the situation, it seemed to me, pointed in the direction I have already indicated—the need for working out solutions in the Middle East in conjunction with the Soviet Union.

Yet no far-reaching agreement about the Middle East was achieved with the Soviet leader Leonid Brezhnev during his visit to Washington in June, 1973.

The fourth Arab-Israeli war, which broke out five months after the Russian's visit, dramatically illustrated both the need and the opportunities for agreement.

In order to put this war into perspective, one must ask what there was about it that was different from its three predecessors.

First of all, two extraordinary men have played leading roles in this war and its aftermath—President Anwar Sadat of Egypt and Secretary of State Henry Kissinger of the United States.

The Egyptian president took advantage of his reputation for impossible bombast to prepare the war in secrecy. No one really took him seriously. He had talked about a "year of decision" and had done nothing. He had threatened to cross the Canal and had not done so. When Israeli and Washington intelligence officers saw the report of his armed maneuvers, they smiled and turned the page. Once again, the experts were wrong. They were so sure they knew how Sadat and his Egyptians would act that they did not heed the evidence. Sadat succeeded beyond Nasser's wildest dreams in uniting the Arab World, both traditionalist and revolutionary. With an objective that was strictly controlled and limited in his own mind, he did not allow his propagandists to indulge in wild talk about driving the Jews into the sea. From the beginning his objective was to create a situation by which Egypt could get a viable settlement.

As for Henry Kissinger, his negotiating genius expressed itself more brilliantly during and after the Arab-Israeli war than ever before. He got off to a flying start thanks to an invitation from Premier Kosygin of the Soviet Union, who had just returned from Cairo and who doubtless understood that his clients were in military trouble. In two days Dr. Kissinger worked out the fundamental agreement on which the October 22 cease-fire and all subsequent negotiations and agreements are based. The full scope of what Dr. Kissinger worked out with Mr. Brezhnev may not become known for a long time, but one may say that it amply made up for the lack of agreement on the Middle East during the Russian's visit to Washington. From this point on, Dr. Kissinger never stopped moving. He carried the negotiations forward by sheer momentum, deftly obscuring by small classics of diplomatic obfuscation the points that could not be reconciled; for instance, the second point of the agreement requiring the Israelis to return to the October 22 lines. Dr. Kissinger knew the lines of October 22 could probably never be determined and that the Israelis would in any case refuse to go back if told to do so directly. So he made the agreement read that the parties would engage in "immediate discussions to settle the question of the return to the October 22 positions in the framework of agreement on the disengagement and separation of forces under United Nations auspices." What a linguistic swamp, a swamp in which the opposing parties could each find its own interpretation.

Dr. Kissinger succeeded at the beginning in promoting an agreement under which Egypt's 238 Israeli prisoners were exchanged for the 7,852 Egyptians held by Israel. The exchange was carried out under the auspices of the International Red Cross, by aircraft marked with the Red Cross flying between Cairo and Tel Aviv. In return for getting back the prisoners, which the Israelis wanted above all things, Kissinger was able to persuade the Israelis to allow food to go through their lines to the Egyptian Third Army. The Israelis were persuaded also not to insist on the question of the blockade at Bab El Mandeb, their port at the entrance to the Red Sea. The Egyptians said they could not officially call off the blockade because they had not officially proclaimed one, and the Straits were in any case technically the responsibility of the South Yemenis. Here was the kind of imprecise situation which Dr. Kissinger so ably exploits in the interests of more important issues.

By good fortune, Dr. Kissinger's Middle Eastern negotiations fell neatly into the framework of his visit to Peking. What could be better suited to encourage Soviet cooperation with the United States than a cozy visit between Dr. Kissinger and Chou En-lai, who promptly dubbed his visitor "the Middle Eastern cyclone!"

Beyond the remarkable personalities engaged, the next point of difference between this war and its predecessors is the degree of agreement Dr. Kissinger was able to work out during his visit to Moscow. From this foundation, the other points follow.

In a manner quite different from anything that has been seen in U.S.-Israeli relations since 1956, Dr. Kissinger has subtly applied pressure to oblige the Israelis to do what he thinks necessary. The first demonstration of this, almost unnoticed at the time, was the switch in the United States position on whether the cease-fire should be on the October 6 lines or "in place." At a time when the Arabs had made considerable gains and before the Israelis had made their comeback, Kissinger decided that the United States should insist on a cease-fire in place.

The next point concerned the feeding of the Egyptian Third Army. Kissinger saw in a flash that if the Third Army were destroyed there would be no basis for settlement between the Israelis and Egyptians. The whole idea that the Egyptians had regained their self-respect by proving that they could not only fight but hurt the Israelis and could therefore meet them as equals would be swept away. So he told the Israelis they must allow the Third Army to survive even though its survival meant that the Israelis were giving up the victory they had almost in their hands.

In the negotiations at Kilometer 101 about the cease-fire lines, Kissinger had to deal with a microcosm of the larger problem of Israel's withdrawal from Sinai. It was obvious that if there was going to be a settlement, the Israelis would have to go back—if not all the way, at least a great deal farther than they wanted to go.

Another point that makes this war different is that, on the other side, the Russians will have to play a very special role in persuading the Egyptians to go through with the settlement. The Egyptians will have to forego the total recovery of their territory, to sit down and negotiate face to face with the Israelis, to recognize the State of Israel, and to sign with it a peace treaty. This is the meaning, in the final analysis, of "delivering" the Egyptians, which is the responsibility of the Soviet Union much as "delivering" the Israelis is the responsibility of the U.S.

A final point of difference is that the Arabs have used their so-called "oil weapon" and it has been effective, as attested by the resolution of the nine members of the European Common Market calling for the return of the Israelis to the 1967 borders in accordance with Resolution 242 and by Japan's efforts to prove goodwill toward the Arab cause. The oil producers acknowledged the Europeans' position by deciding at a meeting in Vienna in mid-November not to increase the pressure on Europe. They refrained from adding another five percent to the twenty-five percent by which they had already reduced their production for the Europeans. But the total boycott of the United States, Canada, and the Netherlands continued.

One cannot help but wonder what the ultimate Russian intentions may be beyond the agreement made with Dr. Kissinger. What was it that motivated them to threaten, at the height of the war, to send their airborne troops into Egypt? Was it just that they feared that their client might lose its precious territorial gains in Sinai? Or did the Russians really imagine that they could in this manner steal a march and appear suddenly in the Egyptian desert drawn up in full panpoly in fulfillment of a dream that has persisted in the Russian psyche since the days of Catherine the Great?

I would like to think that both superpowers learned a sobering lesson while looking down each other's gun barrels, as it were, during the confrontation, while Soviet and American fleets were drawn up in the Eastern Mediterranean, air transports were ferrying tanks to the Middle East, and airborne troops of both nations were standing poised at battle stations.

As I have said, the final settlement in the Middle East has got to be buttressed by and built upon a United States-Soviet settlement. Here are points that should be included in such an agreement:

1. First, we should agree to restrict arms shipments to the Middle East, not only to Israel and her immediate Arab neighbors, but also to Iran, Iraq, and the other Arab states around the Persian Gulf. The Israelis are perfectly justified in their apprehensions. The contract clauses prohibiting the transfer of arms sold to third countries cannot be enforced—quite apart from the fact that a Phantom can fly 1,600 miles unrefueled. Another side of the question is that the great quantities of arms we ship to the countries around the Persian Gulf amount to an invitation to the Soviet Union to undertake some enormous military program for Iraq. If we do not come to terms with the Russians on this subject, and then draw Britain and France into the agreement as well, we can look forward to ever more dangerous confrontations, to a Vietnam-type limited conflict, eventually even to World War III.

2. As a second step, the United States and the Soviet Union should agree on a just formula for settlement of the conflict between Israel and the Arab countries, including territories from which the Israelis should withdraw, the establishment of demilitarized zones, Arab recognition of Israel, and international guaran-

tees of the new situation. I have explained at length elsewhere why I am sure the Israelis and Arabs can never come to terms directly with one another without Great Power assistance. The Security Council Resolution 242 and the Rogers Plan are indeed now out of date, as the Israelis have maintained so long and so eloquently. They are out of date because the preponderance of Israeli strength is now so great, thanks to American deliveries plus the Israelis' own effort, that the Israelis no longer feel the need even to pay lip service to a balanced solution. The real Israeli policy has been expressed in words attributed to General Dayan: "I would rather have land than peace," which contrasts ironically with one of King Hussein's favorite lines, that "Israel can have land or peace, but not both."

Having arrived at an agreement on a just solution in which the Israelis would withdraw, not from all but from most occupied territories, under which an international force would control critical areas such as the Golan Heights and Sharm el-Sheikh, the Americans and Russians would have to agree also on ways in which to bring pressure to bear on Israel and the Arabs to accept this settlement. I have no doubt that, working in concert, the two Great Powers could succeed. The Chinese would oppose it, as would the Fedayeen and some Israelis. The forces of moderation on both sides could prevail.

3. The agreement establishing new borders between Israel and the surrounding Arab countries should be guaranteed by the Great Powers. It should take the form of renewal of the 1950 Tripartite Agreement, under which the United States, Britain, and France undertook to uphold existing borders in the Middle East and to oppose aggression from whatever source. This agreement would now be expanded to include the Soviet Union. The Soviet Union or its allies would be included without question in any international force designated to patrol the demilitarized critical areas.

The agreement would offer an occasion for the United States overtly to accept coexistence with the Soviet Union in the Middle East, provided the Russians refrained from subversion.

In this connection, I do not favor the idea expounded by Senator William Fulbright that the United States should formalize its implied commitment to the preservation of Israel by signing a treaty with the Israelis. While this might seem logical, it would contribute to the polarization of East-West forces. Some Israelis would doubtless prefer to have it this way, so that Israel would be the sole political and military base of the United States in this part of the Middle East. But I think the same purpose could be achieved in an evenhanded way that would preserve American ties in the Arab world by reviving the principles of the Tripartite Declaration.

4. The American-Russian agreement should acknowledge the desirability of creating an independent Palestinian state on the West Bank of the Jordan plus the Gaza Strip. This state would maintain its own independent political life under the protection of the Great Powers. It would be open economically to Israel on the one hand and to Jordan on the other, rather more than it is at present. The viability of the state would depend on its success in maintaining and expanding these links. At present Jordan accepts imports from the West Bank provided they are certified not to include Israeli products, and Jordanian goods move quite freely to the West Bank. In spite of Israeli occupation, the Jordanian Government still pays the salaries of teachers and many other civil servants. The Israelis accept some West Bank products, insofar as they do not compete with Israeli agriculture, and the West Bankers are free to buy in Israel. Tens of thousand of West Bankers have achieved modest prosperity by accepting jobs in Israel.

If such a state were created there would have to be special arrangements for transportation across Israel between the West Bank and the Gaza Strip so that the new state would have its outlet to the sea at Gaza.

Premier Golda Meir explicitly rejected the idea of a Palestinian state between Israel and Jordan, but this solution has been foreshadowed by other Israelis who have toyed with the establishment of autonomous political institutions on the West Bank, and by King Hussein, who has promised the people of the West Bank that after a political settlement with Israel he would acknowledge their right of self-determination. That is, he acknowledged that they might then choose whether they wished to be part of Jordan, autonomous, or independent. Creation of an autonomous Palestinian state would be a breakthrough toward real peace because it would touch the real core of the problem, namely, the fate of the Palestinian people. One can imagine that once peace and normal exchanges among states developed, a federal relationship between the West Bank State and either or both of its economic partners might develop.

The creation of such a state might outrage the Fedayeen but at the same time go far toward assuaging the outraged sensibilities of a great number of moderate Palestinians.

The commandos reject it with anger because, in their eyes, acceptance of a quarter, or even a half loaf implies that the Israelis are entitled to the rest of the loaf. Yet this is a realistic idea. Unlike the theorizing of Fedayeen intellectuals and Israeli Marxists, it is a thing that might really happen.

I personally have been aware during my many visits to Amman, and during a short visit to the West Bank in the summer of 1970, of the great interest of moderate Palestinians in this idea.

The idea of the West Bank State brings to mind remarks made by King Hussein at a small gathering of journalists at the Jordanian Embassy in London a few months after the 1967 War. He said then that if there could be no "Arab solution" in the Middle East because the Arab rulers could not come to terms with one another, then there would have to be a "Jordanian solution." I took it that this meant that if all else failed, King Hussein would have to come to terms separately with the Israelis. I believe that such a solution would necessarily include the West Bank State.

This brings to mind also the remarks King Hussein made in response to my question at an interview at Blair House in Washington in January, 1972. In what seems to me a most remarkable expression of Hussein's willingness to come to terms with the Israelis, he proposed that Jerusalem be proclaimed an open city, that is, one that would be demilitarized and not be attacked under any circumstances by anyone. Jerusalem, he suggested, would then become the "city of peace": Israel and an Arab state would share Jerusalem as their capital.

In his solution for Jerusalem, the old demarcation line between Israeli and Jordanian territory would be re-established, but only as a principle. The city would be run as a unit, ignoring the line, by a joint Israeli and Jordanian administration under the direction of a mutually acceptable neutral manager. The holy places would, of course, be open and accessible to people of all faiths.

Except for the proposal that Jews and Arabs share Jerusalem as a capital, the idea was almost identical to one that had been outlined to me several years earlier by the chief of the King's personal staff, Zaid Rifai. During a visit to Jerusalem in September, 1972, I also discussed it with Teddy Kollek, an old friend from the days when I was *New York Times* correspondent in Israel and he was a personal aide to Premier Ben-Gurion. He thought it made a lot of sense but was sure it would unfortunately not be acceptable to the Government generally.

5. Closely related to the problems of the Middle East is the problem of rivalry between the United States and the Soviet Union in the Indian Ocean. Because this rivalry is still at an early stage, it could be brought under control by an agreement between the two superpowers to demilitarize the Indian Ocean including the Persian Gulf so far as the Great Powers are concerned. This idea has the enthusiastic backing of the Shah of Iran who would indeed become "Mr. Big" in the area.

In the Mediterranean the presence of the United States and the Soviet Union is too well established and complex to be reversed, but in the Indian Ocean there is a chance.

If the Soviet Union turns down this proposal, as it has in the past, then the United States must be prepared to keep abreast of the growing Soviet presence in the Indian Ocean. If necessary to offset Soviet activities, the United States, together with Britain, should establish a small naval base on the island of Diego Garcia, where they have already, in recent years, set up a joint communications station. The island is uninhabited and offers not only adequate space for the landing of aircraft but also a lagoon forming an ideal harbor.

From such a base, combined with the technique of "at sea" resupply, the United States could make regular sweeps into the Persian Gulf to maintain the United States' presence and offset Soviet activities. In the long run, I believe that a procedure of this kind would prove more satisfactory than maintenance of the existing small facility which the United States inherited from the British at Bahrain. In any case, at the height of the fourth Arab-Israeli war, in October, 1973, the Bahrainis gave the U.S. the required one year's notice to leave this base.

6. President Nixon's leadership in dealing with the energy crisis, which began long before the fourth Arab-Israeli war but was made far more critical by it, has been totally inadequate. Beyond a strict system of rationing of all fuels, the President should launch a crash program of vast proportions to develop alternative sources of energy. This should go well beyond the current program for liquifying and gasifying coal, for building the Alaska pipeline, for expanding the search for gas, for pushing the quest for oil far into the waters of the continental shelf, and for hastening development of nuclear power. This program should reach out to the exotic forms of energy, so that they may no longer be exotic. It should put unprecedented energies behind the expansion of nuclear power, including development of the breeder reactor and, ultimately, of the fusion process. Shale oil and tar sands must be exploited with government subsidies. Research must be pressed on solar energy and means of using the heat of the earth's interior, and the tides and the temperature changes in the sea. By making a very great effort in these as well as in more conventional fields, the United States would confirm and extend its position as the scientific and technological leader of the world and would set itself free from the perils and pressures of oil politics.

If there had been no war, the United States would be spending $20 billion a year for imported oil by 1980. We would begin to set ourselves free from this dependence by putting five times that much —100 billion dollars—into research.

Unfortunately, these terms are unlikely ever to be worked out. The main reason, I venture, is that the Nixon Administration and its successors will boggle at approaching the core of the matter, namely the need to put pressure on Israel.

We are dealing here with one of the globe's most intractable conflicts, more difficult than the Vietnam War because its roots are very old, and religious as well as economic, political, and military.

The issues cut deep into American emotional life. When it comes to the crunch, Dr. Kissinger's brilliance will not be the decisive factor. The real question will be whether the President of the United States is willing to go down the line politically in backing his clever Secretary of State, whether the President after all his internal political travail still has that kind of option. Beyond that the question will be whether the Senate, which has always in the past, like the doting parent of a spoiled child, granted all the wishes of the State of Israel, is capable this time of coming to terms with a new and stern reality. And even further down the line the question will be whether the Zionist organizations will let the Senate be wise, whether they will, as they doubtless could by their influence, frustrate Dr. Kissinger's attempt to reach a settlement, or whether they will help Israelis and the friends of Israel to see the compromise as an opportunity to begin a new era, an era in which the genius of the sons of Ishmael and Isaac will be melded. It would be an era of unheard of harmony and prosperity in which such works as the Eric Johnston plan for development of the Jordan Valley would be carried out at last. The Arab refugees would be compensated or allowed to go home. Israelis and Palestinian enterprise would go hand in hand. The scientific resources of the Jews and the wealth of oil sheikhdoms would intermingle and flourish.

Long before these dreams are fulfilled—right now—Israelis feel that the territorial concessions they are asked to make are unfair in the light of the military success they scored at the last minute in Sinai. Certainly these concessions are going to be profoundly divisive among Israelis, as among Americans. Among Israelis there will be a bitter split between two schools of thought. On the one hand are those who believe that Israel must and can prevail by superior strength. On the other hand, there are those who have come to the conclusion that the great lesson to be drawn from this war is not that Israel must have more space within which to defend herself but that this is a last chance to come to terms with the Arabs.

Among Americans, too, division runs deep. The energy crisis has made Americans aware for the first time of the extent of the burden this country bears for the sake of Israel. Inevitably some

Americans will turn against the Israelis and anti-Jewish expressions may, unfortunately, ensue.

If there is a settlement the strength of the moderates will be consolidated and a period of relative stability will follow. If there is no settlement there will be no consolidation, no stability. Either way, sooner or later, the two leading proponents of settlement among the Arabs, King Hussein and President Sadat, will find themselves more and more under pressure by radical forces. They will be castigated by their enemies as lackeys of the United States, the King for having wiped out the Fedayeen, the heroes of the youth in all Arab lands, the President for having expelled his Russian allies and deprived the Arabs of the military backing they needed to match their Israeli enemy's American support, both for not continuing the struggle against Israel. To what end, King Hussein will be asked, did you make such a bloody sacrifice? To what end, President Sadat will be asked, did you throw away so great an advantage? This sort of situation is made to order for the leftist revolutionaries, the kind of inflammatory ammunition they are looking for.

Fatah, I believe, will disintegrate or become a captive of the moderate regimes, while the radicals in Fatah and the Marxist commando organizations, such as PFLP and PDFLP, will go underground. Their mission, for the next decade, will be to overthrow first the monarchies, then the moderate republics, and finally the "liberated" regimes. In almost every Arab country they will have a fifth column working for them—the frustrated Palestinians. Because they are homeless, because they have aspirations and are frustrated, because they suffer and find no solace, the Palestinians are in the Middle East what the Jews have been in similar situations in other parts of the world: catalysts of revolutionary change.

Whether there is a settlement or not, whether the inevitable revolutions of the Middle East occur sooner or later, one must anticipate further rounds of war between Israel and the Arab states. The Israelis will undoubtedly win each round, although each time less decisively and at greater cost. If the radicals take over Jordan, they will have the best Arab army and they will turn it into the new Palestinian state. If the radicals take over the

Persian Gulf, they will have money enough for their armies. And as they close in on the sources of Arab wealth, no doubt the Chinese will be siding with them, offering them benefits of international support. After that, the question "Will the Arabs find their Mao?" may seem less exotic than at present.

Eventually—no one can possibly know when—the inexorable march of economic and demographic growth and technological development will have given the Arabs massive material and numerical superiority. And Israel, no matter how great her qualitative superiority, would, in a final test of strength, be submerged unless the United States came to her rescue. This could be Armageddon for the Arabs and the Israelis.

The point at which the United States would come to rescue Israel would be the point at which the United States would be most likely to clash with the Soviet Union. This could be World War III —Armageddon for the world.

Long before Armageddon, it may be assumed, United States and Western interests in the Middle East would have been swept away. In fact, the process is already underway in the oil industry. President Qaddafi began with the nationalization of British petroleum holdings in Libya in reprisal for the fact that the British had remained quiescent while Iran occupied some small Arab-owned islands in the Gulf. The Iraqis have also resorted to nationalizing part of the Iraq Petroleum Company's interests. Iran has, in a more "genteel" way, done the same thing to all of the members of the consortium who pump oil in Iran, merely offering them preferred status as purchasers. Meanwhile, the other oil-producing countries have begun imposing on the companies agreements permitting them to "participate" in growing percentages in the ownership of the companies operating in their territories.

There will be very little the United States can do about this. It will be a little too late to find friends in the countries from which most of the oil imported by the United States in the next twenty years is bound to come. Unless we can reconcile the contradiction between our sentimental interest in the Israelis and our economic interest in Arab lands, we will be inexorably drawn into the successive rounds of the Arab-Israeli struggle.

This is an unfinished story, one that is not likely to be finished in our time. Pitting brother against brother and cousin against cousin, with heroism on both sides going for naught, with terror and perfidy on both sides canceling each other out, it is a conflict in which neither side can finally prevail. This is a tragedy, on the classic scale, a family struggle between the sons of Isaac and the sons of Ishmael. Israelis and Arabs and their Great Power sponsors are locked in a struggle which will lead to mutual doom.

Of course we must go on working to postpone Armageddon. If we work hard enough and long enough, the gleam of hope may yet brighten the Middle Eastern horizon. This hope is founded on the assumption of growth on both sides, not economic, military, or demographic, but cultural. I see new generations of Israelis growing up who do not really believe in many of the old Zionist slogans and who want to be part not so much of the Jewish world as of the Middle East. These are the Sabras, those born in the land of Israel, some of whom feel they have more in common with Amman and Damascus than they have with Brooklyn.

On the Arab side, there will be new generations who have grown up in the twentieth, and perhaps the twenty-first, centuries who will equal the Israelis in wealth, in technology, and self-confidence, no longer suffering from any kind of inferiority complex. These generations would perceive Israel as a part of the Middle East rather than as an outpost of worldwide forces. They could deal directly with such an Israel and come to terms.

I like to reflect that if anyone had predicted in 1871 that within one hundred years Germans and Frenchmen would be living as part of a European community linked politically and economically, such a person would have been called mad. But even more mad would have been he who predicted that such an achievement would take place only after the awful bloodletting of a World War I and a World War II.

Index